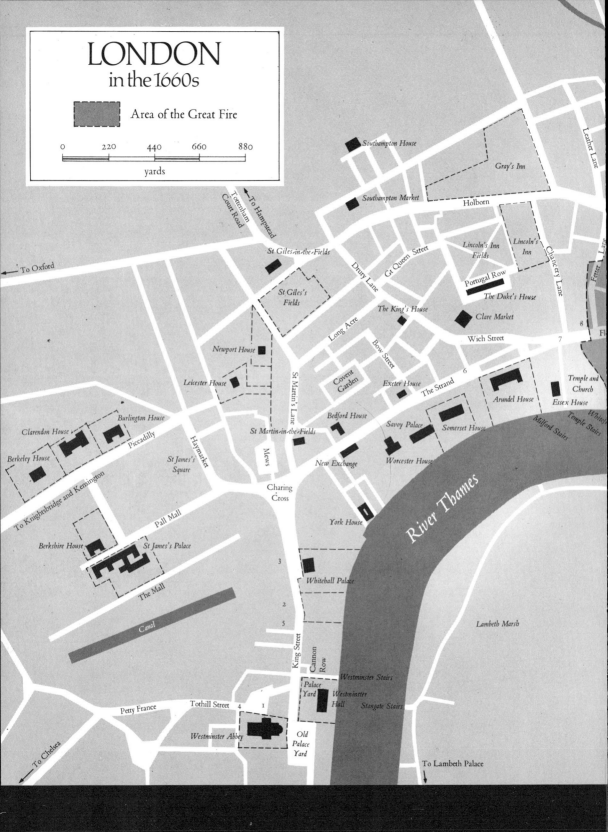

LONDON
in the 1660s

Area of the Great Fire

0   220   440   660   880
yards

To Hampstead
Tottenham Court Road

To Oxford

Southampton House

Gray's Inn

Southampton Market

Holborn

St Giles-in-the-Fields

Drury Lane

Gt Queen Street

Lincoln's Inn Fields

Lincoln's Inn

Chancery Lane

Leather Lane

St Giles's Fields

The King's House

Portugal Row

The Duke's House

Clare Market

Long Acre

Wich Street

Newport House

Bow Street

Covent Garden

Exeter House

The Strand

Arundel House

Essex House

Temple and Church

Whitefriars Temple Stairs

Leicester House

St Martin's Lane

Bedford House

Savoy Palace

Somerset House

Milford Stairs

Clarendon House

Burlington House

Piccadilly

St Martin-in-the-Fields

New Exchange

Worcester House

Berkeley House

Haymarket

St James's Square

Mews

Charing Cross

Berkshire House

Pall Mall

St James's Palace

York House

River Thames

To Knightsbridge and Kensington

The Mall

Canal

Whitehall Palace

Lambeth Marsh

King Street

Cannon Row

Westminster Stairs

To Chelsea

Petty France

Tothill Street

Palace Yard

Westminster Hall

Stangate Stairs

Westminster Abbey

Old Palace Yard

To Lambeth Palace

Fetter Lane

8

7

6

3

2

5

4   1

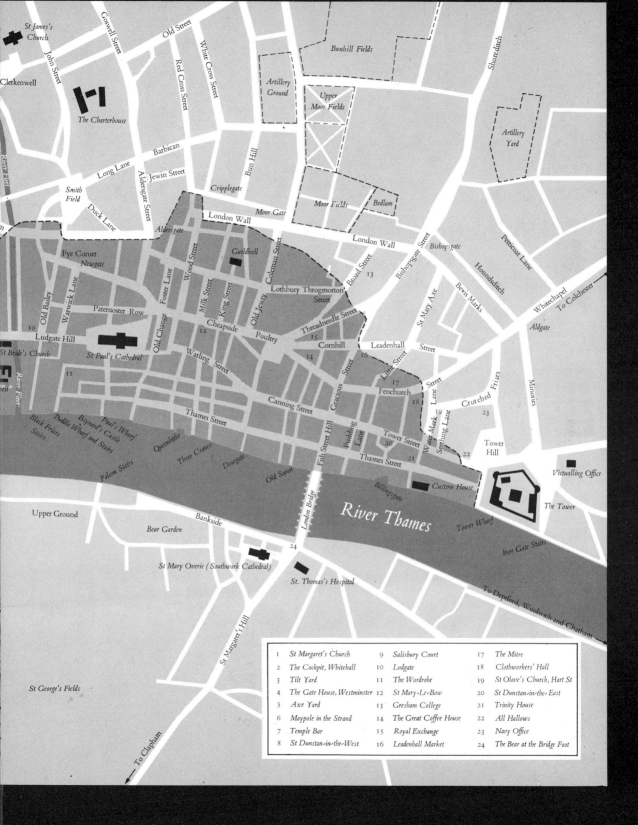

The Illustrated
PEPYS

Selected and edited by Robert Latham, Fellow and Pepys Librarian at Magdalene College, Cambridge. Together with the late Professor William Matthews he is joint editor of the recently completed, definitive edition of the *Diary of Samuel Pepys*.

The Illustrated
PEPYS

Extracts from the Diary

Selected & edited by
ROBERT LATHAM

LONDON
BELL & HYMAN LIMITED

British Library Cataloguing in Publication Data
Pepys, Samuel
[Diary, *Selections*]. The illustrated Pepys.
1. Great Britain – History – Charles II, 1660–1685 – Sources
2. Great Britain – Social life and customs
I. Title   II. The illustrated Pepys   III. Latham, Robert
942.06'6   DA447.P4

ISBN 0–7135–1328–4
First published in 1978
Published in paperback in 1982. Reprinted 1983

This book was designed and produced
by The Rainbird Publishing Group Limited,
40 Park Street, London W1Y 4DE
for Bell & Hyman Limited
37–39 Queen Elizabeth Street, London SE1 2QB

House Editor: Felicity Luard
Picture Researcher: Barbara Fraser
Indexer: Douglas Matthews
Production: Bridget Walsh
Map of London: Tom Stalker Miller

Cover Illustration: Whitehall from St James's Park by Hendrick Danckerts.
Text printed and bound by Mackays of Chatham Ltd
Colour plates originated by Gilchrist Bros Ltd, Leeds

CONTENTS

COLOUR PLATES

The page numbers given are those opposite the colour plates, or, in the case of a double page spread, those on either side of the plate

Introduction

To read Pepys is to be transported immediately into his world. His diary is not so much a record of events as a re-creation of them. Not all the passages are as picturesque as the famous set-pieces in which he describes Charles II's coronation or the Great Fire of London, but there is no entry which does not in some degree display the same power of summoning back to life the events it relates.

How is it done? One explanation is Pepys's close observation and total recall of detail: it is the small touches that achieve the effect. Another is the freshness and flexibility of the language. Pepys writes quickly, in shorthand and for himself alone. The words, often piled on top of each other without much respect for formal grammar, exactly reflect the impressions of the moment. But the most important explanation, is, perhaps, that throughout the diary Pepys writes mainly as an observer of people. It is this that makes him the most human and accessible of diarists, and that gives the diary its special quality as a historical record.

Instead of writing a considered narrative, such as would be presented by the historian or biographer or autobiographer, Pepys shows us hundreds of scenes from life – civil servants in committee, M.P.s in debate, concerts of music, friends on a river outing. Events are jumbled together, sermons with amorous assignations, domestic tiffs with national crises. In this perspective the great personages are reduced to the same dimensions as the rest of us – the King is a tennis player and an amateur of science, the Duke of York a host who recommends a new sauce, the Lord Chancellor an old man who snores during Privy Council meetings. Moreover, because Pepys relates events in the form of daily observations, he registers their flow at something not very different from the rate at which they occurred. He almost persuades us that we are sharing his life.

We are the more willing to be persuaded because Pepys was so frank about himself. Anyone so transparently honest about his own failings convinces us that he is a reliable guide on other matters. He seems to suppress little or nothing about himself. A part of the explanation is that the diary was secret and not designed for publication – such diaries

Illustrations on preliminary pages from
Visscher's *Prospect of London*, 1616,
Greater London Council

were never published in his day. His shorthand was meant to protect the diary from prying eyes – as he makes clear in the last entry. In relating his sexual adventures he took the extra precaution of writing (still in shorthand) a private polyglot composed of English and two or three foreign languages. His frankness also resulted from his being deficient in humour and self-criticism, so that he is not always conscious of showing himself to disadvantage. Thus he failed to recognize the parsimony with which he treated his wife as mean and selfish. But for the most part his frankness was genuine – it was a sort of innocence, a love of truth for truth's sake. He does not flinch, for instance, from recording instances of his own cowardice.

One characteristic stands out above all others in Pepys's self-portrait – his genius for happiness. Anxiety and fear could plague him, but not for long – always his spirits would rise again to their naturally high and steady level. He often remarks with contentment on his good fortune, and thanks God for it. He could extract extraordinary pleasure from ordinary experience – from wearing a new coat, from the company of children, from a morning spent knocking up nails in the house. As a spirited young man, he had the tastes appropriate to his years. He was fond of drinking with friends, and as is well known his sexual appetites were strong – perhaps abnormally strong: they were of a piece with his general vitality. He had an eager curiosity and was always on the lookout for novelty, for something 'observable'. His interests were wide and he pursued them with energy – the private pleasure of collecting books and prints, as well as the more sociable pleasures of music, the theatre and the new sciences. The language of the diary often reflects his excitement; superlatives flow: Frances Stewart is 'the beautifullest creature that ever I saw in my life'; Mrs Knepp 'sings the noblest that ever I heard in my life'; Nell Gwyn's acting is such as 'was never I believe in the world before'. Each successive pleasure was the best.

But one pleasure he came to regard above the rest – the pleasure that comes from hard work; the satisfaction of completing a difficult office memorandum or some long-deferred casting-up of his private accounts. He was a civil servant and work was the means of giving him the wealth and public esteem he coveted. But it was also something more – it gave him the self-discipline and self-fulfilment that his ardent nature required. It is no accident that the diary (which virtually begins with the opening of his public career) has more information about his work than about any other aspect of his life. After the summer of 1660 he was Clerk of the Acts to the Navy Board – he held, that is, a key post in what was in some ways the most important of all government departments. It spent more money than any other and controlled the largest industrial unit in the country – the royal dockyards. His duties brought him into constant contact not only with colleagues in the public service, but with Court and Parliament. He reports cabinet meetings; although not yet an M.P. he summarizes parliamentary debates; he observes political intrigues and relates naval battles. Best of all he tells secrets – of how M.P.s were lobbied and parliamentary estimates doctored, and (most copiously and usefully) of how public servants like himself built up fortunes from the gifts and retainers handed out by government contractors. (They did not thereby necessarily sell their souls. Pepys flattered himself, not always without good reason, that he knew how to accept bribes without becoming corrupt.)

The diary's contents are shaped also by another factor – its geographical setting. It is a

London diary, with only occasional glimpses of the countryside. But as a panorama of the seventeenth-century capital it is incomparable: more comprehensive than Boswell's account of the London of a century later because Pepys moved in a wider world. As luck would have it, Pepys wrote in the decade when London suffered two of its great disasters – the Plague of 1665 and the Great Fire of the following year. His descriptions of both – agonizingly vivid – achieve their effect by being something more than superlative reporting: they are written with compassion. As always with Pepys it is people, not literary effects, that matter.

Pepys was only twenty-seven when he began to keep his diary, and thirty-six when fear of losing his eyesight forced him to end it. Why he kept it we can only guess: he never tells us. No doubt his motives were mixed. He may have been inspired to start it by the political excitement of the later months of 1659 when it was plain to all that the Commonwealth was collapsing; certainly the subject of restoration bulks large in the early entries. He may have been influenced, too, by the Puritan writers and preachers of his youth, who taught the value of a journal as a means of moral discipline. His diary bears traces of that influence in the monthly and annual reckonings in which he summarized the state of his affairs. But the strongest likelihood is that he wrote from a need to organize and discipline himself that was temperamental rather than religious in origin. He was by nature obsessively and compulsively systematic. The neatness of his handwriting is significant. So is his concern for arranging his books by size, and for the regular balancing of his accounts. Yet, with all this passion for order, he was spontaneous and enthusiastic. The diary was perhaps the means of reconciling these opposing qualities. He loved life because it was so varied; at the same time he was worried by disorder. By sieving the untidy events through his memory and marshalling them in the diary's straight and neatly written lines he could impose on them some semblance of control.

He had been born in Salisbury Court, off Fleet Street, on 23 February 1633. His father, John, was a tailor who came from a family of good yeoman stock long settled in Cambridgeshire. Pepys's Elizabethan great-grandfather had married well and acquired the manor of Cottenham. But his father inherited little – he was the third son of a third son – and had gone to London to earn a livelihood. He had married a washmaid, Margaret Kite, and Pepys was the fifth of the eleven children born to them. By the time he was seven he was the oldest surviving child. He was a boy of ability and after a short spell during the Civil War at the grammar school at Huntingdon was sent to St Paul's School and thence, with a leaving exhibition, to Magdalene College, Cambridge. There again he was awarded a scholarship, and took his degree in 1654. Possibly he meant to become a lawyer, which would have been a natural choice of career for a poor but clever young man. But the execution of the King and the establishment of a republic had opened up another career. Edward Mountagu, a distant relative, had become a Councillor of State and a Treasury Commissioner under the newly formed Cromwellian Protectorate. He now took Pepys into his service as a secretary or domestic steward. Shortly afterwards Pepys acquired a clerkship in the Exchequer – a post which made no great demands on his time but gave him a little money – and in 1655 he was able to marry. His bride was Elizabeth St Michel, the fifteen-year-old daughter of a refugee Huguenot who can have provided her with little or no dowry. In March 1658 Pepys was operated on for the stone – a complaint endemic in his family – by Thomas Hollier, a surgeon of St Thomas's. Shortly afterwards he moved to a house in Axe Yard, off King Street, near to the palace of Whitehall. It is in the garret of that house that the opening scene of the diary is set.

In the first few months of the diary the Commonwealth collapsed. In February Pepys witnessed Monck's march to London, which led to the fall of the Rump and the recall of Charles II. Mountagu had been involved in secret negotiations for the King's return, and in April 1660, when a new parliament had decided to invite Charles back, was sent with a fleet to Holland to bring him home. He took with him the young Pepys, making him for this purpose his secretary and treasurer to the fleet. Within a few weeks, from being an obscure Exchequer clerk, Pepys became a functionary of some consequence: issuing commissions to naval captains, drafting resolutions to send to the King, and receiving letters addressed to 'Samuel Pepys, Esquire'. His career and the diary had got off to a flying start. He had an exciting fortnight in Holland and then sailed back in the same ship as the King himself to Dover. In July came his reward: through the influence of Mountagu – himself made Knight of the Garter and Earl of Sandwich – Pepys was appointed Clerk of the Acts to the Navy Board, in the face of the claims of a much more experienced rival championed by Monck.

His flair for organizing was soon evident, and with the outbreak of the Dutch War in 1665 he proved himself the leading member of the Navy Board. In February 1665 he had become treasurer of the committee which supervised the government of Tangier, and though he treated the post mainly as a source of income, it proved a time-consuming one. There were few Sundays free from work in the later years of the diary, and he began to feel the strain. In particular his eyes gave trouble: candlelight was painful and the effort of writing the diary became progressively more difficult. The trouble was almost certainly what would now be recognized and treated as astigmatism, but Pepys was convinced that he was going blind.

His life with Elizabeth had become difficult too. He was fond of her, but they were in many ways incompatible. She was untidy, mismanaged the household, and did not get on with his father. For his part he kept her lonely and short of money; upbraided her for the slightest fault; and was time and time again unfaithful to her. In November 1668 Elizabeth for the first time found him out – caught him *in flagrante* with her young companion, Deb Willet. The Pepyses had once before – previous to the diary period – parted company. They were now close to parting again. After a series of rows and reconciliations (described in a novelist's detail), they patched things up. The diary leaves them on the eve of sailing off on a holiday to France and the Low Countries to cure Pepys's eyes and maybe mend their marriage.

The rest of Pepys's life after the spring of 1669 – some thirty-four years – is not recorded in a diary. To some extent it is recorded in history. He was promoted Secretary to the Admiralty in 1673 and in the same year became a member of parliament. He commanded the naval organization during the Dutch War of 1672–4, and was responsible for some important developments after it – a shipbuilding programme of unprecedented dimensions, and the introduction of half-pay for officers which, together with other reforms, laid the basis for a professional naval service for the first time in English history. In 1679 he suffered a sudden unwarranted eclipse. Through his association with the Duke of York he fell into disfavour during the panic of the Popish Plot, and lay in the Tower for six weeks under suspicion of treason (though his enemies shrewdly enough did not bring a formal charge against him). He returned to office in 1684 as the King's 'Secretary for Admiralty Affairs': a post akin to that of a secretary of state invented for him and never held by anyone else. He served in that office throughout the reign of his old master, now James II, putting right the things that had gone wrong in his years out of power, and left public service in 1689 shortly after James's flight to France.

His wife had died in October 1669 from a complaint contracted on their trip to the continent. They had had no children, and he never married again. From about 1670 until his death in 1703 his household was presided over by Mary Skinner, to whom he left a grateful legacy in recognition of her 'Steddy friendship and assistances' to him. Since 1679 he had lived in a house in Buckingham Street, Westminster, owned by Will Hewer, his oldest friend, once his clerk and now a rich bachelor. In retirement he continued to live there, making occasional visits to the rural retreat at Clapham which Hewer also owned. In 1690 he published a short book defending his conduct of naval administration since 1684 – his *Memoires Relating to the State of the Royal Navy*. For the rest – apart from two abortive attempts to re-enter parliament – he steered clear of public affairs after leaving office, and fought off without difficulty the attempts made in 1689 and 1690 to brand him a Jacobite plotter. He had once meant to write a history of the navy; that plan was abandoned, but he now had time to read, to make music, to meet and exchange letters with his friends. Among their number were eminent scholars and virtuosi such as Evelyn, Wallis, Newton and Wren: some had sat under him on the council of the Royal Society when he was its President from 1684 to 1686. Most of his leisure he now spent on his library. He intensified his search for books and prints, setting himself a target of 3,000 volumes. New and better copies replaced old ones; friends and agents were conscripted to help; his nephew and heir John Jackson was despatched on a tour of France, Italy and Spain with lists of wanted items, which were shipped at intervals by the trunkful to London. Pepys and his library clerk devised a great three-volumed catalogue; collated Pepysian copies with those in other collections; adorned volume upon volume with exquisite title pages written calligraphically by scribes; pasted prints into their guard-books; inserted indexes and lists of contents. The work was in sight of completion by the time that his health began to deteriorate seriously in 1700, with renewed attacks of the stone; only a handful of books remained to be bought to complete the scheme. In 1701 he moved to the Clapham house, and died there two years later, on 26 May 1703, his life's work done.

The library survives at Magdalene College, to which it was bequeathed under conditions that ensure that its contents remain intact and unaltered – still housed in the glazed bookcases that Pepys over the years had had made for them by dockyard joiners, and still arranged in the order in which he and his heir had left them. In the first of the bookcases, on the back row of the second shelf, are the volumes of the diary.

Pepys earned his place in history by his work for the navy. But perhaps these diary volumes and the library containing them are his most eloquent memorials. They speak, as no other relics can, of the man himself.

THE MANUSCRIPT AND ITS PUBLICATION

The original manuscript of the diary survives in the Pepys Library at Magdalene College, Cambridge, and consists of six leather-bound volumes neatly written in ink. The writing is in shorthand, with occasional words (mostly personal and place names) in longhand. The shorthand Pepys used was a system invented by Thomas Shelton, who published his first manual of instruction in 1626. The art of shorthand is an old one – the Greeks knew it – and although it did not become a widespread accomplishment until its use in business in the later nineteenth century, it was in demand in England from Elizabethan times onwards – among lawyers and their clerks, for instance, as a means of recording evidence and case-reports, and among the general public for a variety of purposes, but particularly (with the growth of Puritanism) as a method of taking notes of sermons. Pepys learned it as an undergraduate and used it throughout his life for his office work. In 1680 he used it to write down at the King's dictation the story of his escape after the battle of Worcester in 1651. Isaac Newton employed the same system.

Pepys wrote the diary from rough notes at irregular intervals, but always within a few days at most after the events to which it relates. He never revised it – an act of self-control rare among diarists – never even filling in the occasional blank left where he had momentarily forgotten a name. The symbols are clear, but not always easy to interpret because they may represent only the first syllable of a word. Usually all forms of certain common verbs (e.g. 'have', 'give') are represented by the initial letter: whether Pepys meant 'has' or 'hath', 'give' or 'gave', has to be determined from a consideration of his linguistic habits at the time. These can be determined from his longhand writings elsewhere – e.g. from his letters. Similarly his longhand words are often abbreviated and have to be filled out by a process of informed guesswork. From the context, for example, it is usually possible to tell whether 'Exch' stands for 'Exchequer' or 'Exchange', and whether 'WH' stands for 'Will Hewer' or 'Will Howe'. Occasionally in both the longhand and the shorthand the writing is obscure and two or more readings are possible. No transcription can claim to be absolutely accurate: all are reconstructions rather than copies.

The presence of the diary volumes in the Pepys Library was hardly noticed until the diary of his friend John Evelyn was published in 1818. The Master of Magdalene then arranged for a few pages to be transcribed by his uncle, the statesman Lord Grenville, who had learned a shorthand similar to the Shelton as a law student. With this to help him, an undergraduate of St John's College, John Smith, performed the gigantic task of transcribing the whole diary, except for certain passages he labelled 'objectionable'. A small selection from his fifty-four notebooks was published by Lord Braybrooke, the Master's brother, in 1825. It had an immediate and phenomenal success. But it was Braybrooke's third edition of 1848–9, published at about the same time as Macaulay's *History*, which established the diary's popularity with the Victorian reading public. Another transcription, by the Rev. Mynors Bright, a Fellow of Magdalene, was published (again in severely shortened form) in six volumes in 1875–9. It was reissued in ten volumes, with some revision and much better footnotes, by H. B. Wheatley in 1893–9. About nine-tenths of the diary was now made public: Wheatley deliberately omitted only the erotic passages, and those could hardly have been published in Victorian England without offence. It was from a broader point of view more regrettable that the text, as Wheatley printed it, had a host of remediable faults and that his commentary was thin and uneven.

The text used for this selection is that of the large edition published in 1970–7 by Bell in London and by the University of California Press in North America, and edited by the late Professor William Matthews and myself. This was the first edition in which the entire text was printed and a comprehensive commentary attempted.

EDITOR'S NOTES

1. The original diary has an entry for every day of the period it covers, except for eleven days in September–October 1668 which Pepys spent in East Anglia. In this edition a few entries are reproduced in full, but a large number have been omitted in whole or in part, with the result that, all told, this selection contains about one-twelfth of the original. In particular, most of Pepys's references to his official business in the Navy Office have been omitted since these would require fairly elaborate editorial explanation. At some points the text has been reduced by telescoping. Thus at 14 February 1667 the words here italicized are omitted: 'Thence away by coach with Sir H. Cholmly *and Fitzgerald and Creed, setting down the two latter at the New Exchange; and H. Cholmly and I* to the Temple and there walked in the dark in the walks, *talking of news*; and he surprizes me with the certain news that the King did last night in council declare his being in treaty with the Dutch'. Neither at this nor at any other point are marks of omission used. In general the aim has been to retain as much as possible of the variety of the original and to keep to a minimum the discontinuities that are created by compression.

2. Where Pepys's meaning is obscure in the original or has been made obscure by compression, the editor has inserted a word or phrase within square brackets.

3. To bridge gaps created by compression the editor has occasionally interpolated passages in his own words. These are printed in italics.

4. The spelling is as far as possible Pepys's own. The words that he wrote out completely in longhand are reproduced as he wrote them. If he abbreviated a word in longhand, it is extended in what we know (from the evidence of his usages in the diary and in his other writings) to have been his preferred spelling. (Like all seventeenth-century writers he was far from consistent. Ben Jonson said that it was a dull man who could spell a word only one way.) Similarly some of his shorthand words are printed as he would probably have spelt them, where we have enough information from his longhand usages. In other cases the shorthand itself, being phonetic, establishes the spelling – 'then' for 'than', 'themselfs' for 'themselves', 'fallow' for 'follow', etc. But in those cases where we have no phonetic guidance from the shorthand and no evidence from his longhand habits, shorthand words are spelt out in modern English style. To this there is no alternative, since there was no standard seventeenth-century orthography.

5. Most of the punctuation is editorial; Pepys used almost none, except for full stops (which he mostly represented by a triangle of dots) since the marks could often be confused with his shorthand symbols. Where he used full stops to mark off phrases rather than sentences – as he often did – they have usually been represented by dashes.

6. Capitalization follows modern usage. Pepys's ways with upper- and lower-case letters are random and seem to have no significance. He could use lower-case for the initial letter of a personal or place name; equally he could insert an upper-case letter into its middle. It would be confusing as well as pointless to follow his example in all cases.

7. The paragraphing is almost always editorial, since the reduction of the text has altered the design of Pepys's paragraphs.

8. The Index and Glossary, as well as providing a guide to the contents of the volume, carries short identifications of persons, books and plays, and definitions of words which may give difficulty. (The definitions do not cover all Pepys's usages). The reader should be warned that some words have changed their meaning – in Pepys's usage, for instance, 'presently' meant 'immediately', and 'amused' could mean 'bemused'.

9. The illustrations are chosen so that they may play as full a part as possible in setting the scene for the text. They are necessarily taken from a wider period than the ten years covered by the diary itself: with few exceptions the limits are those of Pepys's lifetime. Some contemporary Dutch and French pictures are included, wherever these do not give a misleading impression of English life.

· ·

The editor and publisher are grateful to Philippa Glanville of the Museum of London for her help with the illustrations and captions.

From Pepys's calligraphical collection.

1660

Pepys is a young man of 26, married since 1655 to Elizabeth St Michel. They have lived since 1658, when he was operated on for the stone (his 'old pain'), in Axe Yard, off King Street, Westminster, a little to the north of the present-day Downing Street. Their maid Jane Birch remains a friend throughout the diary. Pepys is a clerk in the Exchequer employed by George Downing (after whom Downing Street was later to be named), and also serves Edward Mountagu ('my Lord') as his man of business. Mountagu is shortly to become a general-at-sea and an important figure in the moves towards a restoration of the King.

The Rump Parliament (in control after the fall of Richard Cromwell in April 1659) had been sent packing by the army officers under Major-General Lambert in October, but, as Lambert's support melts away, has just reassembled on Boxing Day. Lawson, in command of the fleet and stationed in the Thames, has declared for parliament, and Monck, at the head of the army in Scotland, who has made no secret for some months of his support of the civil authority, is about to march to London. He crosses the border on New Year's Day, to be greeted by declarations from all parts of the country in favour of a 'free Parliament'. Lambert's army, in Northumberland, offers no resistance. In early February, backed by the civic authorities of London, Monck insists that the Rump shall admit the moderate members excluded in 1648, and that it shall arrange for free elections. Everyone knows that this will mean the return of the King.

Blessed be God, at the end of the last year I was in very good health, without any sense of my old pain but upon taking of cold. I lived in Axe Yard, having my wife and servant Jane, and no more in family then us three. My wife, after the absence of her terms for seven weeks, gave me hopes of her being with child, but on the last day of the year she hath them again. The condition of the state was thus. Viz. the Rump, after being disturbed by my Lord Lambert, was lately returned to sit again. The officers of the army all forced to yield. Lawson lie[s] still in the river and Monke is with his army in Scotland. Only my Lord Lambert is not yet come in to the Parliament; nor is it expected that he will, without being forced to it. The new Common Council of the City doth speak very high; and hath sent to Monke their sword-bearer, to acquaint him with their desires for a free and full Parliament, which is at present the desires and the hopes and expectation of all: My own private condition very handsome; and esteemed rich, but endeed very poor, besides my goods of my house and my office, which at present is somewhat uncertain. Mr Downing master of my office.

1 January. This morning (we lying lately in the garret) I rose, put on my suit with great skirts, having not lately worn any other clothes but them. Went to Mr Gunnings church at Exeter House, where he made a very good sermon. Dined at home in the garret, where my wife dressed the remains of a turkey, and in the doing of it she burned her hand.

The opening pages of the diary. Pepys writes in Shelton's system of shorthand, with occasional words in longhand. The double year date (1659/60) was used between 1 January and 25 March (Old New Year's Day) until the reform of the calendar in 1752.

. . . .

5 January. [I] wrote a letter to my Lord, and told him the news that the Parliament hath this night voted that the members that was discharged from setting in the years 1648 and 49 was duly discharged, and that there should be writs issued presently for the calling of others in their places. And that Monke and Fairfax were commanded up to town, and that lodgings were to be provided for Monke at Whitehall.

14 January. Nothing to do at our office. Went to the coffee-house and heard exceeding good argument against Mr Harrington's assertion that overbalance of propriety was the foundation of government.

15 January. Having been exceedingly disturbed in the night with the barking of a dog of one of our neighbours, that I could not sleep for an hour or two, I slept late; and then in the morning took physic, and so stayed within all day. At noon my brother John came to me, and I corrected as well as I could his Greek speech against the Apposition [*at St Paul's School*], though I believe he himself was as well able to do it as myself. After that, my wife and I in pleasant discourse till night that I went to supper, and after that to make an end of this week's notes in this book, and so to bed. It being a cold day and a great snow, my physic did not work so well as it should have done.

16 January. To the Greene Dragon on Lambeth Hill, both the Mr Pinknys, Smith, Harrison, Morrice that sang the bass, Sheply and I, and there we sang of all sorts of things and I ventured with good success upon things at first sight and after that played on my flagelette; and stayed there till 9 a'clock, very merry and drawn on with one song after another till it came to be so late. After that, Sheply, Harrison and myself, we went towards Westminster on foot, and at the Golden Lion, near Charing Cross, we went in and drank a pint of wine, and so parted; and thence home, where I found my wife and maid a-washing. I sat up till the bell-man came by with his bell, just under my window as I was writing of this very line, and cried, 'Past one of the clock, and a cold, frosty, windy morning.' I then went to bed and left my wife and the maid a-washing still.

18 January. All the world is now at a loss to think what Monke will do: the City saying that he will be for them, and the Parliament saying he will be for them.

25 January. I called at Paul's Churchyard, where I bought Buxtorfes Hebrew Grammar and read a declaration of the gentlemen of Northamptonshire which came out this afternoon. So [to] my Lady Wright to speak with her, but she was abroad; so Mr Evans, her butler, had me into his buttery and gave me sack and a lesson on his lute, on which he played very well. Hence I went to my Lord's and got most things ready against tomorrow, as fires and laying the cloth, and my wife was making of her tarts and larding of her pullets till 11 a'clock.

26 January. Home from my office to my Lord's lodgings, where my wife had got ready a very fine dinner: viz. a dish of marrow bones; a leg of mutton; a loin of veal; a dish of fowl; three pullets, and two dozen of larks, all in a dish; a great tart; a neat's tongue; a dish of anchoves; a dish of prawns, and cheese. My company was my father, my uncle Fenner, his two sons, Mr Pierce, and all their wifes, and my brother Tom. We were as merry as I could frame myself to be in that company.

29 January. I spent the afternoon in casting up of my accounts; and do find myself to be worth 40*l* and more, which I did not think, but am afraid that I have forgot something.

3 February. I and Joyce went walking all over Whitehall, whither Generall Monke was newly come and we saw all his forces march by in very good plight and stout officers.

7 February. Boys do now cry 'Kiss my Parliament!' instead of 'Kiss my arse!' so great and general a contempt is the Rump come to among all men, good and bad.

11 February. I walked in [Westminster] Hall, where I heard the news of a letter from Monke, who was now gone into the city again and did resolve to stand for the sudden filling up of the House; and it was very strange how the countenance of men in the Hall was all changed with joy in half an hour's time. Thence we took coach for the city to Guildhall, where the hall was full of people expecting Monke and Lord Mayor to come thither, and all very joyful. And endeed I saw many people give the soldiers drink and money, and all along in the streets cried, 'God bless them!' and extraordinary good words. In Cheapside there was a great many bonfires, and Bow bells and all the bells in all the churches as we went home were a-ringing. Hence we went homewards, it being about 10 a-clock. But the common joy that was everywhere to be seen! The number of bonfires, there being fourteen between St Dunstan's and Temple Bar. And at Strand Bridge I could at one view tell thirty-one fires. In King Streete, seven or eight, and all along burning and roasting and drinking for rumps – there being rumps tied upon sticks and carried up and down. The buchers at the Maypole in the Strand rang a peal with their knifes when they were going to sacrifice their rump. On Ludgate Hill there was one turning of the spit, that had a rump tied upon it, and another basting of it. Indeed, it was past imagination, both the greatness and the suddenness of it. At one end of the street, you would think there was a whole lane of fire, and so hot that we were fain to keep still on the further side merely for heat.

6 March. Shrove Tuesday. [My Lord] bade me look out now, at this turn, some good place; and he would use all his own and all the interest of his friends that he hath in England to do me good. And asked me whether I could without too much inconvenience go to sea as his Secretary, and bade me think of it. He also begin to talk of things of state, and told me that he should now want one in that capacity at sea that he might trust in.

. . . .

(*Below left*) Edward Mountagu, Pepys's patron ('My Lord'), soon to be made 1st Earl of Sandwich and Knight of the Garter; after Lely.
(*Below right*) James, Duke of York, Lord High Admiral, by Samuel Cooper 1661. Pepys became one of his most valued naval servants.

And therefore he would have me to go. Everybody now drink the King's health without any fear, whereas before it was very private that a man dare do it.

22 March. I went forth about my own business to buy a pair of riding gray serge stockings, a sword, and belt and shoes. And after that took Wotton and Brigden to the Popes Head tavern in Chancery Lane, where Gilb. Holland and Shelston was; and we dined and drank a great deal of wine, and they paid all. Strange how these people do now promise me anything; one a rapier, the other a vessel of wine or a gown, and offered me his silver hatband to [do] him a courtesy. I pray God keep me from being proud or too much lifted up hereby.

23 March. My Lord and the Captain in one [barge], and W. Howe and I and Mr Ibbott and Mr Burr in the other, to the Long Reach, where the *Swiftsure* lay at anchor (in our way we saw the great breach which the late high water had made, to the loss of many 1000*l* to the people about Limehouse). As soon as my Lord on board, the guns went off bravely from the ships; and a little while after comes the Vice-Admirall, Lawson, and seemed very respectful to my Lord, and so did the rest of the comanders of the frigates that were thereabouts. I to the cabbin allotted for me, which was the best that any had that belonged to my Lord. I got out some things out of my chests for writing, and to work presently, Mr Burr and I both. After that to bed in my cabin, which was but short; however, I made shift with it and slept very well; and the weather being good, I was not sick at all; yet I know not when I shall be.

26 March. This day it is two years since it pleased God that I was cut of the stone at Mrs Turner's in Salisbury Court. And did resolve while I live to keep it a festival, as I did the last year at my house, and for ever to have Mrs Turner and her company with me. But now it pleases God that I am where I am and so am prevented to do it openly; only, within my soul I can and do rejoice and bless God, being at this time, blessed be His holy name, in as good health as ever I was in my life.

27 March. Early in the morning at making a fair new establishment of the fleet to send to the Council. This morning the wind came about and we fell into the Hope, and in our passing by the Vice-Admirall, he and the rest of the frigates with him did give us abundance of guns and we them, so much that the report of them broke all my windows in my cabbin and broke off the iron bar that was upon it to keep anybody from creeping in at the scuttle.

On 2 April Mountagu shifts his flag from the Swiftsure *to the* Naseby, *and on the 5th the fleet begins to fall down the river. On the 9th it anchors in the Downs, and lies there during the parliamentary elections which Monck and the City have forced the Rump to arrange. The new Parliament meets on 25 April and on the morning of 1 May receives messages from the King at Breda; in the afternoon the two Houses pass identical resolutions for the restoration of the monarchy. The King's letters from Breda are read to the fleet on 3 May, and it sets sail for Holland to bring him home on the 11th.*

7 April. This day, about 9 a'clock in the morning, the wind grew high; and we being among the sands, lay at anchor. I begin to be dizzy and squeamish. After dinner and all the afternoon I walked upon the deck to keep myself from being sick; and at last, about 5 a'clock, went to bed and got a caudle made me, and sleep upon it very well.

8 April. Lords Day. We had a brave wind all the afternoon. And overtook two good merchantmen that overtook us yesterday, going to the East Indys, and the Lieutenant and I lay out of his window with his glass, looking at the women that were on board them, being pretty handsome.

14 April. What with the goodness of the bed and the rocking of the ship, I slept till almost 10 a'clock – with Mr Sheply, which occasioned my thinking upon the happy life that I live now, had I nothing to care for but myself.

23 April. In the evening, the first time that we have had any sport among the seamen; and indeed, there was extraordinary good sport after my Lord had done playing at ninepins. After that, W. Howe and I went to play two trebles in the great cabbin below; which my Lord hearing, after supper he called for our instruments and played a set of Lock's, two trebles and a bass. And that being done, he fell to singing of a song made upon the Rump, with which he pleased himself well – to the tune of 'The Blacksmith'.

3 May. This morning my Lord showed me the King's declaration and his letter to be communicated to the fleet. The commanders all came on board, and the council set in the coach (the first council of war that hath been in my time), where I read the letter and declaration; and while they were discoursing upon it, I seemed to draw up a vote; which being offered, they passed. Not one man seemed to say no to it, though I am confident many in their hearts were against it. After this was done, I went up to the quarterdeck with my Lord and the commanders, and there read both the papers and the vote; which done, and demanding their opinion, the seamen did all of them cry out 'God bless King Charles!' with the greatest joy imaginable. After dinner, to the rest of the ships (I stayed at the *Assistance* to hear the harper a good while) quite through the fleet. Which was a very brave sight, to visit all the ships and to be received with the respect and honour that I was on board them all. And much more to see the great joy that I brought to all men; not one through the whole fleet showing the least dislike of the business. In the evening, as I was going on board the Vice-Admirall, the Generall begun to fire his guns, which he did all that he had in the ship; and so did all the rest of the commanders, which was very gallant, and to hear the bullets go hissing over our heads as we were in the boat.

12 May. My Lord did give order for weighing anchor; which we did, and sailed all day. In our way in the morning, coming in the midway between Dover and Callis, we could see both places very easily, and very pleasant it was to me, but the farther we went the more we lost sight of both lands.

14 May. In the morning, when I waked and rose, I saw myself out of the scuttle close by the shore, which afterwards I was told to be the Duch shore. The Hague was clearly to be seen by us. Some masty Duchmen came on board to proffer their boats to carry things from us on shore &c., to get money by us. Before noon, some gentlemen came on board from the shore to kiss my Lords hands. And by and by Mr North and Dr Clerke went to kiss the Queen of Bohemia's hands from my Lord, with a dozen of attendants from on board to wait on them; among which I sent my boy – who, like myself, is with child to see any strange thing. Mr Creed and I went in the fore-part of a coach, wherein there was two very pretty ladies, very fashionable and with black paches, who very merrily sang all the way and that very well. And were very free to kiss the two blades that were with them. I took out my flagelette and piped. The Hague is a most neat place in all respects. The houses so neat in all places and things as is possible. Here we walked up and down a great while, the town being now very full of Englishmen. We walked up and down the town and Court to see the place; and by the help of a stranger, an Englishman, we saw a great many places and were made to understand many things, as the intention of the maypoles which we saw there standing at every great man's door, of different greatness according to the quality of the person.

18 May. [Delft] is a most sweet town, with bridges and a river in every street. Observing that in every house of entertainment there hangs in every room a poor man's box and desirous to know the reason thereof, it was told me that it is their custom to confirm all bargains by putting something into the poor people's box, and that that binds as fast as anything. We saw likewise the Guesthouse, where it was very pleasant to see what neat preparation there is for the poor. We saw one poor man a-dying there. Back by water, where a pretty sober Duch lass sat reading all the way, and I could not fasten any discourse upon her.

19 May. [At Lausdune] I met my old chamberfellow Mr Ch. Anderson and a friend of his (both physicians), Mr Wright, who took me to a Duch house where there was an exceeding pretty lass and right for the sport; but it being Saturday, we could not have much of her company; but however, I stayed with them till 12 at night; by that time Charles was almost drunk; and then broke up, he resolving to go thither again (after he had seen me at my lodging) and lie with the girl, which he told me he had done in the morning. Going to my lodging, we met with the bell-man, who strikes upon a clapper, which I took in my hand and it is just like the clapper that our boys fright the birds away from the corn with in summer time in England. To bed.

23 May. The King, with the two Dukes [his brothers, the Dukes of York and Gloucester], the Queen of Bohemia [his aunt, Elizabeth, Dowager Queen], Princesse Royalle, and Prince of Orange [his sister Mary and her son, later William III of England], came on board; where I in their coming in kissed the Kings, Queen and Princesses hands, having done the other before. Infinite shooting off of the guns, and that in a disorder on purpose, which was better then if it had been otherwise. Dined in a great deal of state, the royall company by themselves in the coach, which was a blessed sight to see. We weighed ancre, and with a fresh gale and most happy weather we set sail for

England – all the afternoon the King walking here and there, up and down (quite contrary to what I thought him to have been), very active and stirring. Upon the quarterdeck he fell in discourse of his escape from Worcester. Where it made me ready to weep to hear the stories that he told of his difficulties that he had passed through. As his travelling four days and three nights on foot, every step up to his knees in dirt, with nothing but a green coat and a pair of country breeches on and a pair of country shoes, that made him so sore all over his feet that he could scarce stir.

25 May. By the morning we were come close to the land and everybody made ready to get on shore. The King and the two Dukes did eat their breakfast before they went, and there being set some shipps diet before them, only to show them the manner of the shipps diet, they eat of nothing else but pease and pork and boiled beef. I spoke with the Duke of York about business, who called me Pepys by name, and upon my desire did promise me his future favour. I went, and Mr Mansell and one of the King's footmen, with a dog that the King loved (which shit in the boat, which made us laugh and me think that a King and all that belong to him are but just as others are) went in a boat by ourselfs; and so got on shore when the King did, who was received by Generall Monke with all imaginable love and respect at his entrance upon the land at Dover. Infinite the croud of people and the gallantry of the horsemen, citizens, and noblemen of all sorts. The Mayor of the town came and gave him his white staffe, the badge of his place, which the King did give him again. The Mayor also presented him from the town a very rich Bible, which he took and said it was the thing that he loved above all things in the world.

1 June. Mr Cooke brought us word that the Parliament had ordered the 29 of May, the King's birthday, to be for ever kept as a day of thanksgiving for our redemption from tyranny and the King's return to his government, he entering London that day.

2 June. My Lord told me that he hoped to do me a more lasting kindness, if all things stand as they are now between him and the King – but says 'We must have a little patience and we will rise together. In the meantime I will do you all the good jobbs I can.' Which was great content for me to hear from my Lord.

22 June. To bed, the first time since my coming from sea, in my own house, for which God be praised.

Mountagu is now appointed to the Privy Council, raised to the peerage as Earl of Sandwich, and given court office (with a house) as Master of the King's Wardrobe. For Pepys he obtains a post in the civil administration of the Navy. During the Interregnum its administration had been in the hands of commissioners; now the traditional Navy Board, dating back to Henry VIII's time, is restored, staffed by the 'Principal Officers of the Navy' – the Treasurer (Sir George Carteret), the Comptroller (Sir Robert Slingsby, soon replaced on his death by Sir John Mennes), the Surveyor of the Ships (Sir William Batten), and the Clerk of the Acts (Pepys). To these, two new-style commissioners are added – Sir William Penn and Peter Pett. Pepys now has a house in Seething Lane in the city in the block of buildings that houses the office and some of the staff. It happens that

Thomas Barlow, who had been appointed Clerk for life before the Civil War, is still alive. He is persuaded to surrender his claims in return for an annuity.

29 June. Up and to Whitehall, where I got my warrant from the Duke to be Clerk of the Acts. Also, I got my Lord's warrant from the Secretary for his Honour of Earle of [Sandwich] and Vicount Mountagu of Hinchingbrooke. I was told by Mr Huchinson at the Admiralty that Mr Barlow my predecessor, Clerk of the Acts, is yet alive and coming up to town to look after his place – which made my heart sad a little. At night told my Lord thereof and he bade me to get possession of my patent; and he would do all that could be done to keep him out.

1 July. This morning came home my fine camlott cloak with gold buttons – and a silk suit; which cost me much money and I pray God to make me be able to pay for it. I went to the cook's and got a good joint of meat, and my wife and I dined at home alone. So to see for Mr Creed, to speak about getting a copy of Barlow's patent.

. . . .

Palace of Whitehall, *c.* 1694. The Banqueting House is in the centre with the Horse Guards to its right and the Privy Garden on the left. The buildings were used both as official lodgings and as government offices. Across St James's Park, and close by the recently constructed ornamental water, lies Arlington House (occupying roughly the site of the modern Buckingham Palace), and (to the right), St James's Palace.

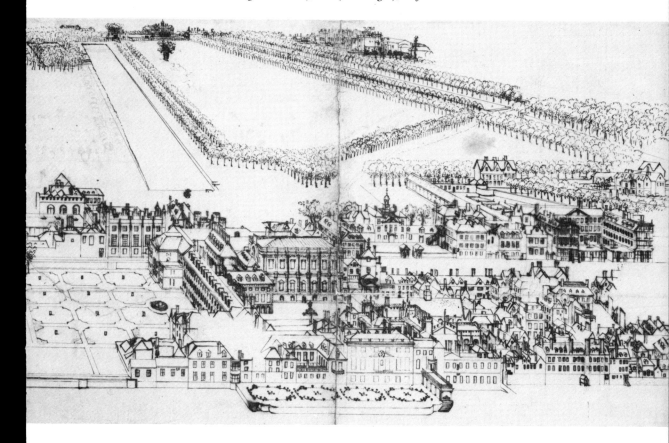

3 July. In the afternoon my heart was quite pulled down by being told that Mr Barlow was to enquire today for Mr Coventry. But at night I met with my Lord, who told me that I need not fear, for he would get me the place against the world. And when I came to W. Howe, he told me that Dr Petty hath been with my Lord and did tell him that Barlow was a sickly man and did not entend to execute the place himself; which put me in great comfort again.

8 July. Lords Day. To Whitehall to chapel, where I got in with ease by going before the Lord Chancellor with Mr Kipps. Here I heard very good musique, the first time that I remember ever to have heard the organs and singing-men in surplices in my life.

13 July. Up early, the first day that I put on my black camlott coat with silver buttons. To Mr Spong, whom I found in his nightgown writing of my patent; and so carried it to Mr Beale for a dockett. But he was very angry, and unwilling to do it, because he said it was ill-writ (because I had got it writ by another hand and not by him); but by much importunity I got Mr Spong to go to his office and make an end of my patent, and in the meantime Mr Beale to be preparing my dockett; which being done, I did give him two pieces, after which it was strange how civil and tractable he was to me. From thence I went to the Navy Office, where we despatched much business and resolved of the houses for the Officers and Commissioners, which I was glad of, and I got leave to have a door made me into the leads.

17 July. There came to my house before I went out, Mr Barlow, an old consumptive man and fair-conditioned – with whom I did discourse a great while; and after much talk, I did grant him what he asked – viz., *50l* per annum if my salary be not encreased and 100*l* per annum in case it be to 350*l*; at which he was very well pleased to be paid as I received my money, and not otherwise.

31 July. To Whitehall, where my Lord and the Principal Officers met and had great discourse about raising of money for the Navy; which is in very sad condition, and money must be raised for it.

10 August. Never since I was a man in the world was I ever so great a stranger to public affairs as now I am, having not read a newsbook or anything like it, or enquired after any news, or what the Parliament doth or in any wise how things go. Many people look after my house in Axe Yard to hire it of me, so that I am troubled with them; and I have a mind to get the money to buy goods for my house at the Navy Office.

. . . .

(*Opposite*) 'With a fresh gale and most happy weather we set sail for England.' (23 May 1660.) Charles II sails from Scheveningen, attributed to J. Lingelbach (detail). (*Overleaf*) The King's procession from the Tower to Whitehall (detail). 'My Lord Monke rode bare after the King, and led in his hand a spare horse, as being Maister of the Horse. The King, in a most rich imbroidered suit and cloak, looked most nobly.' (22 April 1661.)

16 August. This morning my Lord (all things being ready) carried me by coach to Mr Crews, in the way talking how good he did hope my place would be to me and, in general, speaking that it was not the salary of any place that did make a man rich, but the opportunities of getting money while he is in the place.

18 August. To the Cockepitt play, the first that I have had time to see since my coming from sea, *The Loyall Subject*, where one Kinaston, a boy, acted the Dukes sister but made the loveliest lady that ever I saw in my life – only, her voice not very good. After the play done, we three went to drink, and by Captain Ferre[r]s means, Mr Kinaston and another that acted Archas the Generall came to us and drank with us. Thence home by coach; and after being trimmed, leaving my wife to look after her little bich, which was just now a-whelping, I to bed.

4 September. To Axeyard to my house; where standing at the door, Mrs Diana comes by, whom I took into my house upstairs and there did dally with her a great while, and find that in Latin *nulla puella negat*. So home by water; and there sat up late, putting my papers in order and my money also, and teaching my wife her musique lesson, in which I take great pleasure. So to bed.

11 September. At Sir W. Battens with Sir W. Pen we drank our morning draught, and from thence for an houre in the office and despatch a little business. Dined at Sir W. Battens; and by this time I see that we are like to have a very good correspondency and neighbourhood, but chargeable. All the afternoon at home looking over my carpenters. At night I called Tho. Hater out of the office to my house to sit and talk with me. After he was gone I caused the girle to wash the wainscote of our parler, which she did very well; which caused my wife and I good sport. Up to my chamber to read a little, and write my diary for three or four days past.

22 September. [Llewellyn and I] walked to Fleetstreete, where at Mr Standings in Salsbury Court we drank our morning draught and had a pickled herring. Among other discourse here, he told me how the pretty woman that I always loved at the beginning of Cheapeside that sells children's coates was served by the Lady Bennett (a famous strumpet), who by counterfeiting to fall into a swoune upon the sight of her in her shop, became acquainted with her and at last got her ends of her to lie with a gallant that had hired her to procure this poor soul for him.

25 September. To the office, where Sir W. Batten, Collonell Slingsby, and I sat a while; and Sir R. Ford coming to us about some business, we talked together of the interest of this kingdom to have a peace with Spain and a war with France and Holland – where Sir R. Ford talked like a man of great reason and experience. And afterwards did send for a cupp of tee (a China drink) of which I never had drank before) and went away.

(*Opposite*) Lady Castlemaine, studio of Lely. 'But strange it is, how for her beauty I ... pity her ... though I know well enough she is a whore.' (16 July 1662.)

28 September. All the afternoon at home among my workmen; work till 10 or 11 at night; and did give them drink and were very merry with them – it being my luck to meet with a sort of drolling workmen upon all occasions. To bed.

29 September. All day at home to make an end of our dirty work of the playsterers; and indeed, my kitchin is now so handsome that I did not repent of all the trouble that I have been put to to have it done.

13 October. I went out to Charing Cross to see Major-Generall Harrison hanged, drawn, and quartered – which was done there – he looking as cheerfully as any man could do in that condition. He was presently cut down and his head and his heart shown to the people, at which there was great shouts of joy. It is said that he said that he was sure to come shortly at the right hand of Christ to judge them that now have judged him. And that his wife doth expect his coming again. Thus it was my chance to see the King beheaded at Whitehall and to see the first blood shed in revenge for the blood of the King at Charing Cross.

20 October. This morning one came to me to advise with me where to make me a window into my cellar in lieu of one that Sir W. Batten had stopped up; and going down my cellar to look, I put my foot into a great heap of turds, by which I find that Mr Turners house of office is full and comes into my cellar, which doth trouble me; but I will have it helped. To my Lord's where I dined. He was very merry and did talk very high how he would have a French cooke and a Master of his Horse, and his lady and child to wear black paches; which methought was strange, but he is become a perfect courtier; and among other things, my Lady saying that she would have a good merchant for her daughter Jem, he answered that he would rather see her with a pedlar's pack at her back, so she married a gentleman rather then that she should marry a citizen.

29 October. I up earely, it being my Lord Mayors Day (Sir Rich. Browne); and neglecting my office, I went to the Wardrobe, where I met my Lady Sandwich and all the children. Where after drinking of some strang and incomparable good clarett of Mr Rumballs, he and Mr Townsend did take us and set the young Lords at one Mr Nevills, a draper in Pauls Churchyard; and my Lady and my Lady Pickering and I to one Mr Isackson's, a linendraper at the Key in Cheapside – where there was a company of fine ladies and we were very civilly treated and had a very good place to see the pageants; which were many and I believe good for such kind of things, but in themselfs but poor and absurd.

1 November. This morning Sir W. Pen and I were mounted early. And have very merry discourse all the way [to Walthamstow], he being very good company. We came to Sir Wm. Battens, where he lives like a prince and we were made very welcome. Among other things, he showed us a chaire which he calls King Harrys chair, where he that sits down is catched with two irons that come round about him, which makes good sport. Here dined with us two or three more country gentlemen; among the rest, Mr Christmas my old schoolfellow, with whom I had much talk. He did remember that I was a great Roundhead when I was a boy, and I was much afeared that he would have remembered the words that I said the day that the King was beheaded (that were I to preach upon him, my text should be: 'The memory of the wicked shall rot'); but I found afterward that he did go away from schoole before that time. He did make us good sport in imitating Mr Case, Ash, and Nye, the ministers – which he did very well. But a deadly drinker he is, and grown exceeding fat.

2 November. To my Lord's, where he was come and I supt with him, he being very merry, telling merry stories of the country mayors how they entertained the King all the way as he came along, and how the country gentlewomen did hold up their heads to be kissed by the King, not taking his hand to kiss as they should do.

11 November. Lords Day. To church into our new gallery (the first time that ever it was used and it not being yet quite finished); there came after us Sir W. Pen, Mr Davis, and his eldest son. There being no women this day, we sat in the foremost pew and behind us our servants; but I hope it will not be always so, it not being handsome for our servants to sit so equal with us. This day also did Mr Mills begin to read all the Common Prayer, which I was glad of.

13 November. Home to dinner. Where I find my wife making of pyes and tarts to try her oven with (which she hath never yet done); but not knowing the nature of it, did heat it too hot and so did a little overbake her things, but knows how to do better another time.

20 November. Mr Sheply and I to the new playhouse near Lincolnes Inn Fields (which was formerly Gibbons's tennis court), where the play of *Beggers' Bush* was newly begun. And so we went in and saw it. It was well acted (and here I saw the first time one Moone, who is said to be the best actor in the world, lately come over with the King); and endeed it is the finest playhouse, I believe, that ever was in England. And so home, where I found the house in a washing pickle; and my wife in a very joyful condition when I told her that she is to see the Queene next Thursday. Which puts me in mind to say that this morning I found my Lord in bed late, he having been with the King, Queene, and Princesse at the Cockpitt all night, where Generall Monke treated them; and after supper, a play – where the King did put a great affront upon Singleton's musique, he bidding them stop and bade the French musique play – which my Lord says doth much outdo all ours.

22 November. Mr Fox did take my wife and I to the Queenes Presence Chamber. Where he got my wife placed behind the Queenes chaire and I got into the crowd, and by and by the Queen and the two Princesses came to dinner. The Queen, a very little plain old woman, and nothing more in her presence in any respect, nor garbe, then any ordinary woman. The Princess of Orange I have often seen before. The Princess Henriettee is very pretty, but much below my expectation – and her dressing of herself with her haire frized short up to her eares did make her seem so much the less to me. But my wife, with two or three black paches on and well dressed, did seem to me much handsomer than she.

1661

At the end of the last and the beginning of this year I do live in one of the houses belonging to the Navy Office as one of the Principall Officers – and have done now about half a year. After much trouble with workmen, I am now almost settled – my family being, myself, my wife, Jane, Will Ewre, and Wayneman, my girl's brother. Myself in a constant good health – and in a most handsome and thriving condition. Blessed be Almighty God for it. I am now taking of my sister Paulina to come and live with me. As to things of state – the King settled and loved of all. The Duke of Yorke lately matched to my Lord Chancellor's daughter, which doth not please many. The Queene upon her return to France, with the Princess Henrietta. The Princesse of Orange lately dead, and we into new mourning for her. The Parliament, which hath done all this great good to the King, beginning to grow factious, the King did dissolve it December 29 last – and another likely to be chosen speedily. I take myself now to be worth 300*l* clear in money. And all my goods and all manner of debts paid, which are none at all.

3 January. To the Theatre, where was acted *Beggars Bush* – it being very well done; and here the first time that ever I saw women come upon the stage.

6 January. Lords Day and Twelfeday. My wife and I to church this morning; and so home to dinner to a boiled leg of mutton – all alone. To church again; where before sermon, a long psalm was set that lasted an hour while the sexton gathered his year's contribucion through the whole church.

17 January. We went through Ham Creeke to the *Soverayne* (a goodly sight – all the way to see the brave ships that lie here) first, which is a most noble ship I never saw before. My Lady Sandwich, my Lady Jemimah, Mrs Browne, Mrs Grace, and Mary and the page, my lady's servants, and myself, all went into the lanthorne together. From thence to the *Charles*, where my Lady took great pleasure to see all the rooms and to hear me tell her how things are when my Lord is there. After we had seen all, then the officers of the ship have prepared a handsome breakfast for her; and while she was pledging my Lord's health, they gave her five guns. That done, we went off; and then they gave us thirteen guns more. I confess it was a great pleasure to myself to see the ship that I begun my good fortune in.

28 January. To the Theatre, where I saw again *The Lost Lady*, which doth now please me better then before. And here, I sitting behind in a dark place, a lady spat backward upon me by a mistake, not seeing me. But after seeing her to be a very pretty lady, I was not troubled at it at all.

8 February. To the Exchange. Here I met with many sea-commanders; and among others, Captain Cuttle, and Curtis and Mootham; and I went to the Fleece tavern to drink and there we spent till 4 a-clock telling stories of Algier and the manner of the life of slaves there; and truly, Captain Mootham and Mr Dawes (who have been both slaves there) did make me full acquainted with their condition there. As, how they eat nothing but bread and water. At their redempcion, they pay so much for the water that they drink at the public fountaynes during their being slaves. How they are beat upon the soles of the feet and bellies at the liberty of their padron. How they are all at night called into their master's bagnard, and there they lie. How the poorest men do use their slaves best. How some rogues do live well, if they do endent to bring their masters in so much a week by their industry or theft and then they are put to no other work at all. And theft there is counted no great crime at all.

17 February. Lords Day. A most tedious, unseasonable, and impertinent sermon by an Irish Doctor. His text was 'Scatter them, O Lord, that delight in warr'. Sir Wm. Batten and I very much angry with the parson.

19 February. To my Lord's and found him dined; and so I lost my dinner. But I stayed and played with him and Mr Childe &c. some things of four partes; and so it raining hard and bitter cold (the first winter day we have yet had this winter), I took coach home and spent the evening in reading of a Latin play, the *Naufragium joculare*. And so to bed.

18 March. To bed with my head and mind full of business, which doth a little put me out of order. And I do find myself to become more and more thoughtful about getting of money than ever heretofore.

6 April. Met with Mr Townsend, who told of his mistake the other day to put his legs through one of his knees of his breeches, and went so all day.

Pepys spends 8–10 April at Chatham inspecting the dockyard with his colleague Sir William Batten.

8–9 April. To the Hill House at Chatham. Here we supped very merry and late to bed; Sir Wm., telling me that old Edgeborow, his predecessor, did die and walk in my chamber, did make me somewhat afeared but not so much as for mirth sake I did seem. So to bed in the Treasurer's chamber and lay and sleep well – till 3 in the morning, and then waking; and by the light of the moon I saw my pillow (which overnight I flung from me) stand upright, but not bethinking myself what it might be, I was a little afeared. But sleep overcame all, and so lay till high morning – at which time I had a caudle brought me and a good fire made. And in generall, it was a great pleasure all the time I stayed here, to see how I am respected and honoured by all people; and I find that I begin to know now how to receive so much reverence, which at the beginning I could not tell how to do.

10 April. So to Captain Allens (where we was last night and heard him play of the harpsicon; and I find him to be a perfect good musician); and there, having no mind to leave Mrs Rebecca, I did, what with talk and singing (her father and I), Mrs Turner and I stayed there till 2 a'clock in the morning and was most exceeding merry; and I had the opportunity of kissing Mrs Reb. very often. Among other things, Captain Pett was saying that he thought that he had got his wife with childe since I came thither. Which I tooke hold of and was merrily asking him what he would take to have it said for my honour that it was of my getting? He merrily answered that he would, if I would promise to be godfather to it if it did come within the time just; and I said that I would. So that I must remember to compute it when the time comes.

13 April. To Whitehall to the Banquet House and there saw the King heale, the first time that ever I saw him do it – which he did with great gravity; and it seemed to me to be an ugly office and a simple one.

22 April. King's going from the Tower to Whitehall. Up earely and made myself as fine as I could, and put on my velvet coat, the first day that I put it on though made half a year ago: and being ready, Sir W. Batten, my Lady, and his two daughters and his son and wife, and Sir W. Penn and his son and I went to Mr Young's the flagg-maker in Cornhill; and there we had a good room to ourselfs, with wine and good cake, and saw the shew very well – in which it is impossible to relate the glory of that this day, expressed in the clothes of them that rid, and their horses and horse cloths. Among others, my Lord Sandwich. Imbroidery and diamonds were ordinary among them. The Knights of the Bath was a brave sight of itself. Remarquable was the two men that represent the two Dukes of Normandy and Aquitane. The Bishops came next after the Barons, which is the higher place; which makes me think that the next parliament they will be called to the House of Lords. My Lord Monke rode bare after the King, and led in his hand a spare horse, as being Maister of the Horse. The King, in a most rich imbroidered suit and cloak, looked most nobly. Wadlow, the vintner at the Devil in Fleetstreet, did lead a fine company of souldiers, all young comely men, in white doublets. There fallowed the Vice-Chamberlin, Sir G. Carteret, a company of men all like Turkes; but I know not yet what they are for. The streets all gravelled; and the houses, hung with carpets before them, made brave show, and the ladies out of the windows. One of which, over against us, I took much notice of and spoke of her, which made good sport among us. So glorious was the show with gold and silver, that we were not able to look at it – our eyes at last being so much overcome with it. Both the King and the Duke of Yorke took notice of us as he saw us at the window.

23 April. Coronacion Day. I lay with Mr Sheply, and about 4 in the morning I rose. And got to the Abby, where I fallowed Sir J. Denham the surveyor with some company that he was leading in. And with much ado, by the favour of Mr Cooper his man, did get up into a great scaffold across the north end of the Abby – where with a great deal of patience I sat from past 4 till 11 before the King came in. And a pleasure it was to see the Abbey raised in the middle, all covered with red and a throne (that is a chaire) and footstoole on the top of it. And all the officers of all kinds, so much as the very fidlers, in red vests. At last comes in the Deane and Prebends of Westminster with the Bishops (many of them in cloth-of-

30

(*Left*) 'I . . . saw the King heale, the first time that ever I saw him do it – which he did with great gravity.' (13 April 1661.) Charles II revived the ceremony of touching for the King's Evil (scrofula, a glandular disease); the ceremony went out of use under the Hanoverians. (*Right*) 'A pleasure it was to see the Abbey raised in the middle, all covered with red and a throne (that is a chaire) and footstoole on the top of it.' (23 April 1661.) The Crowning and Enthronement of Charles II, from J. Ogilby's *The Entertainment of . . . Charles II* 1662.

. . . .

gold copes); and after them the nobility all in their parliament robes, which was a most magnificent sight. Then the Duke and the King with a scepter (carried by my Lord of Sandwich) and sword and mond before him, and the crowne too. The King in his robes, bareheaded, which was very fine. And after all had placed themselfs, there was a sermon and the service. And then in the quire at the high altar he passed all the ceremonies of the coronacion – which, to my very great grief, I and most in the Abbey could not see. The crowne being put upon his head, a great shout begun. And he came forth to the throne and there passed more ceremonies: as, taking the oath and having things read to him by the Bishopp, and his lords (who put on their capps as soon as the King put on his crowne) and Bishopps came and kneeled before him. And three times the King at Armes went to the three open places on the scaffold and proclaimed that if any one could show any reason why Ch. Steward should not be King of England, that now he should come and speak. And a generall pardon also was read by the Lord Chancellor; and meddalls flung up and down by my Lord Cornwallis – of silver, but I could not come by any. But so great a noise, that I could make but little of the musique; and endeed, it was lost to everybody. But I had so great a list to pisse, that I went out a little while before the King had done all his ceremonies and went round the Abby to Westminister Hall, all the way within rayles, and ten thousand people, with the ground covered with blue cloth – and scaffolds all the way. Into the hall I got, where it was very fine with hangings and scaffolds, one upon another, full of brave ladies. And my wife in one little one on the right hand. Here I stayed walking up and down; and at last, upon one of the sidestalls, I stood and saw the King come in with all the persons (but the souldiers) that were yesterday in the cavalcade; and a most pleasant sight it was to see them in their several robes. And the King came in with his crowne on and his sceptre in his hand – under a canopy borne up by six silver staves, carried by Barons of the Cinqueports – and little bells at every end. And after a long time he got up to the farther end, and all set themselfs down at their several tables – and that was also a rare sight. And the King's first course carried up by the Knights of the Bath. And many fine ceremonies there was of the Heralds leading up people before him and bowing; and my Lord of Albimarles going to the kitchin and eat a bit of the first dish that was to go to the King's table. But above all was these three Lords, Northumberland and Suffolke and the Duke of Ormond, coming before the courses on horseback, and staying so all dinner-time; and at last, to bring up (Dymock) the King's Champion, all in armor on horseback, with his speare and targett carried before him. And a herald proclaim that if any dare deny Ch. Steward to be lawful King of England, here was a Champion that would fight with him; and with those words the Champion flings down his gantlet; and all this he doth three times in his going up toward the King's table. At last, when he is come, the King drinkes to him and then sends him the cup, which is of gold; and he drinks it off and then rides back again with the cup in his hand. I went from table to table to see the Bishops and all others at their dinner, and was infinite pleased with it. And at the Lords' table I met with Wll. Howe and he spoke to my Lord for me and he did give him four rabbits and a pullet; and so I got it, and Mr Creed and I got Mr Michell to give us some bread and so we at a stall eat it, as everybody else did what they could get. I took a great deal of pleasure to go up and down and look upon the ladies – and to hear the musique of all sorts; but above all, the twenty-four viollins. And strange it is, to think that these two days have held up fair till now that all is done and the King gone out of the Hall; and then it fell a-raining and thundering and lightening as I have not seen it do some years – which people did take great notice of God's blessing of the work of these two days – which is a foolery, to take too much notice of such things. Mr Hunt and I went in with Mr Thornbury (yeoman of the wine cellar to the King) to his house; and there, with his wife and two of his sisters and some gallant sparks that were there, we drank the King's health and nothing else, till one of the gentlemen fell down stark drunk and there lay speweing. And I went to my Lord's pretty well. But no sooner a-bed with Mr Sheply but my head begun to turne and I to vomitt, and if ever I was foxed it was now – which I cannot say yet, because I fell asleep and sleep till morning – only, when I waked I found myself wet

⌐ with joy everywhere.

he pleasure of the sight of these glorious things,
r objects, or for the future trouble myself to see
:ver to see the like again in this world.

my head in a sad taking through the last night's
. So rise and went out with Mr Creed to drink our
,ive me in chocolate to settle my stomach.

rse with Mr Ashmole, wherein he did assure me that
often fall from the sky ready-formed.

made myself fine and put six spoons and
W. Pen and I took coach and
:owe. And being come thither,
/ho is yet a mere boy) preach upon
turned,' &c: he reads all, and his
o dinner to Sir Wms; and then after

a walk ... n's, where Sir W. Pen and I were
godfathers and Mrs ... ers to her boy. And there, before and
after the christening, we were ... ove in her chamber; but whether we
carried ourselfs well or ill, I know not – ... as directed by young Mrs Batten. One
passage, of a lady that eate wafers with her dog, did a little displease me. I did give the
midwife 10s and the nurse 5s and the maid of the house 2: but for as much as I expected
to give the name of the childe, but did not, it being called John, I forbore then to give my
plate – till another time, after a little more advice.

5 June. It being very hot weather, I took my flagilette and played upon the leads in the
garden, where Sir W. Penn came out in his shirt into his leads and there we stayed talking
and singing and drinking of great draughts of clarret and eating botargo and bread and
butter till 12 at night, it being moonshine. And so to bed – very near fuddled.

28 June. Sir W. Penn in his coach and I, we went to Moorefields and there walked; and
stood and saw the wrestling, which I never saw so much of before – between the North
and West countrymen.

*Pepys's Uncle Robert, his father's brother, who lived at Brampton, near Huntingdon, now dies,
leaving no children. He bequeathes a life-interest in his house and land to Pepys's father, after whose
death Pepys is to inherit the house and a half-interest in the estate. Legal disputes follow over the claims
of Robert's brother Thomas, and other matters, but the house is to prove a valuable country home for
Pepys's family. Pepys pays several visits to it and in 1663 settles his parents and sister there.*

6 July. Waked this morning with news, brought me by a messenger on purpose, that my
Uncle Robert is dead – and died yesterday. So I rose – sorry in some respect; glad in my

expectations in another respect. So I made myself ready. Went and told my Uncle Wight, my Lady, and some others thereof. And bought me a pair of boots in St Martins and got myself ready; and then to the post-house and set out about 11 or 12 a-clock, taking the messenger with me that came to me; and so we rode and got well by 9 a-clock to Brampton, where I find my father well. My uncles corps in a coffin, standing upon joynt-stools in the chimny in the hall; but it begun to smell, and so I caused it to be set forth in the yard all night and wached by two men. My aunt I find in bedd in a most nasty ugly pickle, made me sick to see it. My father and I lay together tonight, I greedy to see the will but did not aske to see it till tomorrow.

7 July. Lords Day. In the morning my father and I walked in the garden and read the will; where though he gives me nothing at present till my father's death, or at least very little, yet I am glad to see that he hath done so well for us all – and well to the rest of his kindred.

26 July. Having the beginning of this week made a vowe to myself to drink no wine this week (finding it to unfit me to look after business), and this day breaking of it against my will, I am much troubled for it – but I hope God will forgive me.

29 September. Lords Day. At dinner and supper, I drank, I know not how, of my owne accord, so much wine, that I was even almost foxed and my head aked all night. So home, and to bed without prayers, which I never did yet since I came to the house of a Sonday night: I being now so out of order that I durst not read prayers, for fear of being perceived by my servants in what case I was. So to bed.

28 October. I to the Theatre and there saw *Argalus and Parthenia*; where a woman acted Parthenia and came afterward on the stage in man's clothes, and had the best legs that ever I saw; and I was very well pleased with it.

3 November. Lords Day. At night my wife and I had a good supper, of a pullet hashed; which pleased me much to see my condition come to allow ourselfs a dish like that.

29 November. To Whitehall to the Duke, who met us in his closett; and there he did desire of us to know what hath been the common practice about making of forrayne ships to strike sail to us: which they did all do as much as they could, but I could say nothing to it, which I was sorry for; so endeed, I was forced to study a lie; and so after we were gone from the Duke, I told Mr Coventry that I had heard Mr Selden often say that he could prove that in Henry the 7ths time he did give commission to his captains to make the King of Denmark's ships to strike to him in the Baltique.

30 December. I at the Miter, whither I had invited all my old acquaintance of the Exchequer to a good chine of beefe – which, with three barrels of oysters and three pullets and plenty of wine and mirth, was our dinner. There was about twelve of us. And here I made them a foolish promise to give them one this day twelvemonth, and so for ever while I live. But I do not entend it.

31 December. After supper and my barber had trimmed me, I sat down to end my journall for this year; and my condition at this time, by God's blessing, is thus: My health (only upon ketching cold, which brings great pain in my back and making of water, as it use to be when I had the stone) very good, and so my wife's in all respects. My servants, W. Hewer, Sarah, Nell, and Waynman. My house at the Navy Office. I suppose myself to be worth about 500*l* clear in the world, and my goods of my house my owne, and what is coming to me from Brampton when my father dies – which God defere. But by my uncles death, the whole care and trouble of all and settling of all lies upon me; which is very great because of lawsuits. My chiefest thoughts is now to get a good wife for Tom – there being one offered by the Joyces, a cousin of theirs, worth 200*l* in ready money. I am also upon writing a little treatise to present to the Duke, about our privilege in the seas as to other nations striking their flags to us. But my greatest trouble is that I have for this last half-year been a very great spendthrift in all manner of respects, that I am afeared to cast up my accounts, though I hope I am worth what I say above. But I will cast them up very shortly. I have newly taken a solemne oath about abstaining from plays and wine, which I am resolved to keep according to the letter of the oath, which I keepe by me.

Early in the year a marriage had been arranged between Charles II and a Portuguese infanta, Catherine of Braganza. She brought a dowry consisting not only of money but also of two colonies – Bombay and Tangier. With the latter Pepys is soon to be involved, as Treasurer of the committee which supervised its government. Meantime Sandwich has sailed to Tangier to take possession in the King's name, and is now waiting in Tangier roads to go to Lisbon to bring home the new Queen. Another fleet is about to carry English troops to Portugal to help in the War of Independence against Spain.

The fleete hath been ready to sail for Portugall, but hath lack[ed] wind, this fortnight. And by that means my Lord is forced to keep at sea all this winter till he brings home the Queen – which is the expectacion of all now – and the greatest matter of public talk.

. . . .

Charles II coronation mug.

1662

1 January. Waking this morning out of my sleep on a sudden, I did with my elbow hit my wife a great blow over her face and nose, which waked her with pain – at which I was sorry. And to sleep again.

6 January. Twelfe Day. To dinner to Sir Wm. Pens (it being a solemn feast day with him, his wedding day; and we have, besides a good chine of beef and other good cheer, eighteen mince pies in a dish, the number of the years that he hath been married); where Sir W. Batten and his Lady and daughter was, and Collonell Treswell and Major Holmes, who I perceive would fain get to be free and friends with my wife; but I shall prevent it.

16 January. Captain Stokes told us that notwithstanding the country of Gambo is so unhealthy, yet the people of that place live very long, so as the present King there is 150 years old, which they count by raynes because every year it rains continually four months together. He also told us that the kings there have above a hundred wifes apiece, and offered him the choice of any of his wifes to lie with, and so he did Captain Holmes.

31 January. I did by night set many things in order, which pleased me well and puts me upon a resolution of keeping within doors and minding my business and the business of the office – which I pray God I may put in practice.

8 February. All the morning in the sellar with the colliers, removing the coles out of the old coal-hole into the new one, which cost me 8s. the doing; but now the cellar is done and made clean, it doth please me exceedingly, as much as anything that was ever yet done to my house. I pray God keep me from setting my mind too much upon it. About 3 a-clock, the colliers having done, I went up to dinner (my wife having often urged me to come, but my mind is so set upon these things that I cannot but be with the workmen to see things done to my mind; which if I am not there is seldom done); and so to the office.

15 February. With the two Sir Wms. to the Trinity House; and after dinner I was sworne a Younger Brother, Sir W. Rider being Deputy-Maister for my Lord Sandwich; and after I was sworn, all the Elder Brothers shake me by the hand; it is their custome it seems.

23 February. This day, by God's mercy I am twenty-nine years of age, and in very good health and like to live and get an estate; and if I have a heart to be contented, I think I may reckon myself as happy a man as any is in the world – for which God be praised. So to prayers and to bed.

Elizabeth Pepys, engraving by Thomson 1828; the original portrait (by J. Hayls) has
disappeared. Elizabeth is represented as St Catherine, with a wheel and martyr's palm
– a mode of portraiture made fashionable by Queen Catherine.

28 February. Earely with Sir W. Pen by coach to Whitehall, to the Duke of Yorkes chamber; and there I presented him from my Lord a fine map of Tanger, done by one Captain Beckman, a Swede that is with my Lord. We stayed looking it over a great while with the Duke after he was ready.

1 March. My wife and I by coach to the Opera and there saw *Romeo and Julett,* the first time it was ever acted. But it is the play of itself the worst that ever I heard in my life, and the worst acted that ever I saw these people do; and I am resolved to go no more to see the first time of acting, for they were all of them out more or less.

2 March. Lords Day. With my mind much eased, talking long in bed with my wife about our frugall life for the time to come, proposing to her what I could and would do if I were worth 2000*l*; that is, be a knight and keep my coach – which pleased her. To church in the morning; none in the pew but myself. So home to dinner. And after dinner came Sir Wm. [Penn] and talked with me till church-time; and then to church, where at our going out I was at a loss by [his] putting me upon it whether to take my wife or Mrs Martha [Batten] (who alone was there); and I begun to take my wife, but he jogged me and so I took Martha and led her down before him and my wife.

3 March. I set to make some strict rules for my future practice in my expenses, which I did bind myself in the presence of God by oath to observe, upon penaltys therein set down. And I do not doubt but hereafter to give a good account of my time and to grow rich – for I do find a great deal more of content in those few days that I do spend well about my business then in all the pleasures of a whole week.

5 March. To the pewterers to buy a poore's box to put my forfeites in, upon breach of my late vowes.

23 March. Lords Day. This morning was brought me my boyes fine livery, which is very handsome, and I do think to keep to black and gold lace upon gray, being the colour of my armes, for ever. To church in the morning. And so home with Sir W. Batten and there eat some boiled great oysters; and so home, and while I was at dinner with my wife, I was sick and was forced to vomitt up my oysters again, and then I was well.

26 March. Up earely – this being, by God's great blessing, the fourth solemne day of my cutting for the stone this day four year. And am by God's mercy in very good health, and like to do well, the Lord's name be praised for it. To the office and Sir G. Carterets all the morning, about business. At noon came my good guest[s] Madam Turner, The[ophila] and Cosen Norton, and a gentleman, one Mr Lewin of the King's Lifeguard. I had a pretty dinner for them – viz.: a brace of stewed carps, six roasted chicken, and a jowle of salmon hot, for the first course; a tanzy and two neats' tongues and cheese the second. And were very merry all the afternoon, talking and singing and piping on the flagelette. In the evening they went with great pleasure away; and I with great content, and my wife, walked half an houre in the garden; and so home to supper and to bed.

11 April. To Greenwich by water; and there, while something is dressing for our dinner, Sir Wm and I walked into the Parke, where the King hath planted trees and made steps in the Hill up to the Castle, which is very magnificent. So up and down the house, which is now repayring in the Queenes lodgings. So to dinner at the Globe, and Captain Lambert of the Dukes pleasure boat came to us and dined with us – and were merry. And I in the evening to the Exchange and spoke with Uncle Wight; and so home and walked with my wife on the leads late; and so the barber came to me; and so to bed very weary, which I seldom am.

3 May. To dinner to my Lady Sandwich; and Sir Tho. Crewes children coming thither, I took them and all my Lady's to the Tower and showed them the lions and all that was to be shown, and so took them to my house and there made much of them; Sir Th. Crewes children being as pretty and the best behaved that ever I saw of their age.

4 May. Lords Day. Lay long, talking with my wife. Then up and Mr Holliard came to me and let me blood, about 16 ounces, I being exceedingly full of blood, and very good. I begun to be sick; but lying upon my back, I was presently well again and did give him 5s for his pains; and so we parted. And I to my chamber to write down my journall.

7 May. Sir Tho. Crew and I talked together; and among other instances of the simple light discourse that sometimes is in the Parliament House, he told me how in the late business of chymny money, when all occupyers were to pay, it was questioned whether women were under that name to pay, and somebody rose and said that they were not occupiers, but occupied.

20 May. This being a very pleasant life that we now lead, and have long done; the Lord be blessed and make us thankful. But though I am much against too much spending, yet I do think it best to enjoy some degree of pleasure, now that we have health, money and opportunities, rather then to leave pleasures to old age or poverty, when we cannot have them so properly.

21 May. Walking into Whitehall garden, in the Privy Garden saw the finest smocks and linen petticoats of my Lady Castlemaynes, laced with rich lace at the bottomes, that ever I saw; and did me good to look upon them.

25 May. Lords Day. At the Triumph taverne some Portugall Ladys which are come to towne before the Queene. They are not handsome, and their farthingales a strange dress. Many ladies and persons of quality come to see them. I find nothing in them that is pleasing. And I see they have learnt to kiss and look freely up and downe already, and I do believe will soon forget the recluse practice of their own country. They complain much for lack of good water to drink.

3 June. At the office all the morning, and Mr Coventry brought his patent and took his place with us this morning. Upon our making a contract, I went, as I use to do, to draw

The Navy Office, Crutched Friars, 1714. Built to replace Pepys's Navy Office, which was destroyed by fire in 1673.

the heads thereof; but Sir W. Pen most basely told me that the Controller is [to] do it, and so begun to imploy Mr Turner about it, at which I was much vexed and begun to dispute; and what with the letter of the Dukes orders, and Mr Barlows letter, and the practice of our predecessors, which Sir G. Carteret knew best when he was Comptroller, it was ruled for me. What Sir J. Minnes will do when he comes I know not, but Sir W. Penn did it like a base raskall, and so I shall remember him while I live.

12 June. This morning I tried on my riding cloth suit with close knees, the first that ever I made, and I think they will be very convenient – if not too hot to wear any other open knees after them. At the office all the morning – where we have a full Board, viz., Sir G. Carteret, Sir John Mennes, Sir W. Batten, Mr Coventry, Sir W. Pen, Mr Pett and myself. Among many other businesses, I did get a vote signed by all concerning my issuing of warrants, which they did not smell the use I entend to make of it; but it is to plead for my clerks to have their right of giving out all warrants, in which I am not a little pleased. Thence to dinner, by Mr Gaudens invitation, to the Dolphin where a good dinner. But which is to myself a great wonder, that with ease I passed the whole dinner without drink[ing] a drop of wine.

18 June. [Pett] and I walked to Lillys the painter's; where we saw, among other rare thing[s], the Duchesse of Yorke her whole body, sitting in state in a chair in white sattin. And another of the King's that is not finished; most rare things. I did give the fellow something that showed them us, and promised to come some other time and he would show me my Lady Castlemaynes, which I could not then see, it being locked up. Thence to Wrights the painter's; but Lord, the difference that is between their two works.

19 June. At the office, preparing papers and things; and endeed, my head hath not been so full of business a great while and with so much pleasure, for I begin to see the pleasure of it. God give me health. So to bed.

Officers of the Navy Board. (*From left to right*) Sir George Carteret, Treasurer, by Lely; Sir John Mennes, Comptroller, after Van Dyck; (Sir) William Coventry, Commissioner, by Riley; Sir William Penn, Commissioner, by Lely.

21 June. I having from my wife and the maids complaints made of the boy, I called him up and with my whip did whip him till I was not able to stir, and yet I could not make him confess any of the lies that they tax him with. At last, not willing to let him go away a conqueror, I took him in task again and pulled off his frock to his shirt, and whipped him till he did confess that he did drink the whay, which he hath denied. And pulled a pinke, and above all, did lay the candlesticke upon the ground in his chamber, which he hath denied this quarter of this year. I confess it is one of the greatest wonders that ever I met with, that such a little boy as he could be able to suffer half so much as he did to maintain a lie. But I think I must be forced to put him away. So to bed, with my arme very weary.

25 June. I into Thames Street beyond the bridge and there enquired among the shops the price of tarr and oyle; and do find great content in it and hope to save the King money.

28 June. My mind is now in a wonderful condition of quiet and content, more than ever in all my life – since my minding the business of my office, which I have done most constantly; and I find it to be the very effect of my late oaths against wine and plays; which, if God please, I will keep constant in. For now my business is a delight to me and brings me great credit, and my purse encreases too.

30 June. Up betimes and to my office, where I find Griffens girl making it clean; but God forgive me, what a mind I have to her, but did not meddle with her. She being gone, I fell upon boring holes for me to see from my closet into the great office without going forth, wherein I please myself much.

3 July. Up by 4 a,clock and to my office till 8 o'clock, writing over two copys of our contract with Sir Wm. Rider &c. for 500 ton of hempe; which, because it is a secret, I have the trouble of writing over, as well as drawing. Then home to dress myself and so to

41

the office – where another fray between Sir Rich: Ford and myself about his yarne, wherein I find the Board to yield on my side.

4 July. Up by 5 a-clock; and after my journall put in order, to my office about my business, which I am resolved to fallow, for every day I see what ground I get by it. By and by comes Mr Cooper, mate of the *Royall Charles*, of whom I entend to learn mathematiques; and so begin with him today, he being a very able man. After an hour's being with him at arithmetique, my first attempt being to learn the multiplicacion table, Sir W. Warren did come to me about business and did begin to instruct me in the nature of firre, timber and deals, telling me the nature of every sort; and from that, we fall to discourse of Sir W. Batten's corruption and the people that he imploys, and from one discourse to another of that kind; I was much pleased with his company and so stayed talking with him all alone at my office till 4 in the afternoon, without eating or drinking all day; and then parted and I home to eat a bit, and so back again to my office.

7 July. My morning's work at the office was to put the new books of my office into order and writing on the backsides what books they be and transferring out of some old books some things into them.

8 July. At the office all the morning, and dined at home; and after dinner in all haste to make up my accounts with my Lord, which I did with some trouble, because I had some hopes to have made a profit to myself in this account, above what was due to me (which God forgive me in); but I could not.

9 July. Up by 4 a-clock and at my multiplication table hard, which is all the trouble I meet withal in my arithmetique. Dined at home, and so to the office again, my wife with me; and while I was for an hour making a hole behind my seat in my closet, to look into the office, she was talking to me about her going to Brampton. Then to my business till night; then Mr Cooper and I to our business, and then came Mr Mills the minister to see me – which he hath but rarely done to me, though every day almost to others of us; but he is a cunning fellow and knows where the good victualls is and the good drink, at Sir W. Batten. However, I used him civilly, though I love him as I do the rest of his coat.

11 July. To St James's and at Mr Coventrys chamber, which is very neat and fine, we had a pretty neat dinner; and after dinner fell to discourse of business and regulation and do think of many things that will put matters into better order. And upon the whole, my heart rejoices to see Mr Coventry so ingenious and able and studious to do good, and with much frankness and respect to Mr Pett and myself perticularly.

15 July. In the evening comes Cooper, and I took him by water, on purpose to tell me things belonging to ships, which was time well spent, and so home again.

16 July. This day I was told that my Lady Castlemayne (being quite fallen out with her husband) did yesterday go away from him with all her plate, jewells and other best things;

and is gone to Richmond to a brother of hers; which I am apt to think was a design to get out of town, that the King might come at her the better. But strange it is, how for her beauty I am willing to conster all this to the best and to pity her wherein it is to her hurt, though I know well enough she is a whore.

17 July. Find much business to lie upon my hand; and was late at the office, writing letters by candlelight, which is rare at this time of the year. But I do it with much content and joy, and then I do please me to see that I begin to have people direct themselfs to me in all businesses.

21 July. To Woolwich to the ropeyard; and there looked over the several sorts of hemp, and did fall upon my great survey of seeing the working and experiments of the strength and the charge in the dressing of every sort; and I do think have brought it to so great a certainty as I have done the King great service in it. And do purpose to get it ready against the Dukes coming to towne, to present to him. Thence to the dock, where we walked in Mr Sheldens garden, eating more fruit and drinking and eating figs, which were very good, and talking, while the *Royall James* was bringing towards the docke; and then we went out and saw the manner and trouble of dockeing such a ship; which yet they could not do, but only brought her head into the docke and so shored her up till next tide. But, good God, what a deal of company was there from both yards to help to do it, when half the company would have done it as well; but I see it is impossible for the King to have things done as cheap as other men.

31 July. I drank but two glasses of wine this day, and yet it makes my head ake all night, and indisposed me all the next day – of which I am glad.

1 August. At the office all the afternoon, till evening to my chamber; where, God forgive me, I was sorry to hear that Sir W. Pens maid Betty was gone away yesterday, for I was in hopes to have had a bout with her before she had gone, she being very pretty. I have also a mind to my own wench, but I dare not, for fear she should prove honest and refuse and then tell my wife.

8 August. Up by 4 a-clock in the morning and at 5 by water to Woolwich, there to see the manner of tarring; and all the morning looking to see the several proceedings in making of cordage and other things relating to that sort of works, much to my satisfaccion. At noon came Mr Coventree on purpose from Hampton Court to see the same. And dined with Mr Falconer; and after dinner, to several experiments of hempe. [Mr Coventry] told me the passage of a Frenchman through London Bridge; where when he saw the great fall, he begun to cross himself and say his prayers in the greatest fear in the world; and as soon as he was over, he swore 'Morbleu! c'est le plus grand plaisir du mond!' – being the most like a French humour in the world.

20 August. Up earely and to my office. And thence to my Lord Sandwich, who I find in bed and he sent for me in; and among other talk, doth tell me that he hath put me into commission with a great many great persons in the business of Tanger, which is a very great honour to me and may be of good concernment to me. By and by comes in Mr Coventry to us, who my Lord tells that he is also put into the commission, and that I am there; of which he said he was glad and did tell my Lord that I was endeed the life of this office, and much more to my commendation, beyond measure. So that on all hands, by God's blessing, I find myself a very rising man.

23 August. I offered 8*s* for a boat to attend me this afternoon and they would not, it being the day of the Queenes coming to town from Hampton Court. So we fairly walked it to Whitehall; and through my Lord's lodgings we got into Whitehall garden, and so the bowling greene and up to the top of the new banquetting house there over the Thames, which was a most pleasant place as any I could have got. And all the show consisted chiefly in the number of boats and barges – and two pageants, one of a King and another of a Queene, with her maydes of honour sitting at her feet very prettily. And they tell me the Queene is Sir Rich. Fords daughter. Anon came the King and Queene in a barge under a canopy, with ten thousand barges and boats I think, for we could see no water for them – nor discern the King nor Queen. And so they landed at Whitehall Bridge and the great guns on the other side went off. But that which pleased me best was that my Lady Castlemayne stood over against us upon a piece of Whitehall – where I glutted myself with looking on her. But methought it was strange to see her Lord and her upon the same place, walking up and down without taking notice one of another; only, at first entry, he put off his hat and she made him a very civil salute – but afterwards took no notice one of another. But both of them now and then would take their child, which the nurse held in her armes, and dandle it. One thing more; there happened a scaffold below to fall, and we feared some hurt but there was none; but she, of all the great ladies only, run down among the common rabble to see what hurt was done, and did take care of a child that received some little hurt; which methought was so noble. Anon there came one there, booted and spurred, that she talked long with. And by and by, she being in her haire, she put on his hat, which was but an ordinary one, to keep the wind off. But methought it became her mightily, as everything else do.

5 September. To Mr Bland's the merchant, by invitation, and among other pretty discourse, some was of Sir Jerom Bowes, Embassador from Queene Elizabeth to the Emperor of Russia – who, because some of the noblemen there would go up the stairs to the Emperor before him, he would not go up till the Emperor had ordered those two men to be dragged downstair, with their heads knocking upon every stair till they were killed. And when he was come up, they demanded his sword of him before he entered the room; he told them, if they would have his sword, they should have his boots too; and so caused his boots to be pulled off and his nightgown and nightcap and slippers to be sent for, and made the Emperor stay till he could go in his nightdress, since he might not go as a soldier.

25 September. This evening I sat a while at Sir W. Batten's with Sir J. Mennes &c., where he told us, among many other things, how in Portugall they scorn to make a seat for a house of office. But they do shit all in pots and so empty them in the river.

44

'Anon came the King and Queene in a barge under a canopy, with ten thousand barges and boats I think, for we could see no water for them – nor discern the King nor Queene.' (23 August 1662.) The Queen's Journey from Hampton Court to Whitehall. Alongside the royal procession are the barges of the city livery companies.

. . . .

29 September. Michaelmas Day.   To the King's Theatre, where we saw *Midsummer's Nights Dreame*, which I have never seen before, nor shall ever again, for it is the most insipid ridiculous play that ever I saw in my life. I saw, I confess, some good dancing and some handsome women, which was all my pleasure.

2 November.   Lay long with pleasure, talking with my wife – in whom I never had greater content, blessed by God, then now; she continuing with the same care and thrift and innocence (so long as I keep her from occasions of being otherwise) as ever she was in her life, and keeps house as well. Then to church; and there being a lazy preacher, I sleep out the sermon and so home. To my office, preparing things against tomorrow for the Duke; and so home and to bed, with some pain in making water, having taken cold this morning in staying too long barelegged to pare my cornes.

25 November.   Great talk among people how some of the fanatiques do say that the end of the world is at hand and that next Tuesday is to be the day – against which, whenever it shall be, good God fit us all.

31 December.   Mr Povy and I, to Whitehall, he carrying me thither on purpose to carry me into the Ball this night before the King. By and by comes the King and Queen, the Duke and Duchesse, and all the great ones; and after seating themselfs, the King takes out the Duchess of Yorke, and the Duke the Duchesse of Buckingham, the Duke of Monmouth my Lady Castlemayne, and so other lords other ladies; and they danced the bransle. After that, the King led a lady a single coranto; and then the rest of the lords, one after another, other ladies. Very noble it was, and great pleasure to see. Then to country dances; the King leading the first which he called for; which was says he, 'Cuckolds all a-row' – the old dance of England. The manner was, when the King dances, all the ladies in the room, and the Queen herself, stands up; and endeed he dances rarely and much better then the Duke of Yorke. Having stayed here as long as I thought fit, to my infinite content, it being the greatest pleasure I could wish now to see at Court.

1663

Pepys and his wife have just spent two nights at Sandwich's lodgings in Whitehall palace. They now return home.

6 January. Myself somewhat vexed at my wife's neglect in leaving of her scarfe, waistcoat, and nightdressings in the coach today that brought us from Westminster, though I confess she did give them to me to look after – yet it was her fault not to see that I did take them out of the coach. This night making an end wholly of Christmas, with a mind fully satisfyed with the great pleasures we have had by being abroad from home. And I do find my mind so apt to run its old wont of pleasures, that it is high time to betake myself to my late vows, which I will tomorrow, God willing, perfect and bind myself to, that so I may for a great while do my duty, as I have well begun, and encrease my good name and esteem in the world and get money, which sweetens all things and whereof I have much need.

7 January. Up pretty earely; that is, by 7 a'clock, it being not yet light before or then. So to my office all the morning, signing the Treasurers ledger, part of it where I have not put my hand. And then eat a mouthful of pie at home to stay my stomach; and so with Mr Waith by water to Deptford and there, among other things, viewed old paybooks and find that the comanders did never heretofore receive any pay for the rigging-time but only for sea-time, contrary to what Sir J. Minnes and Sir W. Batten told the Duke the other day. I also searched all the ships in the wett docke for fire and found all in good order – it being very dangerous for the King that so many of his ships lie together there. I was among the canvas in stores also with Mr Harris the saylmaker, and learnt the difference between one sort and another to my great content. And so by water home again.

8 January. Dined at home; and there being the famous new play acted the first time today, which is call[ed] *The Adventures of Five Houres*, at the Duke's House, being they say made or translated by Collonell Tuke, I did long to see it and so made my wife to get her ready, though we were forced to send for a smith to break open her trunke, her maid Jane being gone forth with the keyes. And so we went; and though earely, were forced to sit almost out of sight at the end of one of the lower formes, so full was the house. And the play, in one word, is the best, for the variety and the most excellent continuance of the plot to the very end, that ever I saw or think ever shall. And all possible, not only to be done in that time, but in most other respects very admittible and without one word of ribaldry. And the house, by its frequent plaudites, did show their sufficient approbacion.

9 January. Waking in the morning, my wife begun to speak of the necessity of her keeping somebody to bear her company; for her familiarity with her servants is it that spoils them all, and other company she hath none (which is too true); and called for Jane to reach her out of her trunk, giving her the keys to that purpose, a bundle of papers; and pulls out a paper, a copy of what, a pretty while since, she had writ in a discontent to me, which I would not read but burned. She now read it, and was so picquant, and wrote in English and most of it true, of the retirednesse of her life and how unpleasant it was, that being writ in English and so in danger of being met with and read by others, I was vexed at it and desired her and then commanded her to teare it – which she desired to be excused it; I forced it from her and tore it, and withal took her other bundle of papers from her and leapt out of the bed and in my shirt clapped them into the pockets of my breeches, that she might not get them from me; and having got on my stockings and breeches and gown, I pulled them out one by one and tore them all before her face, though it went against my heart to do it, she crying and desiring me not to do it.

13 January. My poor wife rose by 5 a'clock in the morning, before day, and went to market and bought fowle and many other things for dinner – with which I was highly pleased. Things being put in order and the cooke come, I went to the office, where we sat till noon; and then broke up and I home – whither by and by comes Dr Clerke and his lady, his sister and a she-cosen, and Mr Pierce and his wife, which was all my guest[s]. I had for them, after oysters – at first course, a hash of rabbits and lamb, and a rare chine of beef; next, a great dish of roasted fowl, cost me about 30s, and a tart; and then fruit and

. . . .

The Restoration housewife: recipes and domestic scenes from Hannah Wolley, a seventeenth-century Mrs Beeton.

cheese. My dinner was noble and enough. I had my house mighty clean and neat, my room below with a good fire in it – my dining room above, and my chamber being made a withdrawing chamber, and my wife's a good fire also. I find my new table very proper, and will hold nine or ten people well, but eight with great room. After dinner, the women to cards in my wife's chamber and the doctor [and] Mr Pierce in mine, because the dining room smokes unless I keep a good charcole fire, which I was not then provided with. At night to supper; had a good sack posset and cold meat and sent my guests away about 10 a-clock at night – both them and myself highly pleased with our management of this day. And endeed, their company was very fine and Mrs Clerke a very witty, fine lady, though a little conceited and proud. So weary to bed. I believe this day's feast will cost me near 5l.

4 February. To Paul's schoole and went up to see the head forms posed in Latin, Greek and Hebrew, but I think they do not answer in any so well as we did; only in geography they did pretty well. With Mr Elborough (he being all of my old acquaintance that I could meet with here) to a cookes shop to dinner, but I find him a fool as he ever was, or worse.

6 February. To my Lord Sandwich and there stayed, there being a committee to sit upon the contract for the molle [at Tangier], which I dare say none of us that were there understood; but yet they agreed of things as Mr Cholmly and Sir J. Lawson demanded, who are the undertakers; and so I left them to go on to agree, for I understood it not.

18 February. To my office, all the morning casting up with Captain Cocke their accounts of 500 tons of hemp brought from Riga, and bought by him and parteners upon account, wherein are many things worth my knowledge. So at noon to dinner, taking Mr Hater with me because of losing time; and in the afternoon he and I alone at the office, finishing our account of the extra charge of the Navy not properly belonging to the Navy since the King's coming in to Christmas last; and all extra things being abated, I find that the true charge of the Navy to that time hath been after the rate of 374,743l a year. I made an end by 11 a-clock at night, and so home to bed, almost weary.

21 February. Up and to the office, where Sir John Minnes (most of the rest being at the Parliament House); all the morning [an]swering petitions and other business.

What follows concerns an action brought against Pepys by Edward Field of Wapping for failing to act on information from Field (probably a professional informer) about an alleged case of embezzlement of government timber. Field was awarded £30 damages.

Towards noon there comes a man in, as if upon ordinary business, and shows me a writt from the Exchequer, and tells me that I am his prisoner – in Fields business. Which methought did strike me to the heart, to think that we could not sit safe in the middle of the King's business. I told him how and where we were imployed and bid him have a care; and perceiving that we were busy, he said he would and did withdraw for an houre – in which time Sir J. Minnes took coach and to Court to see what he could do from thence. I stayed in my closet, till by and by the man and four more of his fellows came to know what

I would do; I told them stay till I heard from the King or my Lord Chief Baron, to both whom I had now sent. With that they consulted and told me that if I would promise to stay in the house they would go and refresh themselfs, and come again and know what answer I had. So they away and I home to dinner. Before I had dined, the baylys came back again with the constable, and at the office knock for me but found me not there; and I hearing in what manner they were come, did forbear letting know where I was. So they stood knocking and enquiring for me. By and by at my parlour window comes Sir W. Batten's Mingo to tell me that his Maister and Lady would have me come to their house through Sir J. Mennes's lodgings, which I could not do; but however, by lathers did get over the pale between our yards and so to their house, where I find them (as they have reason) to be much concerned for me – my Lady especially. The fellows stayed in the yard swearing with one or two constables; and some time we locked them into the yard and by and by let them out again, and so keeped them all the afternoon, not letting them see me or know where I was. One time, I went up to the top of Sir W. Batten's house and out of one of their windows spoke to my wife out of one of ours – which methought, though I did it in mirth, yet I was sad to think what a sad thing it would be for me to be really in that condition. By and by comes Sir J. Mennes, who (like himself and all that he doth) tells us that he can do no good, but that my Lord Chancellor wonders that we did not cause the seamen to fall about their eares – which we wished we could have done without our being seen in it; and Captain Grove being there, he did give them some affront and would have got some seamen to have drubbed them, but he had not time nor did we think it fit to have it done, they having executed their commission. Well, at last they went away; and I by advice took occasion to go abroad, and walked through the street to show myself among the neighbours, that they might not think worse then the business is.

27 February. Up and to my office, whither several persons came to me about office business. About 11 a'clock Comissioner Pett and I walked to Chyrurgeons Hall (we being all invited thither and promised to dine there), where we were led into the Theatre; and by and by came the Reader, Dr Tearne, with the Maister and Company, in a very handsome manner; and all being settled, he begun his lecture, this being the second upon the kidnys, ureters, and yard, which was very fine; and his discourse being ended, we walked into the Hall; and there being great store of company we had a fine dinner and good learned company, many doctors of physique, and we used with extraordinary great respect. After dinner Dr Scarborough took some of his friends, and I went along with them, to see the body alone; which we did; he was a lusty fellow, a seaman that was hanged for a robbery. I did touch the dead body with my bare hand; it felt cold, but methought it was a very unpleasant sight.

3 April. Going out of Whitehall, I met Captain Grove, who did give me a letter directed to myself from himself; I discerned money to be in it and took it, knowing, as I found it to be, the proceed of the place I have got him, to have the taking up of vessells for Tanger. But I did not open it till I came home to my office; and there I broke it open, not looking into it till all the money was out, that I might say I saw no money in the paper if ever I should be questioned about it. There was a piece in gold and 4*l* in silver.

'Spent the morning till the barber came in reading in my chamber . . . and being by and by trimmed – to church.' (5 April 1663.) (*Left*) A contemporary French engraving. (*Right*) A barber's plate *c.* 1680.

. . . .

5 April. Lords Day. Up and spent the morning till the barber came in reading in my chamber part of Osborne's *Advice to his Son* (which I shall not never enough admire for sense and language); and being by and by trimmed – to church, myself, wife, Ashwell, &c.; and home to dinner, it raining. While that was prepared, to my office to read over my vowes, with great affection and to very good purpose. So to dinner, and very well pleased with it. Then to church again, where a simple bawling young Scott preached. So home to my office alone till dark, reading some part of my old *Navy precedents*, and so home to supper. And after some pleasant talk, my wife, Ashwell and I – to prayers and to bed.

7 April. To dinner, where I find my wife hath been with Ashwell at La Roches to have her tooth drawn, which it seems akes much. But my wife could not get her to be contented to have it drawn after the first twich, but would let it alone; and so they came home with it undone, which made my wife and me good sport. After dinner to the office, where Sir J. Mennes did make a great complaint to me alone, how my clerk Mr Hater had entered in one of the seabookes a ticket to have been signed by him before it had been examined; which makes the old foole mad almost, though there was upon enquiry the greatest reason in the world for it – which though it vexes me, yet it is most to see from day to day what a coxcomb he is, and that so great a trust should lie in the hands of such a foole.

17 April. Up by 5 a'clock, as I have long done, and to my office all the morning; at noon home to dinner with my father with us. Our dinner, it being Goodfriday, was only sugar sopps and fish; the only time that we have had a Lenten dinner all this Lent. This morning Mr Hunt the instrument-maker brought me home a basse viall to see whether I like it, which I do not very well; besides, I am under a doubt whether I had best buy one yet or no, because of spoiling my present mind and love to business.

'A little angry with my wife for minding nothing now but the dancing maister.'
(12 May 1663.) *The Dancing Master* 1652.

22 April. Up betimes and to my office; very busy all the morning there, entering things into my book manuscript, which pleases me very much. So to the Change and thence to my uncle Wights; whither my father, wife and Ashwell came – where we had but a poor dinner and not well dressed; besides, the very sight of my aunts hands and greasy manner of carving did almost turn my stomach. After dinner, by coach to the King's Playhouse, where we saw but part of *Witt without Mony* – which I do not much like; but coming late put me out of tune, and it costing me four half-crownes for myself and company.

29 April. W. Stankes [of Brampton] is come with my father's horses. But it is very pleasant to hear how he rails at the rumbling and ado that is in London over it is in the country, that he cannot endure it.

30 April. But Lord, what a stir Stankes makes with his being crowded in the streets and wearied in walking in London, and would not be woo'd by my wife and Ashwell to go to a play nor to Whitehall or to see the lyons, though he was carried in a coach. I never could have thought there had been upon earth a man so little curious in the world as he is.

12 May. A little angry with my wife for minding nothing now but the dancing maister [Pembleton], having him come twice a day, which is a folly.

15 May. I sat talking with [Sir T. Crew] all the afternoon, from one discourse to another. The most was upon the unhappy posture of things at this time; that the King doth mind nothing but pleasures and hates the very sight or thoughts of business. That my Lady Castlemayne rules him; who he says hath all the tricks of Aretin that are to be practised to give pleasure – in which he is too able, hav[ing] a large —. [*sic*]

Home – where I find it almost night and my wife and the dancing maister alone above, not dancing but walking. Now, so deadly full of jealousy I am, that my heart and head did so cast about and fret, that I could not do any business possibly, but went out to my office. I am ashamed to think what a course I did take by lying to see whether my wife did wear drawers today as she used to do, and other things to raise my suspicion of her; but I found no true cause of doing it.

16 May. To my office and there setting all the morning; and at noon dined at home. After dinner comes Pembleton again; and I being out of humour, would not see him, pretending business; but Lord, with what jealousy did I walk up and down my chamber, listening to hear whether they danced or no or what they did.

19 May. To the office till the evening; we sat and then by water (taking Pembleton with us) over the water to the Halfway House, where we played at ninepins; and there my damned jealousy took fire, he and my wife being of a side and I seeing of him taking her by the hand in play; though I now believe he did only in passing and sport.

24 May. Lords Day. To church, and over against our gallery I espied Pembleton and saw him leer upon my wife all the sermon, I taking no notice of him, and my wife upon him; and I observed she made a curtsey to him at coming out, without taking notice to me at all of it; which, with the consideration of her being desirous these two last Lords Days to go to church both forenoon and afternoon, doth really make me suspect something more then ordinary, though I am loath to think the worst. But I must have patience and get her into the country, or at least to make an end of her learning to dance as soon as I can.

26 May. Nothing could get the business out of my head, I fearing that this afternoon, by my wife's sending every[one] abroad and knowing that I must be at the office, she hath appointed [Pembleton] to come. This is my devilish jealousy; which I pray God may be false, but it makes a very hell in my mind; which the God of Heaven remove, or I shall be very unhappy. So to the office, where we sat a while. By and by, my mind being in great trouble, I went home to see how things were; and there I find as I doubted, Mr Pembleton with my wife and nobody else in the house, which made me almost mad. And Lord, how my jealousy wrought so far, that I went saftly up to see whether any of the beds were out of order or no, which I found not; but that did not content me, but I stayed all the evening walking, and though anon my wife came up to me and would have spoke of business to me, yet I construed it to be but impudence; and though my heart was full, yet I did say nothing, being in great doubt what to do. So at night suffered them to go all to bed, and late put myself to bed in great discontent, and so to sleep.

27 May. So I waked by 3 a-clock, my mind being troubled; and so took occasion by making water to wake my wife, and after having lain till past 4 a-clock, seemed going to rise, though I did it only to see what she would do; and so going out of the bed, she took hold of me and would know what ayled me; and after many kind and some cross words, I begun to tax her discretion in yesterday's business, but she quickly told me my owne, knowing well enough that it was my old disease of jealousy; which I disowned, but to no purpose. After an hour's discourse, sometimes high and sometimes kind, I find very good reason to think that her freedom with him was very great and more then was convenient, but with no evil intent.

29 May. To my brother [Tom's] to speak with him, and so home and in my way did take two turns forward and backward through the Fleete Ally to see a couple of pretty whores that stood off the doors there; and God forgive me, I could scarce stay myself from going into their houses with them, so apt is my nature to evil, after once, as I have these two days, set upon pleasure again.

30 May. To my brother's and there I find my aunt James, a poor, religious, well-meaning, good, humble soul, talking of nothing but God Almighty, and that with so much innocence that mightily pleased me. Here was a fellow that said Grace so long, like a prayer; I believe the fellow is a cunning fellow, and yet I by my brother's desire did give him a crowne, he being in great want and it seems a parson among the fanatiques and a cousin of my poor aunts – whose prayers, she told me, did do me good among the many good souls that did by my father's desires pray for me when I was cut of the stone, and which God did hear; which I also in complaisance did owne, but God forgive me, my mind was otherwise. I had a couple of lobsters and some wine for her.

31 May. Lords Day. My whole family lying longer this morning then was fit, and besides, Will having neglected to brush my cloak as he ought to do till I was ready to go to church, and not then till I bid him, I was very angry; and seeing him make little matter of it, but seeming to make a matter indifferent whether he did it or no, I did give him [a] box on the eare, and had it been another day had done more.

1 June. With Sir J. Mennes to the Strand Maypole and there I light out of his coach and walked to the new theatre, which, since the King's players are gone to the royall one, is this day begun to be imployed by the fencers to play prizes at. And here I came and saw the first prize I ever saw in my life; and it was between one Mathews, who did beat at all weapons, and one Westwicke, who was soundly cut several times both in the head and legs, that he was all over bloody. And other deadly blows they did give and take in very good earnest, till [Westwicke] was in a most sad pickle. They fought at eight weapons, three boutes at each weapon. It was very well worth seeing, because I did till this day think that it had only been a cheat; but this being upon a private quarrell, they did it in good earnest; and I felt one of their swords and find it to be very little, if at all, blunter on the edge then the common swords are. Strange to see what a deal of money is flung to them both upon the stage between every boute. But a woeful rude rabble there was and such noises, made my head ake all this evening. So, well pleased for once with this sight, I walked home.

6 June. Met by appointment Mr Deane in the Temple church; and he and I over to Mr Blackburys yard and thence to other places; and after that, to a drinking house; in all which places I did so practise and improve my measuring of timber, that I can now do it with great ease and perfection, which doth please me mightily. This fellow Deane is a conceited fellow and one that means the King a great deal of service; but however, I learn much of him and he is, I perceive, of great use to the King in his place, and so I shall give him all the encouragement I can.

29 June. [To Westminster Hall] and fell in talk with Mrs Lane and after great talk that she never went abroad with any man as she used heretofore to do, I with one word got her to go with me and to meet me at the further Rhenish wine-house – where I did give her a lobster and do so towse her and feel her all over, making her believe how fair and good a skin she had; and endeed, she hath a very white thigh and leg, but monstrous fat. When weary, I did give over, and somebody having seen some of our dalliance, called aloud in the street, 'Sir, why do you kiss the gentlewoman so?' and flung a stone at the window – which vexed me; but I believe they could not see my towsing her, and so we broke up and went out the back way, without being observed I think.

30 June. Thus, by God's blessing, end this book of two years. Being in all points in good health, and a good way to thrive and do well. Some money I do and can lay up, but not much; being worth now about 700*l*, besides goods of all sorts. In my office, my repute and understanding good, especially with the Duke and Mr Coventry. Only, the rest of the officers do rather envy then love me, I standing in most of their lights, especially Sir W. Batten, whose cheats I do daily oppose, to his great trouble, though he appears mighty kind and willing to keep friendship with mee, while Sir J. Mennes, like a dotard, is led by the nose by him. My wife and I (by my late jealousy, for which I am truly to be blamed) have not that fondness between us which we used and ought to have, and I fear will be lost hereafter if I do not take some course to oblige her and yet preserve my authority. Public matters are in an ill condition – parliament sitting and raising four subsidys for the King; which is but a little, considering his wants; and yet that parted withal with great hardness – they being offended to see so much money go, and no debts of the public paid, but all swallowed by a luxurious Court.

1 July. Mr Batten telling us of a late triall of Sir Charles Sydly the other day, before my Lord Chief Justice Foster and the whole Bench, for his debauchery a little while since at Oxford Kates; coming in open day into the balcone and showed his nakedness – acting all the postures of lust and buggery that could be imagined, and abusing of scripture and, as it were, from thence preaching a mountebanke sermon from that pulpitt, saying that there he hath to sell such a pouder as should make all the cunts in town run after him – a thousand people standing underneath to see and hear him. And that being done, he took a glass of wine and washed his prick in it and then drank it off; and then took another and drank the King's health. Upon this discourse, Sir J. Mennes and Mr Batten both say that buggery is now almost grown as common among our gallants as in Italy, and that the very pages of the town begin to complain of their masters for it. But blessed be God, I do not to this day know what is the meaning of this sin, nor which is the agent nor which the patient.

54

4 July. A pretty gentleman told us of one wipe the Queene a little while ago did give [Lady Castlemayne], when she came in and found the Queene under the dresser's hands and had been so long – 'I wonder your Majesty', says she, 'can have the patience to sit so long a∕dressing.' 'Oh', says the Queene, 'I have much reason to use patience, that I can very well bear with it.'

17 July. [At Deptford] I was saluted by Bagwell and his wife (the woman I have a kindness for) and they would have me into their little house; which I was willing enough to, and did salute his wife. They had got wine for me and I perceive live prettily; and I believe the woman a virtuous modest woman.

24 July. To Mr Blands, where Mr Povey, Gauden and I were invited to dinner. They have a kinswoman they call daughter in the house, a short, ugly, red∕haired slut that plays upon the virginalls and sings, but after such a country manner, I was weary of it, but yet could not but commend it.

Pepys and his friend Creed have ridden out to Epsom and put up in the village. Pepys had known the district as a boy on visits to Ashtead, where his relative John Pepys (once secretary to Chief Justice Coke) had lived. Who Mrs Hely was we do not know.

26 July. Lords Day. Up and to the Wells, where great store of citizens; which was the greatest part of the company, though there were some others of better quality. I met many that I knew; and we drunk each of us two pots and so walked away – it being very pleasant to see how everybody turns up his tail, here one and there another, in a bush, and the women in their quarters the like. Thence I walked Creede to Durdans and walked round it and within the courtyard and to the bowling green, where I have seen so much mirth in my time; but now no family in it (my Lord Barkely, whose it is, being with his family at London); and so up and down, with great pleasure viewing my old walks and where Mrs Hely and I did use to walk and talk, with whom I had the first sentiments of love and pleasure in woman's company, discourse and taking her by the hand – she being a pretty woman. But Lord, to see how many I met there of citizens that I could not have thought to have seen there, or that they had ever had it in their heads or purses to go down thither.

27 July. Up in the morning about 7 a∕clock. It being much a warmer day then yesterday, there was great store of gallant company, more then then to my greater pleasure. There was at a distance, under one of the trees on the common, a company got together that sung; I, at that distance, and so all the rest, being a quarter of a mile off, took them for the waytes; so I rid up to them and find them only voices – some citizens, met by chance, that sing four or five parts excellently. I have not been more pleased with a snapp of musique, considering the circumstances of the time and place, in all my life anything so pleasant. We drank each of us three cups; and so, after riding up to the horsemen upon the hill where they were making of matches to run, we went away and to Yowell, where we find our breakefast, the remains of our supper last night hasht. And by and by, after the smith had set on two new shoos to Creedes horse, we mounted; and with little discourse, I being intent upon getting home in time, we rode hard home. Only, I do find by my riding a little swelling to arise just by my anus. I had the same the last time I rode, and then it fell again; and now it is up again about the bigness of the bagg of a silke worme.

28 July. Up, after sleeping very well; and so to my office, setting down the journall of this last three days. And so settled to business again – I hope with greater chearefullnesse and successe by this refreshment.

31 July. Before I went to the office, I went to the coffee-house where Sir J. Cutler and Mr Grant came. And there Mr Grant showed me letters of Sir Wm. Pettys, wherein he says that his vessel which he hath built upon two keeles (a modell whereof, built for the King, he showed me) hath this month won a wager of 50*l* in sailing between Dublin and Holyhead with the pacquett boat, the best ship or vessel the King hath there; and he offers to lay with any vessel in the world.

4 August. I went to Jervas's and took him and his wife over the water to their mother Palmers (the woman that speaks in the belly), thinking, because I had heard that she is a woman of that sort, that I might there have light upon some lady of pleasure (for which God forgive me); but blessed be God, there was none nor anything that pleased me – but a poor little house which she hath set out as fine as she can. And for her singing which she pretends to, is only some old bawdy songs, and those sung abominably; only, she pretends to be able to sing both bass and treble; which she doth, something like but not like what I thought formerly and expected now. Nor doth her speaking in her belly take me now as it did then, but it may be that is because I know it and see her mouth when she speaks.

7 August. I walked to Deptford and there found Sir W. Penn; and I fell to measuring of some plank that was serving into the yard; which the people took notice of and the

. . . .

East Indiamen at Deptford, attributed to I. Sailmaker *c.* 1660. One of Pepys's concerns as Clerk of the Acts was to secure the efficiency of the Royal Dockyards. Deptford was a busy yard employing 238 workmen in 1663.

measurer himself was amuzed at, for I did it much more ready than he. And I believe Sir W. Penn would be glad I could have done less, or he more. By and by he went away, and I stayed walking up and down, discoursing with the officers of the yard of several things; and so walked back again, and on my way young Bagwell and his wife waylayd me to desire my favour about getting him a better ship; which I shall pretend to be willing to do for them, but my mind is to know his wife a little better.

10 August. Such a folly I am come to now, that whereas before my delight was in multitude of books and spending money in that and buying alway of other things, now that I am become a better husband and have left off buying, now my delight is in the neatness of everything, and so cannot be pleased with anything unless it be very neat; which is a strange folly. Hither came W. Howe about business; and he and I had a great deal of discourse about my Lord Sandwich, and I find by him that my Lord doth dote upon one of the daughters of Mrs [Becke] where he lies, so that he spends his time and money upon her. I do not wonder at it, [he] being a man amorous enough and now begins to allow himself the liberty that he sees everybody else at Court takes.

17 August. I met Mr Moore and he tells me with great sorrow of my Lord's being debauched, he fears, by this woman at Chelsy; which I am troubled at and resolve to speak to him of it if I can seasonably.

4 September. About 1 o'clock went to Povys; and by and by in comes he, and so we sat down to dinner, and his lady whom I never saw before (a handsome old woman that brought him money, that makes him do as he does); and so we had plenty of meat and drink (though I drunk no wine, though mightily urged to it) and in the exact manner that I never saw in my life anywhere – and he the most full and satisfied in it that man can be in this world with anything. After dinner down to see his new cellars which he hath made so fine, with so noble an arch and such contrivances for his barrels and bottles, and in a room

. . . .

(*Below left*) A ship-chandlery, Dutch etching *c.* 1635. The sailmakers use curved needles and grease to stitch the heavy canvas. (*Below right*) 'Ship's draught', from Sir Anthony Deane's manuscript *The Doctrine of Naval Architecture*, dedicated to Pepys.

next to it such a grotto and fountayne, which in summer will be so pleasant as nothing in the world can be almost. But to see how he himself doth pride himself too much in it, and commend and expect to have all admired, though indeed everything doth highly deserve it, is a little troublesome. Thence Creed and I away, and by his importunity away by coach to Bartholomew Fayre, where I had no mind to go without my wife; and therefore rode through the fair without lighting and away home, leaving him there. And at home made my wife get herself presently ready, and so carried her by coach to the fair and showed her the munkys dancing on the ropes; which was strange, but such dirty sport that I was not pleased with it. There was also a horse with hoofes like rams hornes, a goose with four feet, and a cock with three.

10 September. Up betimes and to my office. And then sat all the morning, making a great contract with Sir W. Warren for 3,000*l* worth of masts; but good God, to see what a man might do were I a knave – the whole business, from beginning to the end, being done by me out of the office, and signed to by them upon but once reading of it to them, without the least care or consultation either of quality, price, number or need of them, only in general that it was good to have a store. But I hope my pains was such as the King hath the best bargain of masts hath been bought these twenty-seven years in this office.

Pepys has travelled to Brampton to attend the manorial court in connection with a dispute about the property inherited from his Uncle Robert. With Thomas Pepys of London – another uncle – he now rides on to Wisbech to enquire about the will of a relative, John Day.

17 September. With much ado through the Fens, along dikes, where sometimes we were ready to have our horses sink to the belly, we got by night, with great deal of stir and hard riding, to Parsons Drove, a heathen place – where I found my uncle and aunt Perkins and their daughters, poor wretches, in a sad poor thatched cottage, like a poor barne or stable, peeling of hemp (in which I did give myself good content to see their manner of preparing hemp), and in a poor condition of habitt; took them to our miserable inne and there, after long stay and hearing of Franke their son, the miller, play upon his treble (as he calls it), with which he earnes part of his living, and singing of a country bawdy song, we set down to supper: the whole crew and Frankes wife and children (a sad company, of which I was ashamed) supped with us. By and by news is brought us that one of our horses is stole out of the stable; which proves my uncles, at which I was inwardly glad; I mean, that it was not mine. And at this we were at a great loss; and they doubting a person that lay at next door, a Londoner, some lawyer's clerk, we caused him to be secured in his bed and made care to be taken to seize the horse; and so, about 12 at night or more, to bed in a sad, cold, nasty chamber; only, the maid was indifferent handsome, and so I had a kiss or two of her, and I to bed. And a little after I was asleep, they waked me to tell me that the horse was found, which was good news; and so to sleep till the morning – but was bit cruelly (and nobody else of our company, which I wonder at) by the gnatts.

24 September. In the afternoon, telling my wife that I go to Deptford, I went by water to Westminster Hall; and there finding Mrs Lane, took her over to Lambeth where we were lately, and there did what I would with her but only the main thing, which she would not consent to, for which God be praised; and yet I came so near, that I was provoked to spend. But trust in the Lord I shall never do so again while I live.

27 September. Lords Day. At night to supper, though with little comfort, I finding myself, both head and breast, in great pain; and which troubles me most, my right eare is almost deaf. It is a cold, which God Almighty in justice did give me while I sat lewdly sporting with Mrs Lane the other day with the broken window in my neck. I went to bed with a posset, being very melancholy in consideration of the loss of my hearing.

2 October. At the Change met with Mr Cutler, and he and I to a coffee-house and there discoursed; and he doth assure me that there is great likelihood of a war with Holland – but I hope we shall be in good condition before it comes to break out.

6 October. Slept pretty well, and my wife waked to ring the bell to call up our maids to the washing about 4 a-clock and I was, and she, angry that our bell did not wake them sooner; but I will get a bigger bell. So we to sleep again till 8 a-clock. At noon, Lewellin coming to me, I took him and Deane, and there met my uncle Thomas and we dined together. But was vexed that it being washing day, we had no meat dressed; but sent to the cook's and my people had so little wit to send in our meat from abroad in the cook's dishes, which were marked with the name of the cooke upon them; by which, if they observed anything, they might know it was not my own dinner.

Finding myself beginning to be troubled with wind, as I used to be, and with pain in making water, I took a couple of pills that I had by me of Mr Hollyards.

7 October. They wrought in the morning and I did keep my bed; and my pain continued on me mightily, that I keeped within all day in great pain, and could break no wind nor have any stool after my physic had done working. So in the evening I took coach and to Mr Hollyards, but he was not at home; and so home again. And whether the coach did me good or no I know not, but having a good fire in my chamber, I begun to break six or seven small and great farts; and so to bed and lay in good ease all night, and pissed pretty well in the morning.

20 October. Up and to the office, where we sat; and at noon Sir G. Carteret, Sir J. Mennes and I to dinner to my Lord Mayors, being invited; where was the farmers of the customes, my Lord Chancellors three sons, and other great and much company, and a very great noble dinner, as this Mayor is good for nothing else. No extraordinary discourse of anything, every man being intent upon his dinner. Thence home and took my wife by coach to Whitehall; and she set down at my Lord's lodgings, I to a Committee of Tanger, and thence with her homeward; called at several places by the way – among others, at Paul's Churchyard; and while I was in Kirtons shop, a fellow came to offer kindness or force to my wife in the coach. But she refusing, he went away, after the coachman had struck him and he the coachman. So I being called, went thither; and the fellow coming out again of a shop, I did give him a good cuff or two on the chops; and seeing him not oppose me, I did give him another; at last, found him drunk, of which I was glad and so left him and home.

26 October. Creed and I to one or two periwegg shops about the Temple (having been very much displeased with one that we saw, a head of greazy and old woman's haire, at Jervas's in the morning); and there I think I shall fit myself of one very handsomely made.

29 October. Up, it being my Lord Mayors Day, Sir Anthony Bateman. This morning, in dressing myself and wanting a band, I found all my bands that were newly made clean, so ill-smoothed that I crumpled them and flung them all on the ground and was angry with Jane, which made the poor girl mighty sad, so that I were troubled for it afterwards. At noon I went forth, and by coach to Guildhall (by the way calling to shit at Mr Rawlinsons) and there was admitted; and meeting with Mr Proby (Sir R. Ford's son) and Lieutenant-Collonell Baron, a city commander, we went up and down to see the tables; where under every salt there was a bill of fare, and at the end of the table the persons proper for that table. Many were the tables, but none in the hall but the Mayors and the lords of the Privy Councell that had napkins or knives – which was very strange. We went into the buttry and there stayed and talked, and then into the hall again; and there wine was offered and they drunk, I only drinking some hypocras, which doth not break my vowe, it being, to the best of my present judgment, only a mixed compound drink, and not any wine – if I am mistaken, God forgive me; but I hope and do think I am not. By and by met with Creed; and we with the others went within the several courts and there saw the tables prepared for the ladies and judges and bishops – all great sign of a great dinner to come. By and by, about 1 a-clock, before the Lord Mayor came, came into the hall, from the room where they were first led into, the Lord Chancellor (Archbishopp before him), with the lords of the Council and other bishopps, and they to dinner. Anon comes the Lord Mayor, who went up to the lords and then to the other tables to bid wellcome; and so all to dinner. I set near Proby, Baron, and Creed at the Merchant Strangers table – where ten good dishes to a messe, with plenty of wine of all sorts, of which I drunk none; but it was very unpleasing that we had no napkins nor change of trenchers, and drunk out of earthen pitchers and wooden dishes. After I had dined, I and Creed rose and went up and down the house, and up to the ladies room and there stayed gazing upon them. But though there were many and fine, both young and old, yet I could not discern one handsome face there, which was very strange. I expected musique, but there was none; but only trumpets and drums, which displeased me. The dinner, it seems, is made by the Mayor and two Sheriffs for the time being, the Lord Mayor paying one half and they the other – and the whole, Proby says, is reckoned to come to about 7 or 800*l* at most. Being wearied with looking upon a company of ugly women, Creed and I went away; and took coach and through Cheapside and there saw the pageants, which were very silly.

31 October. To the office, where busy till night; and then to prepare my monthly account, about which I stayed till 10 or 11 a-clock at night; and to my great sorrow, find myself 43*l* worse then I was the last month; which was then 760*l* and now is but 717*l*. But it hath chiefly arisen from my layings-out in clothes for myself and wife – viz., for her, about 12*l*;

and for myself, 55*l* or thereabouts – having made myself a velvet cloak, two new cloth suits, black, plain both; a new shag gown, trimmed with gold buttons and twist; with a new hat and silk top[s] for my legs, and many other things. And also two periwigs, one whereof costs me 3*l* and the other 40*s*. I have wore neither yet, but will begin next week, God willing. So that I hope I shall not now need to lay out more money a great while, I having laid out in clothes for myself and wife, and for her closet and other things without, these two months (this and the last), besides household expenses of victuals &c., above 110*l*. But I hope I shall with more comfort labour to get more, and with better successe then when, for want of clothes, I was forced to sneak like a beggar.

3 November. By and by comes Chapman the periwig⸌maker, and [upon] my liking it, without more ado I went up and there he cut off my haire; which went a little to my heart at present to part with it, but it being over and my periwig on, I paid him 3*l* for it; and away went he with my own hair to make up another of; and I by and by, after I had caused all my maids to look upon it and they conclude it to become me, though Jane was mightily troubled for my parting with my own hair and so was Besse – I went abroad to the coffee⸌house; and coming back, went to Sir W. Penn and there sat with him and Captain Cocke till late at night, Cocke talking of some of the Roman history very well, he having a good memory. Sir W. Penn observed mightily and discoursed much upon my cutting off my hair, as he doth of everything that concerns me; but it is over, and so I perceive, after a day or two, it will be no great matter.

8 November. Lords Day. Up; and it being late, to church without my wife; and there I saw Pembleton come into the church and bring his wife with him, a good comely plain woman. And by and by my wife came after me all alone, which I was a little vexed at. I found that my coming in a perriwigg did not prove so strange to the world as I was afeared it would, for I thought that all the church would presently have cast their eye all upon me – but I found no such thing.

9 November. [Mr Blackburne] tells me that the King, by name, with all his dignities, is prayed for by them that they call fanatiques, as heartily and powerfully as in any of the other churches that are thought better. And that let the King think what he will, it is them that must help him in the day of warr – for, as they are the most, so generally they are the most substantiall sort of people, and the soberest. And did desire me to observe it to my Lord Sandwich, among other things, that of all the old army now, you cannot see a man begging about the street. But what? You shall have this captain turned a shoemaker; the lieutenant, a baker; this, a brewer; that, a haberdasher; this common soldier, a porter; and every man in his apron and frock, &c., as if they never had done anything else – whereas the [Cavaliers] go with their belts and swords, swearing and cursing and stealing – running into people's houses, by force oftentimes, to carry away something. And this is the difference between the temper of one and the other; and concludes (and I think with some reason) that the spirits of the old Parliament⸌soldier[s] are so quiet and contented with God's providences, that the King is safer from any evil meant him by them, a thousand times more then from his own discontented Cavalier[s].

Since the summer of this year Sandwich's affair with Betty Becke of Chelsea has given rise to scandal. His absence from court has been remarked on, and Pepys feels he must intervene.

18 November. This morning I sent Will with my great letter of reproof to my Lord Sandwich, who did give it into his own hand:–

My Lord,

    I do verily hope that neither the manner nor matter of this advice will be condemned by your Lordshipp, when for my defence in the first I shall allege my double attempt (since your return from Hinchingbrooke) of doing it personally, in both of which your Lordshipps occasions, no doubtfulness of mine prevented me. And that being now fearful of a sudden summons to Portsmouth for the discharge of some ships there, I judge it very unbecoming the duty which (every bit of bread I eat tells me) I owe to your Lordshipp to expose the safety of your honour to the uncertainty of my return. For the matter (my Lord), it is such as could I in any measure think safe to conceal from, or likely to be discovered to you by any other hand, I should not have dared so far to own what from my heart I believe is false, as to make myself but the relater of others discourse. But, Sir, your Lordships honour being such as I ought to value it to be, and finding both in City and Court that discourses pass to your prejudice, too generally for mine or any man's controlling but your Lordships, I shall (my Lord), without the least greatening or lessening the matter, do my duty in laying it shortly before you. People of all conditions (my Lord) raise matter of wonder from your Lordships so little appearance at Court – some concluding thence your disfavour there. To which purpose I have had questions asked me; and endeavouring to put off such insinuacions by asserting the contrary, they have replied that your Lordships living so beneath your quality, out of the way and declining of Court attendance, hath been more then once discoursed about the King. Others (my Lord), when the chief ministers of state, and those most active of the Council have been reckoned up (wherein your Lordship never use to want an eminent place), have said, touching your Lordshipp, that now your turn was served and the King had given you a good estate, you left him to stand or fall as he would. And, perticularly in that of the Navy, have enlarged upon your letting fall all service there. Another sort (and those the most) insist upon the bad report of the house wherein your Lordship (now observed in perfect health again) continues to sojourne. And by name have charged one of the daughters for a common courtizan, alleging both places and persons where and with whom she hath been too well known. And how much her wantonness occasions (though unjustly) scandal to your Lordship; and that as well to gratifying of some enemies as to the wounding of more friends, I am not able to tell. Lastly (my Lord), I find a general coldness in all persons towards your Lordship; such as, from my first dependence on you, I never yet knew. Wherein I shall not offer to interpose any thoughts or advice of mine, well knowing your Lordship needs not any. But, with a most faithful assurance that no person nor papers under Heaven is privy to what I here write, besides myself and this, which I shall be careful to have put into your own hands, I rest confident of your Lordships just construction of my dutiful intents herein, and in all humility take leave.

    May it please your Lordship,

Nov. 17. 1663.

Your Lordships most obedient servant,
S.P.

Memorandum. The letter before going was sent sealed up, and enclosed in this that fallows:–

My Lord,

If this finds your Lordshipp either not alone or not at leisure, I beg the suspending your opening of the enclosed till you shall be both – (the matter very well bearing such a delay) – and in all humility remain,

May it please your Lordshipp,

Nov. 17. 1663.

Your Lordships most obedient servant,

S.P.

My servant hath my directions to put this into your Lordships own hand, but not to stay for any answer.

I pray God give a blessing to it. But I confess I am afeared what the consequence may be to me of good or bad, which is according to the ingenuity that he doth receive it with. However, I am satisfied that it will do him good – and that he needs it.

26 November. Up and to the office, where we sat all the morning; and at noon I to the Change and there met with Mr Cutler the merchant, who would needs have me home to his house by the Dutch church; and there in an old but good house with his wife and mother, a couple of plain old women, I dined; a good plain dinner, and his discourse after dinner with me upon matters of the navy victualling, very good and worth my hearing. And so home to my office in the afternoon, with my mind full of business; and there at it late, and so home to supper to my poor wife and to bed – myself being in a little pain in one of my testicles, by a stroke I did give it in pulling up my breeches yesterday over-eagerly; but I will lay nothing to it till I see whether it will cease of [it]self or no.

28 November. I have been told it two or three times, but today for certain I am told how in Holland publicly they have pictured our King with reproach. One way is with his pockets turned the wrong side outward, hanging out empty – another, with two courtiers picking of his pocket – and a third, leading of two ladies while others abuse him – which amounts to great contempt.

29 November. Lords Day. This morning I put on my best black cloth suit trimmed with scarlett ribbon, very neat, with my cloak lined with velvett and a new beaver, which altogether is very noble, with my black silk knit canons I bought a month ago. I to church alone, my wife not going; and there I find my Lady Batten in a velvet gowne, which vexed me that she should be in it before my wife, or that I am able to put her into one; but what cannot be, cannot be. However, when I came home I told my wife of it; and to see my weakness, I could on the sudden have found my heart to have offered her one, but second thoughts put it by: and endeed, it would undo me to think of doing as Sir W. Batten and his Lady do, who hath a good estate besides his office.

4 December. Up pretty betimes; that is, about 7 a-clock, it being now dark then. And so got me ready with my clothes, breeches and warm stockings, and by water, cold and wet and windy, to Woolwich to a hemp ship there; and stayed looking upon it and giving direction as to the getting it ashore, and so back again, very cold; and at home, without going on shore anywhere, about 12 a-clock, being fearful of taking cold. And so dined at home – and shifted myself, and so all the afternoon at my office till night, and then home to keep my poor wife company; and so to supper and to bed.

10 December. Up, pretty well, the weather being become pretty warm again. And to the office, where we sat all the morning; and I confess, having received so lately a token from Mrs Russell, I did find myself concerned for our not buying some tallow of her (which she bought on purpose yesterday most unadvisedly, to her great loss, upon confidence of putting it off to us); so hard it is for a man not to be warped against his duty and maister's interest that receives any bribe or present, though not as a bribe, from anybody else. But she must be contented, and I to do her a good turn when I can without wrong to the King's service. Thence to St Paul's Churchyard to my booksellers; and having gained this day in the office, by my stationer's bill to the King, about 40s or 3l, I did here sit two or three hours, calling for twenty books to lay this money out upon; and found myself at a great loss where to choose, and do see how my nature would gladly returne to the laying out of money in this trade. I could not tell whether to lay out my money for books of pleasure, as plays, which my nature was most earnest in; but at last, after seeing Chaucer, Dugdales *History of Pauls*, Stow's *London*, Gesner, *History of Trent*, besides Shakespeare, Johnson, and Beaumonts plays, I at last chose Dr Fuller's *Worthys*, the *Cabbala or collections of Letters of State* – and a little book, *Delices de Hollande*, with another little book or two, all of good use or serious pleasure; and *Hudibras*, both parts, the book now in greatest fashion for drollery, though I cannot, I confess, see enough where the wit lies.

11 December. I sat by Mr Harrington and some East Country merchants; and talking of the country about [Königsberg] and thereabouts – he told us himself that for fish, none there, the poorest body, will buy a dead fish; but must be alive, unless it be winter; and then they told us the manner of putting their nets into the water through holes made in the thicke ice; they will spread a net of half a mile long, and he hath known a 130 and 170 barrells of fish taken at one draught. And then the people comes with sledges upon the ice, with snow at the bottome, and lay the fish in and cover them with snow, and so carry them to market. And he hath seen when the said fish have been frozen in the sled, so as that he hath taken a fish and broke a-pieces, so hard it hath been; and yet the same fishes, taken out of the snow and brought into a hot room, will be alive and leap up and down. Swallow often are brought up in their nets out of the mudd from under water, hanging together to some twigg or other, dead in ropes; and brought to the fire, will come to life. Fowl killed in December (Alderman Barker said) he did buy; and putting into the box under his sled, did forget to take them out to eate till Aprill next, and they then were found there and were, through the frost, as sweet and fresh and eat as well as at first killed.

20 December. Lords Day. After a dull sermon of the Scotchman, home; and there I find my brother Tom and my two Cosens Scotts, he and she – the first time they were ever here. And by and by in comes my uncle Wight and Mr Norbury, and they sat with us a while drinking of wine, of which I did give them plenty. But they two would not stay supper, but the other two did; and we were as merry as I could be with people that I do wish well to but know not what discourse either to give them or find from them. We showed them

'Being directed by sight of bills upon the walls, did go to Shooe Lane to see a cocke-fighting at a new pit there – a sport I was never at in my life.' (21 December 1663.) From C. Cotton's *The Compleate Gamster* 1674.

. . . .

our house from top to bottom, and had a good turkey roasted for our supper, and store of wine. And after supper sent them home on foot; and so to prayers and to bed.

21 December. Took coach, and being directed by sight of bills upon the walls, did go to Shooe Lane to see a cocke fighting at a new pit there – a sport I was never at in my life. But Lord, to see the strange variety of people, from Parliament-man to the poorest prentices, bakers, brewers, butchers, draymen, and whatnot; and all these fellows one with another in swearing, cursing, and betting. I soon had enough of it; and yet I would not but have seen it once, it being strange to observe the nature of those poor creatures, how they will fight till they drop down dead upon the table and strike after they are ready to give up the ghost – not offering to run away when they are weary or wounded past doing further. Whereas, where a dunghill brood comes, he will, after a sharp stroke that pricks him, run off the stage, and then they wring off his neck without more ado. Whereas the other they preserve, though their eyes be both out, for breed only of a true cock of the game. One thing more it is strange to see, how people of this poor rank that look as if they had not bread to put in their mouths, shall bet 3 or 4*l* at one bet and lose it, and yet bet as much the next battell, as they call every make of two cocks – so that one of them will lose 10 or 20*l* at a meeting.

25 December. Christmas. Lay long, talking pleasantly with my wife; but among other things, she begin, I know not whether by design or chance, to enquire what she should do if I should by an accident die; to which I did give her some slight answer, but shall make good use of it to bring myself to some settlement for her sake, by making a will as soon as I can. Up and to church, where Mr Mills made an ordinary sermon; and so home and dined with great pleasure with my wife; and all the afternoon, first looking out at window and seeing the boys playing at many several sports in our backyard by Sir W. Pens, which minded me of my own former times; and then I begin to read to my wife upon the globes, with great pleasure and to good purpose, for it will be pleasant to her and to me to have her understand those things.

1664

3 January. Lords Day. Lay long in bed; and then rose and with a fire in my chamber stayed within all day, looking over and settling my accounts in good order – by examining all my books and the kitchen books; and I find that though the proper profit of my last year was but 305*l*, yet I did by other gain make it up 444*l* – which in every part of it was unforeseen of me; and therefore it was a strange oversight for lack of examining my expenses that I should spend 690*l* this year. But for the time to come, I have so distinctly settled all my accounts in writing and the perticulars of all my several layings-out, that I do hope I shall hereafter make a better judgment of my spendings then ever. I dined with my wife in her chamber, she in bed. And then down again and till 11 at night; and broke up and to bed with great content, but could not make an end of writing over my vows as I purposed, but I am agreed in everything how to order myself for the year to come, which I trust in God will be much for my good. So up to prayers and to bed.

4 January. To the Tennice Court (after I had spent a little time in Westminster Hall, thinking to have met with Mrs Lane, but I could not and am glad of it) and there saw the King play at tennis and others. But to see how the King's play was extolled without any cause at all, was a loathsome sight, though sometimes endeed he did play very well and deserved to be commended; but such open flattery is beastly. Afterward to St James's Park, being unwilling to go to spend money at the ordinary, and there spent an hour or two, it being a pleasant day, seeing people play at Pell Mell – it pleased me mightily to hear a gallant, lately come from France, swear at one of his companions for suffering his man (a spruce blade) to be so saucy as to strike a ball while his master was playing on the Mall.

6 January. Twelfth Day. Up and to my office, where very busy all the morning; being endeed overloaded with it through my own desire of doing all I can. At noon to the Change but did little, and so home to dinner with my poor wife; and after dinner read a lecture to her in geography, which she takes very prettily, and with great pleasure to her and me to teach her. And so to the office again, where as busy as ever in my life, one thing after another and answering people's business. Perticularly, drawing up things about Mr Woods masts, which I expect to have a quarrel about with Sir W. Batten before it be ended – but I care not. At night home to my wife to supper, discourse, prayers, and to bed.

This morning I begun a practice which I find, by the ease I do it with, that I shall continue, it saving me money and time – that is, to trimme myself with a razer – which pleases me mightily.

. . . .

'To St James's Park . . . seeing people play at Pell Mell.' (4 January 1664.) This French game became fashionable in England at the Restoration. The modern Mall follows the line of the gravelled Pell Mell ground, at the top of the picture. St James's Park *c.* 1700.

16 January. I by water to Westminster Hall and there did see Mrs Lane and de là, elle and I to the cabaret at the Cloche in the street du Roy; and there, after some caresses, je l'ay foutée sous de la chaise deux times, and the last to my great pleasure; mais j'ai grand peur que je l'ay fait faire aussi elle même. Mais after I had done, elle commençait parler as before and I did perceive that je n'avais fait rien de danger à elle. Et avec ça, I came away; and though I did make grand promises à la contraire, nonobstant je ne la verrai pas long time. So home to supper and to bed – with my mind un peu troublé pour ce que j'ai fait today. But I hope it will be la dernière de toute my vie.

The trial of Col. James Turner had been a recent cause célèbre. *Turner (whom Pepys happened to know) was, or claimed to be, an ex-Cavalry officer who had been befriended by an elderly merchant. He had gagged and bound his benefactor at his house in Lime Street and robbed him of £4,500 in jewels and over £1,000 in cash.*

21 January. Up; and after sending my wife to my aunt Wight's to get a place to see Turner hanged, I to the office, where we sat all the morning. And at noon, going to the Change and seeing people flock in that, I enquired and found that Turner was not yet hanged; and so I went among them to Leadenhall Street at the end of Lyme Street, near where the robbery was done, and to St Mary Axe, where he lived; and there I got for a shilling to stand upon the wheel of a cart, in great pain, above an hour before the execution was done – he delaying the time by long discourses and prayers one after another, in hopes of a reprieve; but none came, and at last was flung off the lather in his cloak. A comely-looked man he was, and kept his countenance to the end – I was sorry to see him. It was believed there was at least twelve or fourteen thousand people in the street.

. . . .

'I got for a shilling to stand upon the wheel of a cart, in great pain, above an hour before the execution was done.' (21 January 1664.) Hanging at Tyburn, attributed to Marcellus Laroon II.

30 January. This evening, being in an humour of making all things even and clear in the world, I tore some old papers; among others, a romance which (under the title of *Love a Cheate*) I begun ten year ago at Cambridge; and at this time, reading it over tonight, I liked it very well and wondered a little at myself at my vein at that time when I wrote it, doubting that I cannot do so well now if I would try.

1 February. To the coffee-house, where I heard Lieutenant-Collonell Baron tell very good stories of his travels over the high hills in Asia above the cloudes. How clear the heaven is above them. How thick, like a mist, the way is through the cloud, that wets like a sponge one's clothes. The ground above the clouds all dry and parched, nothing in the world growing, it being only a dry earth. Yet not so hot above as below the clouds. The stars at night most delicate bright and a fine clear blue sky. But cannot see the earth at any time through the clouds, but the clouds look like a world below you.

2 February. Thence to the Change again, and thence off to the Sun taverne with Sir W. Warren and with him discoursed long and had good advice and hints from him; and among [other] things, he did give me a pair of gloves for my wife, wrapped up in paper; which I would not open, feeling it hard, but did tell him my wife should thank him, and so went on in discourse. When I came home, Lord, in what pain I was to get my wife out of the room without bidding her go, that I might see what these gloves were; and by and by, she being gone, it proves a pair of white gloves for her and 40 pieces in good gold: which did so cheer my heart that I could eat no victuals almost for dinner for joy to think how God doth bless us every day more and more – and more yet I hope he will upon the encrease of my duty and endeavours. I was at great loss what to do, whether tell my wife of it or no; which I could hardly forbear, but yet I did and will think of it first before I do, for fear of making her think me to be in a better condition or in a better way of getting money then yet I am.

3 February. This night late, coming in my coach coming up Ludgate Hill, I saw two gallants and their footmen taking a pretty wench which I have much eyed lately, set up shop upon the Hill, a seller of ribband and gloves. They seem to drag her by some force, but the wench went and I believe had her turn served; but God forgive me, what thoughts and wishes I had of being in their place. In Covent Garden tonight, going to fetch home my wife, I stopped at the great coffee-house there, where I never was before – where Draydon the poet (I knew at Cambridge) and all the wits of the town, and Harris the player and Mr Hoole of our college; and had I had time then or could at other times, it will be good coming thither, for there I perceive is very witty and pleasant discourse.

15 February. This afternoon Sir Tho. Chamberlin came to the office to me and showed me several letters from the East Indys, showing the heighth that the Dutch are come to there; showing scorn to all the English even in our only factory there of Surratt, beating several men and hanging the English standard St George under the Dutch flag in scorn; saying that whatever their masters do or say at home, they will do what they list and will be masters of all the world there, and have so proclaimed themselfs Soveraigne of all the

South Seas – which certainly our King cannot endure, if the parliament will give him money. But I doubt and yet do hope they will not yet, till we are more ready for it.

Commercial rivalry with the Dutch was soon to lead to the outbreak of hostilities. In this same winter of 1663–4 an English force under Holmes destroyed Dutch trading posts in West Africa. There was more fighting before the year ended – in North America where New Netherland fell to the English, and in West Africa where de Ruyter re-established the Dutch position. Attacks on Dutch shipping in the Channel occurred in December, and in the same month Sir Thomas Allin made an unprovoked attack on the Dutch Smyrna fleet off Cadiz. War was declared in March 1665.

17 February. Sir W. Rider come and stayed with me till about 12 at night, having found ourselfs work till that time about understanding the measuring of Mr Woods masts; which though I did so well before as to be thought to deal very hardly against Wood, yet I am ashamed I understood it no better and do hope yet, whatever be thought of me, to save the King some more money. And out of an impatience to break up with my head full of confused confounded notions but nothing brought to a clear comprehension, I was resolved to set up, and did, till now it is ready to strike 4 a-clock, all alone, cold, and my candle not enough left to light me to my own house; and so, with my business however brought to some good understanding and set it down pretty clear, I went home to bed, with my mind at good quiet and the girle setting up for me (the rest all a-bed); I eat and drank a little and to bed, weary, sleepy, cold, and my head akeing.

23 February. This day, by the blessing of God, I have lived 31 years in the world; and by the grace of God I find myself not only in good health in everything, and perticularly [as] to the stone, but only pain upon taking cold; and also in a fair way of coming to a better esteem and estate in the world then ever I expected; but I pray God give me a heart to fear a fall and to prepare for it.

24 February. Ashwednesday. Down to the garden of Somersett House and up and down the new building, which in every respect will be mighty magnificent and costly. I stayed a great while talking with a man in the garden that was sawing of a piece of marble – and did give him 6d to drink. He told me much of the nature and labour of that work; how he could not saw above 4 inch. of the stone in a day; and of a greater, not above one or two. And after it is sawed, then it is rubbed with coarse and then with finer and finer sand till they come to putty, and so polish it as smooth as glass. Their saws have no teeth, but it is the sand only which the saw rubs up and down that doth the thing.

27 February. Before I went to the office there came Bagwell's wife to me to speak for her husband. I liked the woman very well and stroked her under the chin, but could not find in my heart to offer anything uncivil to her, she being I believe a very modest woman.

8 March. Up, with some little discontent with my wife upon her saying that she had got and used some puppy-dog water, being put upon it by a desire of my aunt Wight to get some for her; who hath a mind, unknown to her husband, to get some for her ugly face. I to the office, where we sat all the morning; doing not much business through the multitude of counsellors, one hindering another. Then home, whither Luellin came and dined with me; but we made no long stay at dinner, for *Heraclius* being acted, which my wife and I have a mighty mind to see, we do resolve, though not exactly agreeing with the letter of my vowe, yet altogether with the sense, to see another this month – by going hither instead of that at Court, there having been none conveniently since I made my vow for us to see there, nor like to be this Lent; and besides, we did walk home on purpose to make this going as cheap as that would have been to have seen one at Court; and my conscience knows that it is only the saving of money and the time also that I entend by my oaths, and this hath cost no more of either – so that my conscience before God doth, after good consultation and resolution of paying my forfeit did my conscience accuse me of breaking my vow, I do not find myself in the least apprehensive that I have done any vyolence to my oaths. Walked home, calling to see my brother Tom, who is in bed and I doubt very ill.

15 March. Up and to the office, where we sat all the morning; and at noon comes Madam Turner and her daughter The[ophila] – her chief errand to tell me that she had got Dr Wiverly her Doctor to search my brother's mouth, where Mr Powell says there is an ulcer; from whence he concludes that he hath had the pox. But the Doctor swears there is not, nor ever was any. After dinner we took coach and to my brother's; where, contrary to my expectation, he continues as bad or worse, talking idle and now not at all knowing any of us as before. Here we stayed a great while, I going up and down the house looking after things. About 8 a-clock my brother begun to fetch his spittle with more pain and to speak as much, but not so distinctly; till at last, the phlegm getting the maistery of him and he beginning as we thought to rattle, I had no mind to see him die, as we thought he presently would, and so withdrew and led Mrs Turner home. But before I came back, which was in a quarter of an hour, my brother was dead. I went up and found the nurse holding his eyes shut; and he, poor wretch, lying with his chops fallen, a most sad sight and that which put me into a present very great transport of grief and cries. And endeed, it was a most sad sight to see the poor wretch lie now still and dead and pale like a stone. I stayed till he was almost cold, while Mrs Croxton, Holden, and the rest did strip and lay him out – they observing his corpse, as they told me afterwards, to be as clear as any they ever saw. And so this was the end of my poor brother, continuing talking idle and his lips working even to his last, that his phlegm hindered his breathing; and at last his breath broke out, bringing a flood of phlegm and stuff out with it, and so he died. This evening he talked among other talk a great deal of French, very plain and good; as among others – 'Quand un homme boit quand il n'a poynt d'inclinacion a boire il ne luy fait jamai de bien.' I once begun to tell him something of his condition and asked him whither he thought he should go. He in distracted manner answered me – 'Why, whither should I go? there are but two ways. If I go to the bad way, I must give God thanks for it. And if I go the other way, I must give God the more thanks for it; and I hope I have not been so undutiful and unthankful in my life but I hope I shall go that way.' But all being gone, the corps laid out and my wife at Mrs Turners, I thither; and there, after an hour's talk, we up to bed – my wife and I in the little blue chamber. And I lay close to my wife, being full of disorder and grief for my brother, that I could not sleep nor wake with satisfaction.

'After dinner we took coach and to my brother's; where, contrary to my expectation, he continues as bad or worse, talking idle and not at all knowing any of us as before.' (15 March 1664.) (*Left*) Woodcut 1689. (*Right*) Invitation ticket to a funeral.

. . . .

18 March. Up betimes and walked to my brother's, where a great while putting things in order against anon. Then to Madam Turners and eat a breakfast there. And so to Wotton my shoemaker and there got a pair of shoes blacked on the soles, against anon for me. So to my brother's, and to the church and with the grave-maker chose a place for my brother to lie in, just under my mother's pew. But to see how a man's tombes are at the mercy of such a fellow, that for 6*d* he would (as his own words were), 'I will justle them together but I will make room for him' – speaking of the fullness of the middle isle where he was to lie. And that he would for my father's sake do my brother that is dead all the civility he can; which was to disturb other corps that are not quite rotten to make room for him. And methought his manner of speaking it was very remarkable – as of a thing that now was in his power to do a man a courtesy or not. At noon my wife, though in pain, comes; but I being forced to go home, she went back with me, where I dressed myself and so did Besse; and so to my brother's again, whither, though invited as the custom is at 1 or 2 a-clock, they came not till 4 or 5. But at last, one after another they came – many more then I bid; and my reckoning that I bid was 120, but I believe there was nearer 150. Their service was six biscuits a-piece and what they pleased of burnt claret. My Cosen Joyce Norton kept the wine and cakes above, and did give out to them that served, who had white gloves given them. But above all, I am beholden to Mrs Holding, who was most kind and did take mighty pains, not only in getting the house and everything else ready, but this day in going up and down to see the house filled and served, in order to mine and their great content I think – the men setting by themselfs in some rooms, and women by themselves in others – very close, but yet room enough. Anon to church, walking out into the street to the Conduict and so across the street, and had a very good company along with the corps. And being come to the grave as above, Dr Pierson, the minister of the parish, did read the

(*Left*) Delft tile picture of a coffee boy, the sign from a London coffee house. The first coffee house in London is said to date from 1652; by 1663 there were 82 in the city alone. (*Right*) Coffee pot bearing the London hallmark for 1681–2.

. . . .

service for buriall and so I saw my poor brother laid into the grave; and so all broke up and I and my wife and Madam Turner and her family to my brother's, and by and by fell to a barrell of oysters, cake, and cheese of Mr Honiwoods, with him in his chamber and below – being too merry for so late a sad work; but Lord, to see how the world makes nothing of the memory of a man an hour after he is dead. And endeed, I must blame myself; for though at the sight of him, dead and dying, I had real grief for a while, while he was in my sight, yet presently after and ever since, I have had very little grief for him.

23 March. So to the office, where very busy all the morning; and so to the Change and off thence with Sir W. Ryder to the Trinity House and there dined very well. And good discourse among the old men, of islands now and then rising and falling again in the sea; and that there is many dangers of grounds and rocks that come just up to the edge almost of the sea, that is never discovered and ships perish without the world's knowing the reason of it. Among other things, they observed that there are but two seamen in the Parliament house, viz., Sir W. Batten and Sir W. Pen, and not above twenty or thirty merchants; which is a strange thing in an island, and no wonder that things of trade go no better.

1 April. This day Mrs Turner did lend me, as a rarity, a manuscript of one Mr Wells, writ long ago, teaching the method of building a ship; which pleases me mightily. I was at it tonight but durst not stay long at it, I being come to have a great pain and water in my eyes after candlelight.

2 April. At noon to the coffee-house, where excellent discourse with Sir W. Petty; who proposed it, as a thing that is truly questionable, whether there really be any difference between waking and dreaming – that it is hard not only to tell how we know when we do a thing really or in a dream, but also what the difference between one and the other.

19 April. Walked to the Change and there find the Change full of news from Guiny; some say the Dutch have sunk our ships and taken our fort and others say we have done the same to them. But I find by our merchants that something is done, but is yet a secret.

21 April. To the office; we sat all the afternoon but no sooner sat but news comes my Lady Sandwich was come to see us; so I went out, and running up (her friend however before me) I perceive by my dear Lady's blushing that in my dining room she was doing something upon the pott; which I also was ashamed of and so fell to some discourse, but without pleasure, through very pity to my Lady. She tells me, and I find true since, that the House this day hath voted that the King be desired to demand right for the wrong done us by the Dutch, and that they will stand by him with their lives and fortunes – which is a very high vote, and more than I expected. What the issue will be, God knows.

25 April. I took my wife by coach out through the City, discoursing how to spend the afternoon – and conquered, with much ado, a desire of going to a play. But took her out [to] Whitechapel and to Bednell Green; so to Hackny, where I have not been many a year, since a little child I boarded there. Thence to Kingsland by my nurse's house, Goody Lawrence, where my brother Tom and I was kept when young. Then to Newington Green and saw the outside of Mrs Herberts house where she lived, and my aunt Ellen with her. But Lord, how in every point I find myself to overvalue things when a child.

11 May. My uncle Wight came to me to my office this afternoon to speak with me and from me went to my house to see my wife; and strange to think that my wife should by and by send for me after he was gone, to tell me that he should begin discourse of her want of children and his also, and how he thought it would be best for him and her to have one between them, and he would give her 500*l* either in money or jewell beforehand and make the child his heyre. He commended her body and discoursed that for all he knew the thing

. . . .

The Royal Exchange, by W. Hollar 1644. Pepys was a frequent visitor to the Exchange, which was the best source of foreign and commercial news in London. Each group of merchants trading abroad had its own established meeting point within the courtyard. The upper floor of the building contained shops selling imported luxury goods.

was lawful. She says she did give him a very warm answer, such as he did not excuse himself by saying that he said this in jest but told her that since he saw what her mind was, he would say no more to her of it, and desired her to make no words of it. It seemed he did say all this in a kind of counterfeit laugh; but by all words that passed, which I cannot now so well set down, it is plain to me that he was in good earnest, and that I fear all his kindness is but only his lust to her. What to think of it of a sudden I know not, but I think not to take notice yet of it to him till I have thought better of it.

29 May. With Mr Povy home to dinner, where extraordinary cheer. And after dinner, up and down to see his house. And in a word, methinks for his perspective upon his wall in his garden and the springs rising up – with the perspective in the little closet – his room floored above with woods of several colours, like, but above the best cabinet-work I ever saw – his grotto and vault, with his bottles of wine and a well therein to keep them cool – his furniture of all sorts – his bath at the top of his house – good pictures and his manner of eating and drinking, doth surpass all that ever I did see of one man all my life.

24 June. After dinner to Whitehall and there met with Mr Pierce and he showed me the Queen's bedchamber and her closet, where she had nothing but some pretty pious pictures and books of devotion. And her holy water at her head as she sleeps, with a clock by her bedside wherein a lamp burns that tells her the time of the night at any time. Thence with him to the park and there met the Queen coming from chappell, with her Maids of Honour all in silver lace gowns again; which is new to me and that which I did not think would have been brought up again. Thence he carried me to the King's closet; where such variety of pictures and other things of value and rarity, that I was properly confounded and enjoyed no pleasure in the sight of them – which is the only time in my life that ever I was so at a loss for pleasure in the greatest plenty of objects to give it me.

1 July. I to the Change and thence home to dinner; and so to my office, busy till the evening; and then by agreement came Mr Hill and Andrew and one Cheswicke, a maister who plays very well upon the spinette, and we sat singing psalms till 9 at night, and so broke up with great pleasure; and very good company it is, and I hope I shall now and then have their company. They being gone, I to my office till toward 12 a-clock, and then home and to bed.

11 July. I betimes to bed. And there fell into a most mighty sweat in the night, about 11 a-clock; and there, knowing what money I have in the house and hearing a noise, I begin to sweat worse and worse, till I melted almost to water. I rung, and could not in half an hour make either of the wenches hear me; and this made me fear the more, lest they might be gag'd; and then I begin to think that there was some design in a stone being flung at the window over our stairs this evening, by which the thiefes meant to try what looking there would [be] after them and know our company. These thoughts and fears I had, and do hence apprehend the fears of all rich men that are covetous and have much money by them. At last Jane rose and then I understand it was only the dog wants a lodging and so made a noyse.

(*Left*) A London courtesan, from a drawing by Marcellus Laroon II 1670. (*Right*) 'Mr
Pen to visit me. I perceive something of learning he hath got, but a great deal . . . of the
vanity of the French garbe and affected manner of speech and gait.' (30 August 1664.)
French fashions, 1670.

23 July. Being in an idle and wanton humour, walked through Fleet Alley, and there
stood a most pretty wench at one of the doors. So I took a turn or two; but what by sense of
honour and conscience, I would not go in. But much against my will, took coach and
away to Westminster Hall, and there light of Mrs Lane and plotted with her to go over the
water; so met at Whites Stairs in Channel Row, and over to the old house at Lambeth
Marsh and there eat and drank and had my pleasure of her twice – she being the strangest
woman in talk, of love to her husband sometimes, and sometimes again she doth not care
for him – and yet willing enough to allow me a liberty of doing what I would with her. So
spending 5 or 6s upon her, I could do what I would; and after an hour's stay and more,
back again and set her ashore there again, and I forward to Fleetstreete and called at Fleet
Alley, not knowing how to command myself; and went in and there saw what formerly I
have been acquainted with, the wickedness of those houses and the forcing a man to
present expense. The woman, endeed, is a most lovely woman; but I had no courage to
meddle with her, for fear of her not being wholesome, and so counterfeited that I had not
money enough. It was pretty to see how cunning that jade was; would not suffer me to
have to do in any manner with her after she saw I had no money; but told me then I would
not come again, but she now was sure I would come again – though I hope in God I shall
not, for though she be one of the prettiest women I ever saw, yet I fear her abusing me.

*On 10 July Pepys had attended a christening at the house of Anthony Joyce, whose wife Kate was
Pepys's cousin on his mother's side. He now attends the feast and receives some useful advice.*

26 July. All the morning at the office. At noon to Anth. Joyces to our gossips dinner; I
had sent a dozen and a half of bottles of wine thither and paid my double share besides,
which is 18s. Very merry we were, and when the women were merry and ris from table, I
above with them, ne'er a man but I; I begin discourse of my not getting of children and
prayed them to give me their opinions and advice; and they freely and merrily did give me
these ten among them. 1. Do not hug my wife too hard nor too much. 2. Eat no late

suppers. 3. Drink juyce of sage. 4. Tent and toast. 5. Wear cool holland‑drawers. 6. Keep stomach warm and back cool. 7. Upon my query whether it was best to do at night or morn, they answered me neither one nor other, but when we have most mind to it. 8. Wife not to go too straightlaced. 9. Myself to drink mum and sugar. 10. Mrs Ward did give me to change my plat. The 3rd, 4th, 6th, 7th and 10th they all did seriously declare and lay much stress upon them, as rules fit to be observed indeed, and especially the last: to lie with our heads where our heels do, or at least to make the bed high at feet and low at head.

28 July. At the office all the morning. Dined, after Change, at home, and then abroad and seeing *The Bondman* upon the posts, I consulted my oaths and find I may go safely this time without breaking it; I went thither, notwithstanding my great desire to have gone to Fleete Ally, God forgive me, again. There I saw it acted; it is true, for want of practice they had many of them forgot their parts a little, but Baterton and my poor Ianthe out‑do all the world. There is nothing more taking in the world with me then that play.

7 August. Lords Day. I walked homeward and met with Mr Spong; and he with me as far as the Old Exchange, talking of many ingenuous things, musique, and at last of glasses, and I find him still the same ingenuous man that ever he was; and doth, among other fine things, tell me that by his microscope of his own making he doth discover that the wings of a moth is made just as the feathers of the wing of a bird, and that most plainly and certainly. While we were talking, came by several poor creatures, carried by by constables for being at a conventicle. They go like lambs, without any resistance. I would to God they would either conform, or be more wise and not be ketched.

30 August. Up and to the office, where sat long; and at noon to dinner at home. After dinner comes Mr Pen to visit me, and stayed an hour talking with me. I perceive something of learning he hath got, but a great deal, if not too much, of the vanity of the French garbe and affected manner of speech and gait – I fear all real profit he hath made of his travel will signify little. So he gone, I to my office and there very busy till late at night; and so home to supper and to bed.

Pepys has just engaged a new boy, Tom Edwards, an ex‑chorister of the Chapel Royal. He means to train him up as a clerk. Tom fulfils all his hopes, and, besides becoming a clerk, marries the Pepyses' beloved maid Jane Birch.

4 September. Lords Day. All the afternoon my wife and I above, and then the boy and I to singing of psalms, and then came in Mr Hill and he sung with us a while; and he being gone, the boy and I again to the singing of Mr Porter's mottets, and it is a great joy to me that I am come to this condition, to maintain a person in the house able to give me such pleasure as this boy doth by his thorough understand of music.

29 September. Coming home tonight, I did go to examine my wife's house accounts; and finding things that seemed somewhat doubtful, I was angry; though she did make it pretty plain, but confessed that when she doth misse a sum, she doth add something to other things to make it. And upon my being very angry, she doth protest she will here lay up something for herself to buy her a necklace with – which madded me and doth still trouble me, for I fear she will forget by degrees the way of living cheap and under a sense of want.

30 September. Up, and all day, both morning and afternoon, at my accounts, it being a great month both for profit and layings-out – the last being 89*l* – for kitchen, and clothes for myself and wife, and a few extraordinaries for the house. And my profits, besides salary, 239*l*. So that my balance doth come to 1203*l* for which the Lord's name be praised.

7 October. To my office; and there came Mr Cocker and brought me a globe of glasse and a frame of oyled paper (as I desired), to show me the manner of his gaining light to grave by and to lessen the glaringnesse of it at pleasure, by an oyled paper. This I bought of him, giving him a crowne for it.

10 October. This day by the blessing of God, my wife and I have been married nine years – but my head being full of business I did not think of it, to keep it in any extraordinary manner. But bless God for our long lives and loves and health together, which the same God long continue, I wish from my very heart.

25 November. Up, and at my office all the morning to prepare an account of the charge we have been put to extraordinary by the Dutch already; and I have brought it to appear 852,700*l*; but God knows, this is only a scare to the Parliament, to make them give the more money.

14 December. Up: and after a while at the office, I abroad in several places; among other, to my booksellers and there spoke for several books against New Year's day, I resolving to lay out about 7 or 8*l*, God having given me some profit extraordinary of late. And bespoke also some plate, spoons, and forks. I pray God keep me from too great expenses, though these will still be pretty good money.

15 December. [Mr Cholmley] tells me the King doth hate my Lord Chancellor. And that they, that is the King and my Lord Fitzharding, do laugh at him for a dull fellow, and in all this business of the Duch war doth nothing by his advice, hardly consulting him. Only, he is a good minister in other respects, and the King cannot be without him; but above all, being the Dukes father-in-law, he is kept in; otherwise, Fitzharding were able to fling down two of him. This all the wise and grave lords see, and cannot help it but yield to it.

18 December. Lords Day. To church; where God forgive me, I spent most of my time in looking my new morena at the other side of the church, an acquaintance of Pegg Pen's. So home to dinner and then to my chamber to read Ben. Johnsons *Cateline*, a very excellent piece. And so to church again; and thence we met at the office to hire ships, being in great haste and having sent for several maisters of shipps to come to us. Then home, and there Mr Andrews and Hill came and we sung finely.

19 December. Going to bed betimes last night, we waked betimes. And from our people's being forced to take the key to go out to light a candle, I was very angry and begun to find fault with my wife for not commanding her servants as she ought. Thereupon, she giving me some cross answer, I did strike her over her left eye such a blow, as the poor wretch did cry out and was in great pain; but yet her spirit was such as to endeavour to bite and scratch me. But I cogging with her, made her leave crying, and sent for butter and parsley, and friends presently one with another; and I up, vexed at my heart to think what I had done, for she was forced to lay a poultice or something to her eye all day, and is black – and the people of the house observed it.

20 December. Up and walked to Deptford, where after doing something at the yard, I walked, without being observed, with Bagwell home to his house and there was very kindly used, and the poor people did get a dinner for me in their fashion – of which I also eat very well. After dinner I found occasion of sending him abroad; and then alone avec elle je tentoy à faire ce que je voudrais, et contre sa force je le faisoy, bien que pas à mon contentment. By and by, he coming back again, I took leave and walked home.

27–28 December. I went to bed, leaving my wife and all her folks, and Will also, to come to make Christmas gamballs tonight, I waked in the morning about 6 a-clock, and my wife not come to bed. I lacked a pot but there was none, and bitter cold, so was forced to rise and piss in the chimny, and to bed again. Slept a little longer, and then hear my people coming up and so I rose; and my wife to bed at 8 a-clock in the morning, which vexed me a little, but I believe there was no hurt in it all, but only mirth – therefore took no notice.

31 December. At the office all the morning, and after dinner there again; despatched first my letters, and then to my accounts, not of the month but of the whole year also, and was at it till past 12 at night – it being bitter cold; but yet I was well satisfied with my work and, above all, to find myself, by the great blessing of God, worth 1349*l*, by which, as I have spent very largely, so I have laid up above 500*l* this year above what I was worth this day twelvemonth. The Lord make me for ever thankful to his holy name for it. Thence home to eat a little, and so to bed. As soon as ever the clock struck one, I kissed my wife in the kitchen by the fireside, wishing her a merry New Year, observing that I believe I was the first proper wisher of it this year, for I did it as soon as ever the clock struck one. So ends the old year, I bless God with great joy to me; not only from my having made so good a year of profit, as having spent 420*l* and laid up 540*l* and upward. But I bless God, I never have been in so good plight as to my health in so very cold weather as this is, nor indeed in any hot weather these ten years, as I am at this day and have been these four or five months. My family is my wife, in good health, and happy with her – her woman Mercer, a pretty modest quiet maid – her chambermaid Besse – her cookmaid Jane – the little girle Susan, and my boy which I have had about half a year, Tom Edwards, which I took from the King's Chappell. And a pretty and loving quiet family I have as any man in England. My credit in the world and my office grows daily, and I am in good esteem with everybody I think.

1665

21 January. Mr Povy carried me to Somersett House and there showed me the Queen Mother's chamber and closet, most beautiful places for furniture and pictures; and so down the great stone stairs to the garden and tried the brave eccho upon the stairs – which continues a voice so long as the singing three notes, concords, one after another, they all three shall sound in consort together a good while most pleasantly.

23 January. Home to dinner; and finding Mrs Bagwell waiting at the office after dinner, away elle and I to a cabaret where elle and I have été before; and there I had her company toute l'après-dîner and had mon plain plaisir of elle – but strange, to see how a woman, notwithstanding her greatest pretences of love à son mari and religion, may be vaincue. Thence to the Court of the Turky Company at Sir Andr. Rickard's, to treat about carrying some men of ours to Tanger, and had there a very civil reception, though a denial of the thing, as not practicable with them, and I think so too. So to my office a little; but being minded to make an end of my pleasure today, that I might fallow my business, I did take coach and to Jervas's again, thinking to avoir rencontré Jane; mais elle n'etait pas dedans. So I back again and to my office, where I did with great content faire a vow to mind my business and laisser aller les femmes for a month; and am with all my heart glad to find myself able to come to so good a resolution, that thereby I may fallow my business, which, and my honour thereby, lies a-bleeding. So home to supper and to bed.

7 February. Up, and to my office, where busy all the morning. And at home, at dinner, it being Shrove Tuseday, had some very good fritters. All the afternoon and evening at the office. And at night home to supper and to bed. This day Sir W. Batten, who hath been sick four or five days, is now very bad, so as that people begin to fear his death – and I at a loss whether it will be better for me to have him die, because he is a bad man, or live, for fear a worse should come.

15 February. With Creed to Gresham College – where I had been by Mr Povy the last week proposed to be admitted a member; and was this day admitted, by signing a book and being taken by the hand by the Præsident, my Lord Brunkard, and some words of admittance said to me. But it is a most acceptable thing to hear their discourses and see their experiments; which was this day upon the nature of fire, and how it goes out in a place where the ayre is not free, and sooner out where the ayre is exhausted; which they showed by an engine on purpose. After this being done, they to the Crowne tavern behind the Change, and there my Lord and most of the company to a club supper. Above all, Mr Boyle today was at the meeting, and above him Mr Hooke, who is the most, and promises the least, of any man in the world that ever I saw. Here, excellent discourses till 10 at night, and then home.

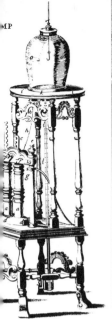

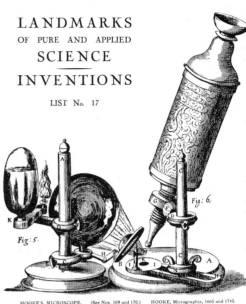

Fig: 5.

Fig: 6.

HOOKE'S MICROSCOPE. (See Nos. 169 and 170.) HOOKE, Micrographia, 1665 and 1745.

(*Left*) 'Their discourses ... was this day upon the nature of fire, which they showed by an engine on purpose. ... Mr Boyle today was at the meeting.' (15 February 1665.) Boyle's Air Pump, presented to the Royal Society in 1660. (*Centre*) Charles II as Patron of the Royal Society, by W. Hollar from Thomas Sprat's *History of the Royal Society* 1667. On the left is the President, Lord Brouncker, and on the right, Francis Bacon. (*Right*) Hooke's microscope from his *Micrographia* 1665. Robert Hooke was 'curator of experiments' to the Royal Society and later its secretary.

. . . .

20 February. By water to Deptford yard, and then down further and so landed at the lower end of the town; and it being dark, did privately entrer en la maison de la femme de Bagwell, and there I had sa compagnie, though with a great deal of difficulty; néanmoins, enfin je avais ma volonté d'elle. And being sated therewith, I walked home to Redriffe, it being now near 9 a-clock; and there I did drink some strong waters and eat some bread and cheese, and so home – where at my office, my wife comes and tells me that she hath hired a chambermaid, one of the prettiest maids that ever she saw in her life, and that she is really jealous of me for her – but hath ventured to hire her from month to month. But I think she means merrily. So to supper and to bed.

21 February. Up, and to the office (having a mighty pain in my forefinger of my left hand, from a strain that it received last night in struggling avec la femme que je mentioned yesterday), where busy till noon; and then, my wife being busy in going with her woman to a hot-house to bath herself, after her long being within doors in the dirt, so that she now pretends to a resolution of being hereafter very clean – how long it will hold, I can guess – I dined with Sir W. Batten and my Lady, they being nowadays very fond of me.

27 February. We to a committee of the Council to discourse concerning pressing of men; but Lord, how they meet; never sit down – one comes, now another goes, then comes another – one complaining that nothing is done, another swearing that he hath been there these two hours and nobody came. At last it came to this: my Lord Annesly, says he, 'I think we must be forced to get the King to come to every committee, for I do not see that we do anything at any time but when he is here.'

1 March. Up – this day being the day that, by a promise a great while ago made to my wife, I was to give her 20*l* to lay out in clothes against Easter. But [I] did boggle mightily at the parting with my money, but at last did give it her; and then she abroad to buy her things, and I to my office, where busy all the morning. At noon I to dinner at Trinity House – and thence to Gresham College, where Mr Hooke read a very curious lecture about the late comett, among other things, proving very probably that this is the very same comett that appeared before in the year 1618, and that in such a time probably it will appear again – which is a very new opinion – but all will be in print. And this day I did pay my admission money – 40*s* – to the Society. Here was very fine discourses and experiments; but I do lack philosophy enough to understand them, and so cannot remember them.

16 March. This afternoon Mr Harris the sayle-maker sent me a noble present of two large silver candlestickes and snuffers, and a slice to keep them upon – which endeed is very handsome. At night came Mr Andrews with 36*l* – the further fruits of my Tanger contract; and so to bed late, and weary with business but in good content of mind.

22 March. Sir Wm. Petty did tell me that in good earnest, he hath in his will left such parts of his estate to him that could invent such and such things – as among others, that could discover truly the way of milk coming into the breasts of a woman, and he that could invent proper characters to express to another the mixture of relishes and tastes. And says that to him that invents gold, he gives nothing for the philosopher's stone – 'for,' says he, 'they that find out that will be able to pay themselfs.'

12 April. Dined at home; and thence to Whitehall again (where I lose most of my time nowadays, to my great trouble, charge, and loss of time and benefit) and there, after the Council rose, Sir G. Carteret, my Lord Brunkard, Sir Tho. Harvy, and myself down to my Lord Treasurer's chamber to him and the Chancellor and the Duke of Albemarle. And there I did give them a large account of the charge of the Navy, and want of money. But strange, to see how they held up their hands, crying, 'What shall we do?' Says my Lord Treasurer, 'Why, what means all this, Mr Pepys? This is true, you say, but what would you have me to do? I have given all I can for my life. Why will not people lend their money? Why will they not trust the King as well as Oliver?'

17 April. To Whitehall; where the King seing me, did come to me, and calling me by name, did discourse with me about the ships in the river; and this is the first time that ever I knew the King did know me personally, so that hereafter I must not go thither but with expectation to be questioned, and to be ready to give good answers.

21 April. This day we hear that the Duke and the fleet are sailed [from Harwich] yesterday: pray God go along with them – that they have good speed.

30 April. Lords Day. In much trouble as to the pains I have taken about the business of Tanger. The fleet, with about 106 ships, upon the coast of Holland, in sight of the Dutch within the Tescell. Great fears of the sickenesse here in the City, it being said that two or three houses are already shut up. God preserve us all.

The sickness was the bubonic plague, which Pepys had never known before – the last outbreak in London having occurred in 1625. This was the worst attack in modern times, though not so widespread and catastrophic as the Black Death of 1348–9. In London it lasted until the summer of 1666 and carried off some 100,000 victims. It spread in early 1666 to other towns, mostly in southern England, but by the end of the year was over. After the 1670s no further cases are known to have occurred in England, and the last serious outbreak in Western Europe was in Marseilles in 1720–1. The bacillus of the disease, which was endemic in the Near East and parts of Africa, was carried by fleas on the rats which infested the ships trading to those areas. No cure was known and the disease was almost always fatal. Pepys regularly reports the fatality statistics which were given in the weekly 'bills of mortality' published by the Parish Clerks' Company of London.

7 June. It being the hottest day that ever I felt in my life, and it is confessed so by all other people the hottest they ever knew in England in the beginning of June – we to the New Exchange and there drunk whey; with much entreaty, getting it for our money, and would not be entreated to let us have one glasse more. So took water, and to Foxhall to the Spring-garden and there walked an hour or two with great pleasure, saving our minds ill at ease concerning the fleet and my Lord Sandwich, that we have no news of them, and ill reports run up and down of his being killed, but without ground. Here stayed, pleasantly walking and spending but *6d*, till 9 at night; and then by water to Whitehall, and there I stopped to hear news of the fleet, but none come, which is strange; and so by water home – where, weary with walking and with the mighty heat of the weather, and for my wife's not coming home – I stayed walking in the garden till 12 at night, when it begun lighten exceedingly through the greatness of the heat. Then, despairing of her coming home, I to bed. This day, much against my will, I did in Drury Lane see two or three houses marked with a red cross upon the doors, and 'Lord have mercy upon us' writ there – which was a sad sight to me, being the first of that kind that to my remembrance I ever saw. It put me into an ill conception of myself and my smell, so that I was forced to buy some roll-tobacco to smell to and chaw – which took away the apprehension.

8 June. Victory over the Dutch. 3 June 1665. This day they engaged – the Dutch neglecting greatly the opportunity of the wind they had of us – by which they lost the benefit of their fireships. The Earl of Falmouth, Muskery, and Mr Rd. Boyle killed on board the Dukes ship, the *Royall Charles*, with one shot. Their blood and brains flying in the Duke's face – and the head of Mr Boyle striking down the Duke, as some say. We have taken and sunk, as is believed, about twenty-four of their best ships. Killed and taken near eight- or ten-thousand men; and lost, we think, not above seven hundred. A great victory, never known in the world. They are all fled; some forty-three got into the Texell and others elsewhere, and we in pursuit of the rest. Had a great bonefire at the gate; and I with my Lady Pens people and others to Mrs Turner's great room, and then down into the street. I did give the boys 4*s* among them – and mighty merry; so home to bed – with my heart at great rest and quiet, saving that the consideration of the victory is too great for me presently to comprehend.

9 June. So abroad to buy several things; and among others, with my taylor to buy a silk suit; which, though I made one lately, yet I do for joy of the good news we have lately had of our victory over the Dutch, which makes me willing to spare myself something extraordinary in clothes.

10 June. Lay long in bed; and then up and at the office all the morning. At noon dined at home, and then to the office, busy all the afternoon. In the evening home to supper, and there to my great trouble hear that the plague is come into the City (though it hath these three or four weeks since its beginning been wholly out of the City); but where should it begin but in my good friend and neighbour's, Dr Burnett in Fanchurch Street – which in both points troubles me mightily. To the office to finish my letters, and then home to bed – being troubled at the sickness, and my head filled also with other business enough, and perticularly how to put my things and estate in order, in case it should please God to call me away – which God dispose of to his own glory.

11 June. Lords Day. I out of doors a little to show forsooth my new suit, and back again; and in going, saw poor Dr Burnets door shut. But he hath, I hear, gained great goodwill among his neighbours; for he discovered it himself first, and caused himself to be shut up of his own accord – which was very handsome. In the evening comes Mr Andrews and his wife and Mr Hill, and stayed and played and sung and supped – most excellent pretty company; so pleasant, ingenious, and harmless, I cannot desire better. They gone, we to bed – my mind in great present ease.

17 June. It stroke me very deep this afternoon, going with a hackney-coach from my Lord Treasurer's down Holborne – the coachman I found to drive easily and easily; at last stood still, and came down hardly able to stand; and told me that he was suddenly stroke very sick and almost blind. So I light and went into another coach, with a sad heart for the poor man and trouble for myself, lest he should have been stroke with the plague – being at that end of the town that I took him up. But God have mercy upon us all.

20 June. Thanksgiving day for Victory over the Dutch. Up, and to the office, where very busy alone all the morning till church time; and there heard a mean sorry sermon of Mr Mills. Then to the Dolphin Taverne, where all we officers of the Navy met with the Comissioners of the Ordnance by agreement and dined – where good musique, at my direction. Our club came to 34*s* a man – nine of us. Thence after dinner I to Whitehall with Sir W. Berkely in his coach. And so I walked to Herberts and there spent a little time avec la mosa, sin hazer algo con ella que kiss and tocar ses mamelles, que me haza hazer la cosa a mi mismo con gran plaisir. Thence by water to Foxhall, and there walked an hour alone, observing the several humours of the citizens that were there this holiday, pulling of cherries and God knows what.

This day I informed myself that there died four or five at Westminster of the plague, in one alley in several houses upon Sunday last – Bell Alley, over against the Palace gate. Yet people do think that the number will be fewer in the town then it was the last week. The Dutch are come out again, with twenty sail under Banker – supposed gone to the norward to meet their East India fleet.

3 July. Late at the office about letters; and so home, resolving from this night forward to close all my letters if possible and end all my business at the office by daylight, and I shall go near to do it and put all my affairs in the world in good order, the season growing so sickly that it is much to be feared how a man can scape having a share with others in it – for which the good Lord God bless me or to be fitted to receive it. So after supper to bed, and mightily troubled in my sleep all night with dreams of Jacke Cole my old schoolfellow, lately dead, who was born at the same time with me, and we reckoned our fortunes pretty equal. God fit me for his condition.

7 July. Up, and having set my neighbour Mr Hudson, wine cooper, at work drawing out a tierce of wine for the sending of some of it to my wife – I abroad, only taking notice to what a condition it hath pleased God to bring me, that at this time I have two tierces of claret; two quarter-cask of canary, and a smaller vessel of sack; a vessel of tent, another of Malaga, and another of white wine, all in my wine cellar together – which I believe none of my friends of my name now alive ever had of his own at one time.

Pepys has helped to arrange a marriage alliance between the families of the Earl of Sandwich and Sir George Carteret – Sandwich's daughter Lady Jemima is to marry Carteret's son Philip. Pepys now takes Philip to Dagnams, the Essex home of Lady Wright, Sandwich's sister-in-law, where the young people are to meet for the first time. Both are excessively shy. Lord Crew was the father-in-law of both Lady Wright and Lady Sandwich.

15 July. Took boat, Mr Carteret and I, to the ferry place at Greenwich and there stayed an hour, after crossing the water to and again to get our coach and horses over, and by and by set out and so toward Dagenham. But Lord, what silly discourse we had by the way as to matter of love matters, he being the most awkerd man I ever met withal in my life as to that business. Thither we came by time it begin to be dark, and were kindly received by my Lady Wright and my Lord Crew; and to discourse they went, my Lord discoursing with him, asking of him questions of travell, which he answered well enough in a few words. But nothing to [Lady Jem] from him at all. To supper, and after supper to talk again, he yet taking no notice of the lady. My Lord would have had me have consented to leaving the young people together tonight to begin their amours, his staying being but to be little. But I advised against it, lest the lady might be too much surprized. So they led him up to his chamber, where I stayed a little to know how he liked the lady; which he told me he did mightily, but Lord, in the dullest insipid manner that ever lover did.

16 July. Lords Day. Having trimmed myself, down to Mr Carteret; and he being ready, we down and walked in the gallery an hour or two, it being a most noble and pretty house that ever for the bigness I saw. Here I taught him what to do; to take the lady alway by the hand to lead her; and telling him that I would find opportunity to leave them two together, he should make these and these compliments, and also take a time to do the like to my Lord Crew and Lady Wright. After I had instructed him, which he thanked me for, owning that he needed my teaching him, my Lord Crew came down and family, the young lady among the rest; and so by coaches to church, four mile off. Thence back again by coach – Mr Carteret having not had the confidence to take his lady once by the hand, coming or going; which I told him of when we came home, and he will hereafter do it. So to dinner. My Lord excellent discourse. Then to walk in the gallery and to sit down. By and by my Lady Wright and I go out (and then my Lord Crew, he not by design); and lastly my Lady Crew came out and left the young people together. And a little pretty daughter of my Lady Wright's most innocently came out afterward, and shut the door to, as if she had done it, poor child, by inspiration – which made us without have good sport to laugh at. They together an hour; and by and by church-time, whither he led her into the coach and into the church; and so at church all the afternoon.

17 July. Before we went, I took my Lady Jem apart and would know how she liked this gentleman and whether she was under any difficulty concerning him. She blushed and hid her face awhile, but at last I forced her to tell me; she answered that she could readily obey what her father and mother had done – which was all she could say or I expect.

The marriage day arrives. Pepys, with the bridegroom's parents, has been delayed by the tide on his way from Deptford, and misses the wedding service. They meet the wedding party returning from church – 'the young lady' looking 'mighty sad... yet I think it was only her gravity.' Then to dinner, 'very merry ... but yet in such a sober way as never almost any wedding was in so great families'.

31 July. At night to supper, and so to talk and, which methought was the most extraordinary thing, all of us to prayers as usual, and the young bride and bridegroom too. And so after prayers, soberly to bed; only, I got into the bridegroom's chamber while he undressed himself, and there was very merry – till he was called to the bride's chamber and into bed they went. I kissed the bride in bed, and so the curtaines drawne with the greatest gravity that could be, and so goodnight. But the modesty and gravity of this business was so decent, that it was to me, endeed, ten times more delightful then if it had been twenty times more merry and joviall.

1 August. Slept and lay long, then up; and my Lord and Sir G. Carteret being gone abroad, I first to see the bridegroom and bride, and found them both up, and he gone to dress himself. Both red in the face and well enough pleased this morning with their night's lodging. Home to the office, where I find all well. And being weary and sleepy, it being very late, I to bed.

11 August. Up, and all day long finishing and writing over my will twice, for my father and my wife. Only in the morning a pleasant rancontre happened, in having a young married woman brought me by her father, old Delkes, that carries pins alway in his mouth, to get her husband off, that he should not go to sea. Uno ombre pouvait avoir done any cosa cum ella, but I did natha sino besar her. I to the Exchequer about striking new tallies; and I find the Exchequer, by proclamacion, removing to Nonesuch. Back again and at my papers, and putting up my books into chests, and settling my house and all things in the best and speediest order I can, lest it should please God to take me away or force me to leave my house.

12 August. The people die so, that now it seems they are fain to carry the dead to be buried by daylight, the nights not sufficing to do it in. And my Lord Mayor commands people to be within at 9 at night, all (as they say) that the sick may have liberty to go abroad for ayre.

On 5 July Pepys had sent his wife out of plague-stricken London to lodge with William Sheldon, Clerk of the Cheque at Woolwich yard. He has just visited her there.

15 August. Up by 4 a-clock and walked to Greenwich, where called at Captain Cockes and to his chamber, he being in bed – where something put my last night's dream into my head, which I think is the best that ever was dreamed – which was, that I had my Lady Castlemayne in my armes and was admitted to use all the dalliance I desired with her, and

. . . .

'The people die so, that now it seems they are fain to carry the dead to be buried by daylight, the nights not sufficing to do it in.' (12 August 1665.) (*Left*) Bill of Mortality for 15–22 August 1665. These bills, published by the Parish Clerks' Company, gave details of deaths from all causes. (*Right*) A plague broadsheet, 1665.

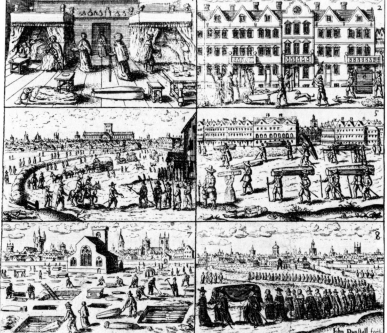

then dreamed that this could not be awake but that it was only a dream. But that since it was a dream and that I took so much real pleasure in it, what a happy thing it would be, if when we are in our graves (as Shakespeere resembles it), we could dream, and dream but such dreams as this – that then we should not need to be so fearful of death as we are this plague-time.

16 August. Up; and after doing some necessary business about my accounts at home, to the office and there with Mr Hater wrote letters. And I did deliver to him my last will, one part of it to deliver to my wife when I am dead. Thence to the Exchange, which I have not been a great while. But Lord, how sad a sight it is to see the streets empty of people, and very few upon the Change – jealous of every door that one sees shut up, lest it should be the plague – and about us, two shops in three, if not more, generally shut up.

On 21 August the Navy Office is moved to Greenwich Palace. Until the New Year Pepys has lodgings nearby, paying occasional visits to his wife at Woolwich and to the office building in London. The Principal Officers now attend service at St Alphege's, the parish church.

3 September. Lords Day. Up, and put on my coloured silk suit, very fine, and my new periwigg, bought a good while since, but darst not wear it because the plague was in Westminster when I bought it. And it is a wonder what will be the fashion after the plague is done as to periwigs, for nobody will dare to buy any haire for fear of the infection – that it had been cut off of the heads of people dead of the plague. Church being done, my Lord Brouncker, Sir J. Mennes, and I up to the vestry at the desire of the Justices of the Peace, Sir Th. Bidolph and Sir W. Boreman and Alderman Hooker – in order to the doing something for the keeping of the plague from growing; but Lord, to consider the madness of people of the town, who will (because they are forbid) come in crowds along with the dead corps to see them buried. But we agreed on some orders for the prevention thereof.

5 September. Home with my Lord Brouncker to dinner, where very merry with him and his doxy. After dinner comes Collonell Blunt in his new charriott made with springs, as that was of wicker wherein a while since we rode at his house. And he hath rode, he says, now this journy, many mile in it with one horse, and outdrives any coach and outgoes any horse, and so easy he says. So for curiosity I went into it to try it; and up the hill to the heath and over the cartrutts went to try it, and found it pretty well, but not so easy as he pretends.

10 September. Lords Day. There happened news to come to me [at Woolwich] by an expresse from Mr Coventry, telling me the most happy news of my Lord Sandwiches meeting with part of the Dutch; his taking two of their East India ships and six or seven others, and very good prize – and that he is in search of the rest of the fleet, which he hopes to find upon the Well Bancke – with the loss only of the *Hector*, poor Captain Cuttle. This news doth so overjoy me, that I know not what to say enough to express it; but the better to do it, I did walk to Greenwich; and there sending away Mr Andrews, I to Captain Cocke's, where I find my Lord Brouncker and his mistress and Sir J. Mennes –

where we supped (there was also Sir W. Doyly and Mr Eveling); but the receipt of this news did put us all into such an extasy of joy, that it inspired into Sir J. Mennes and Mr Eveling such a spirit of mirth, that in all my life I never met with so merry a two hours as our company this night was. Among other humours, Mr Eveling's repeating of some verses made up of nothing but the various acceptations of 'may' and 'can', and doing it so aptly, upon occasion of something of that nature, and so fast, did make us all die almost with laughing, and did so stop the mouth of Sir J. Mennes in the middle of all his mirth (and in a thing agreeing with his own manner of genius) that I never saw any man so outdone in all my life; and Sir J. Mennes's mirth too, to see himself outdone, was the crown of all our mirth. In this humour we sat till about 10 at night; and so my Lord and his mistress home, and we to bed – it being one of the times of my life wherein I was the fullest of true sense of joy.

13 September. Up, and walked to Greenwich, taking pleasure to walk with my minute wach in my hand, by which I am now come to see the distances of my way from Woolwich to Greenwich. And do find myself to come within two minutes constantly to the same place at the end of each quarter of an hour.

Sandwich's recent capture of the two Dutch East Indiamen was to lead to trouble. He had allowed his officers and men to rifle the goods before they were declared prize. His friends on shore – Capt. Cocke and Pepys among them – now prepare to share in the plunder. Pepys grows nervous and in the end sells out to Cocke. Sandwich's enemies at court make the most of the scandal. In February 1666 he is packed off to Spain as ambassador and does not return until September 1668.

23 September. Up, and to my Lord Sandwich – who did advise alone with me how far he might trust Captain Cocke in the business of the prize goods – my Lord telling me that he hath taken into his hands 2 or 3000*l* value of them. It being a good way, he says, to get money, and afterward to get the King's allowance thereof – it being easier, he observes, to keep money when got of the King, then to get it when it is too late. I advised him not to trust Cocke too far. And did thereupon offer him ready money for a thousand pound or two, which he listens to and doth agree to – which is great joy to me, hoping thereby to get something. Thence by coaches to Lambeth, his Lordshipp and all our office, and Mr Eveling, to the Duke of Albemarle. Here we dined, and I did hear my Lord Craven whisper (as he is mightily possessed with a good opinion of me) much to my advantage, which my good Lord did second; and anon my Lord Craven did speak publicly of me to the Duke, in the hearing of all the rest, and the Duke did say something of the like advantage to me; I believe, not much to the satisfaction of my brethren – but I was mightily joyed at it. Thence down to Greenwich to the office, and there wrote several letters; and so to my Lord Sandwich and mighty merry, and he mighty kind to me in the face of all, saying much in my favour; and after supper I took leave and with Captain Cocke set out in the yacht about 10 a clock at night. And after some discourse and drinking a little – my mind full of what we are going about, and jealous of Cocke's out doing me – so to sleep upon beds brought by Cocke on board, mighty handsome, and never slept better then upon this bed upon the floor in the cabbin.

24 September. Lords Day. Waked, and up and drank and then to discourse. And then being about Grayes and a very calme curious morning, we took our wherry, and to the fishermen and bought a great deal of fine fish – and to Gravesend to Whites and had part of it dressed. And in the meantime, we to walk about a mile from the town, and so back again. And there, after breakfast, one of our watermen told us he had heard of a bargain of cloves for us. And we went to a blind alehouse at the further end of the town, to a couple of wretched, dirty seamen, who, poor wretches, had got together about 37 lb of cloves and 10 lb of nuttmeggs. And we bought them of them – the first at 5s 6d per lb, and the latter at 4s – and paid them in gold; but Lord, to see how silly these men are in the selling of it, and easily to be persuaded almost to anything – offering a bag to us, to pass as 20 lb of cloves, which upon weighing proved 25 lb. But it would never have been allowed by my conscience to have wronged the poor wretches, who told us how dangerously they had got some and dearly paid for the rest of these goods. By and by to dinner about 3 a-clock. And then I in the cabin to writing down my journall for these last seven days, to my great content – it having pleased God that in this sad time of the plague everything else hath conspired to my happiness and pleasure, more for these last three months then in all my life before in so little time. God long preserve it, and make me thankful for it. After finishing my journall, then to discourse and to read, and then to supper and to bed, my mind not being at full ease, having not fully satisfied myself how Captain Cocke will deal with me as to the share of the profits.

25 September. Found ourselfs come to the fleet; and so aboard the *Prince*, and there, after a good while in discourse, we did agree a bargain of 5000*l* with Sir Rog. Cuttance for my Lord Sandwich, for silk, cinnamon, nutmegs and indico. And I was near signing to an undertaking for the payment of the whole sum, but I did by chance escape it, having since, upon second thoughts, great cause to be glad of it, reflecting upon the craft and not good condition, it may be, of Captain Cocke. I could get no trifles for my wife. Took our wherry toward Chatham; but it growing dark, we were put to great difficultys, our simple yet confident waterman not knowing a step of the way; and we found ourselfs to go backward and forward, which, in that dark night and a wild place, did vex us mightily. At last we got a fisher boy by chance and took him into the boat; and being an odd kind of boy, did vex us too, for he would not answer us aloud when we spoke to him; but did carry us safe thither, though with a mistake or two, but I wonder they were not more. In our way I was [surprised], and so we were all, at the strange nature of the sea water in a dark night; that it seemed like fire upon every stroke of the oare – and they say is a sign of winde. We went to the Crowne Inne at Rochester, and there to supper and made ourselfs merry with our poor fisher boy, who told us he had not been in a bed in the whole seven year since he came to prentice, and hath two or three year more to serve.

26 September. Up by 5 a-clock and got post-horses and so set out for Greenwich, calling and drinking at Dartford. Being come to Greenwich, and shifting myself, I to the office; and after some letters, down to Woolwich, where I have not lain with my wife these eight days I think, or more. After supper, and telling her my mind about my trouble in what I have done as to buying of these goods – we to bed.

2 October. Walked to Chatham, and there with Comissioner Pett viewed the Yard; and among other things, a teame of four horses came close by us, he being with me, drawing a piece of timber that I am confident one man would easily have carried upon his back; I made the horses be taken away and a man or two take the timber away with their hands. This the Comissioner did see, but said nothing; but I think had cause to be ashamed of. We walked, he and I and Cocke, to the Hill House, where we find Sir Wm. Pen in bed, and there much talk and much dissembling of kindness from him; but he is a false rogue and I shall not trust him. But my being there did procure his consent to have his silk carried away before the money received, which he would not have done for Cocke I am sure. Thence to Rochester; walked to the Crowne, and while dinner was getting ready, I did there walk to visit the old castle ruines, which hath been a noble place; and there going up, I did upon the stairs overtake three pretty maids or women and took them up with me, and I did besarlas muchas vezes et tocar leur mains and necks, to my great pleasure: but Lord, to see what a dreadful thing it is to look down præcipices, for it did fright me mightily and hinder me of much pleasure which I would have made to myself in the company of these three if it had not been for that. The place hath been very noble, and great and strong in former ages. So to walk up and down the Cathedrall, and thence to the Crowne whither Mr Fowler, the Mayor of the towne, was come in his gowne, and is a very reverend magistrate.

5 October. To Mr Evelings to discourse of our confounded business of prisoners and sick and wounded seamen, wherein he and we are so much put out of order. And here he showed me his gardens, which are, for variety of evergreens and hedge of holly, the finest things I ever saw in my life. Thence in his coach to Greenwich, and there to my office, all the way having fine discourse of trees and the nature of vegetables.

11 October. A fine company at my lodgings at Woolwich, where my wife and Mercer and Mrs Barbara danced, and mighty merry we were, but especially at Mercer's dancing a jigg, which she does the best I ever did see, having the most natural way of it and keeps time the most perfectly I ever did see. This night is kept, in lieu of yesterday, for my wedding day of ten yeares – for which God be praised – being now in an extreme good condition of health and estate and honour, and a way of getting more money – though at this hour under some discomposure, rather then dammage, about some prize goods that I have bought of the fleete in partenership with Captain Cocke – and for the discourse about the world concerning my Lord Sandwich, that he hath done a thing so bad; and indeed it must needs have been a very rash act for a General to take what prizes he pleases – and the giving a pretence to take away much more then he entended, and all will be upon him.

Pepys visits London for the day.

16 October. But Lord, how empty the [city] streets are, and melancholy, so many poor sick people in the streets, full of sores, and so many sad stories overheard as I walk, everybody talking of this dead, and that man sick, and so many in this place, and so many in that. And they tell me that in Westminster there is never a physitian, and but one apothecary left, all being dead – but that there are great hopes of a great decrease this week: God send it.

20 October. Busy all the morning; and at noon to Cocke and dined there – he and I alone – vexed that we are not rid of all our trouble about our goods; but it is almost over. And in the afternoon to my lodging and there spent the whole afternoon and evening with Mr Hater, discoursing of the business of the office – where he tells me that among other, Tho. Willson doth now and then seem to hint that I do take too much business upon me, more then I can do, and that therefore some doth lie undone. This, I confess to my trouble, is true; but it arises from my being forced to take so much on me, more then is my proper task.

29 October. Lords Day. Up, and being ready, set out with Captain Cocke in his coach toward Erith, Mr Deane riding along with us – where we dined and were very merry. After dinner we fell to discourse about the Dutch, Cocke undertaking to prove that they were able to wage war with us three year together – which, though it may be true, yet, not being satisfied with his arguments, my Lord and I did oppose the strength of his arguments, which brought us to a great heat – he being a conceited man but of no logique in his head at all, which made my Lord and I mirth. I was set down at Woolwich town's end and walked through the town in the dark, it being now night. But in the street did overtake and almost run upon two women, crying and carrying a man's coffin between them: I suppose the husband of one of them, which methinks is a sad thing. Being come to Sheldens, I find my people in the dark in the dining room, merry and laughing, and I thought sporting one with another; which God help me, raised my jealousy presently. I came in in the dark, and one of them touching me (which afterward I found was Su), made them shreeke; and so went out upstairs, leaving them to light a candle – and to run out. I went out and was very vexed, till I found my wife was gone with Mr Hill and Mercer this day to see me at Greenwich, and these people were at supper; and the candle on a sudden falling out of the candlestick (which I saw as I came through the yard), and Mrs Barbary being there, I was well at ease again – and so bethought myself what to do, whether to go to Greenwich or stay there. At last, go I would; and so with a lantern and three or four people with me, among others, Mr Browne who was there, would go, I walked with a lanthorne – and discoursed with him about painting and the several sorts of it. I came in good time to Greenwich, where I found Mr Hill with my wife – and very glad I was to see him. To supper and discourse of musique, and so to bed, I lying with him, talking till midnight about Berchenshaws music rules.

30 October. Up, and to my office about business. At noon to dinner, and after some discourse of music, he and I, I to the office awhile, and he to get Mr Coleman if he can, against night. By and by, I back again home, and there find him return[ed] with Mr Coleman (his wife being ill) and Mr Laneare – with whom, with their lute, we had excellent company and good singing till midnight, and a good supper I did give them. But Coleman's voice is quite spoiled; and when he begins to be drunk, he is excellent company, but afterward, troublesome and impertinent. Laneare sings, in a melancholy method, very well, and a sober man he seems to be. They being gone, we to bed.

1 November. Lay very long in bed, discoursing with Mr Hill of most things of a man's life, and how little merit doth prevail in the world, but only favour – and that for myself, chance without merit brought me in, and that diligence only keeps me so, and will, living as I do among so many lazy people, that the diligent man becomes necessary, that they cannot do anything without him.

3 November. Was called up about 4 a-clock, and in the dark by lanthorn took boat, and to the ketch and set sail – sleeping a little in the cabbin till day; and then up, and fell to reading of Mr Eveling's book about paynting, which is a very pretty book. Carrying good victuals, and Tom with me, I to breakfast about 9 a-clock, and then to read again, and came to the fleet about 12 – where found my Lord (the Prince being gone in) on board the *Royall James*, Sir Tho. Allen commander; and with my Lord an hour alone, discoursing, which was my chief and only errand, about what was advisable for his Lordshipp to do in this state of things, himself being under the Duke of York and Mr Coventrys envy and a great many more – and likely never to do anything honourably but he shall be envied, and the honour taken as much as can be from it. His absence lessens his interest at Court – and which is worst, we never able to set out a fleet fit for him to command; or if out, to keep them out, or fit them to do any great thing; or if that were so, yet nobody at home minds him or his condition when he is abroad; and lastly, the whole affairs of state looking as if they would all on a sudden break in pieces, and then what a sad thing it would be for him to be out of the way. My Lord did concur in everything, and thanked me infinitely.

5 November. Lords Day. Up, and after being trimmed, by boate to the Cockepitt, where I heard the Duke of Albemarle's chaplain make a simple sermon. Among other things, reproaching the imperfection of humane learning, he cried – 'All our physicians can't tell what an ague is, and all our arithmetique is not able to number the days of a man' – which, God knows, is not the fault of arithmetique, but that our understandings reach not that thing. To dinner, where a great deal of silly discourse. But the worst is, I hear that the plague encreases much at Lambeth, St Martins, and Westminster, and fear it will all over the City. Thence I to the Swan, there thinking to have seen Sarah, but she was at church; and so by water to Deptford, and there made a visit to Mr Evelings, who, among other things, showed me most excellent painting in little, in distemper, Indian incke, water colours, graveing; and above all, the whole secret of mezzotinto and the manner of it, which is very pretty, and good things done with it. He read me part of a play or two of his making, very good, but not as he conceits them I think, to be. He showed me his *Hortus Hyemalis*; leaves laid up in a book of several plants, kept dry, which preserve colour however, and look very finely, better than any herball. In fine, a most excellent person he is, and must be allowed a little for a little conceitedness; but he may well be so, being a man so much above others. He read me, though with too much gusto, some little poems of his own, that were not transcendent, yet one or two very pretty epigrams. Here comes in in the middle of our discourse, Captain Cocke, as drunk as a dog, but could stand and talk and laugh. He did so joy himself in a brave woman that he had been with all the afternoon, and who should it be but my Lady Robinson. But very troublesome he is with his noise and talk and laughing, though very pleasant. With him in his coach to Mr Glanvills, where he sat with Mrs Penington and myself a good while, talking of this fine woman again, and then went away. Then the lady and I to very serious discourse; and among other things, of what a bonny lass my Lady Robinson is, who is reported to be kind to the prisoners, and hath said to Sir G. Smith, who is her great chrony: 'Look, there is a pretty man; I could be contented to break a commandment with him' – and such loose expressions she will have often. After an hour's talk, we to bed – the lady mightily troubled about a little pretty bitch she hath, which is very sick and will eat nothing. And the jest was, I could hear her in her chamber bemoaning the bitch; and by and by taking her to bed with her, the bitch pissed and shit abed, and she was fain to rise and had coals out of my chamber to dry the bed again.

9 November. At noon by water to the King's Head at Deptford, where Captain Taylor invites Sir W. Batten, Sir Jo. Robinson (who came in with a great deal of company from hunting and brought in a hare alive, and a great many silly stories they tell of their sport, which pleases them mightily, and me not at all, such is the different sense of pleasure in mankind) and others, upon the score of a survey of his new ship. And strange it is, to see how a good dinner and feasting reconciles everybody, Sir W. Batten and Sir Jo. Robinson being now as kind to him, and report well of his ship and proceedings and promise money, and Sir W. Batten is a solicitor for him, that it is a strange thing to observe – they being the greatest enemies he had, and yet I believe hath, in the world in their hearts. Thence after dinner stole away, and to my office, where did a great deal of business till midnight.

The Bill of Mortality, to all our griefs, is encreased 399 this week, and the encrease general through the whole city and suburbs, which makes us all sad.

13 November. Up, and to my office, where busy all the morning; and at noon to Captain Cockes to dinner as we had appointed, in order to settle our business of accounts. He did undertake under his hand to secure me in 500*l* profit for my share of the profit of what we bought of the prize goods; we agreed upon the terms, which were easier on my side then I expected; and so, with extraordinary inward joy, we part till the evening.

16–17 November. Up, and fitted myself for my journy down to the fleete; and sending my money and boy down by water to Eriffe, I borrowed a horse and rode to Eriffe; where after making a little visit to Madam Williams, who did give me information of W. Hows having bought eight bags of precious stones, taken from about the Dutch Viceadmirall's neck, of which there were eight dyamonds, which cost him 4000*l* sterling in India and hoped to have made 12000*l* here for them – and that this is told by one that sold him one of the bags, which hath nothing but rubys in it, which he hath for 35*s* – and that it will be proved he hath made 125*l* of one stone that he bought. So I on board my Lord Bruncker, and there he and Sir Edmd Pooly carried me down into the hold of the India shipp, and there did show me the greatest wealth lie in confusion that a man can see in the world – pepper scatter[ed] through every chink, you trod upon it; and in cloves and nutmegs, I walked above the knees – whole rooms full – and silk in bales, and boxes of copper plate, one of which I saw opened. Having seen this, which was as noble a sight as ever I saw in my life, I away on board and got under sail, and had a good bedd; and so sailed all night and got down to Quinbrough water, where all the great ships are now come; and there on board my Lord, and was soon received with great content. And after some little discourse, he and I on board Sir W. Pen and there held a council of warr about many wants of the fleet, but chiefly how to get slopps and victuals for the fleet now going out to convoy our Hambrough ships, that have been so long detained, for four or five months, for want of convoy; which we did accomodate one way or other, and so after much chatt, Sir W. Penn did give us a very good and neat dinner, neater I think then ever I did see at his own house at home in my life, and so was the other I eat with him. After dinner, much talk; and among other things, he and I about his money for his prize goods, wherein I did give him a cool answer but so as we did not disagree in words much; and so let that fall, and so fallowed my Lord Sandwich, who was gone a little before me on board the *Royall James*. And there spent an hour, my Lord playing upon the gittarr, which he now commends above all musique in the world, because it is bass enough for a single voice, and is so portable, and manageable without much trouble.

22 November. I heard this day that the plague is come [this week] very low; that is, 600 and odd – and great hopes of a further decrease, because of this day's being a very exceeding hard frost – and continues freezing. This day the first of the *Oxford Gazettes* came out, which is very pretty, full of news, and no folly in it – wrote by Williamson.

23 November. Up betimes, and so being trimmed, I to get papers ready against Sir H. Cholmly come to me by appointment, he being newly come over from Tanger. He did by and by come, and we settled all matters about his money; and he is a most satisfied man in me, and doth declare his resolution to give me 200*l* per annum. It continuing to be a great frost (which gives us hope for a perfect cure of the plague), he and I to walk in [Greenwich] park, and there discoursed with grief of the calamity of the times; how the King's service is performed, and how Tanger is governed by a man [Lord Belasyse], who, though honourable, yet doth mind his ways of getting, and little else compared, which will never make the place flourish. I brought him home and had a good dinner for him; and there come by chance Captain Cuttance – who tells me how W. How is laid by the heels, and confined to the *Royall Katharin* and his things all seized. And how also, for a quarrell (which endeed my Lord the other night told me), Captain Ferrers, having cut all over the back of another of my Lord's servants, is parted from my Lord. I sent for little Mrs Fr. Tooker; and after they were gone, I sat dallying with her an hour, doing what I would with my hand about her – and a very pretty creature it is. So in the evening parted, and I to the office, where late writing letters; and at my lodging later, writing for the last twelve days my journall, and so to bed.

24 November. Up, and after doing some business at the office, I to London; and there in my way, at my old oyster shop in Gracious Streete, bought two barrels of my fine woman of the shop, who is alive after all the plague – which now is the first observation or enquiry we make at London concerning everybody we knew before it. So to the Change, where very busy with several people, and mightily glad to see the Change so full, and hopes of an abatement still the next week. Off the Change, I went home with Sir G. Smith to dinner, sending for one of my barrel[s] of oysters, which were good, though come from Colchester, where the plague hath been so much. Here a very brave dinner, though no invitation; and Lord, to see how I am treated, that come from so mean a beginning, is matter of wonder to me. But it is God's great mercy to me – and His blessing upon my taking pains and being punctual in my dealings. After dinner, Captain Cocke and I about some business; and then with my other barrel of oysters home to Greenwich, sent them by water to Mrs Penington, while he and I landed and visited Mr Eveling – where most excellent discourse with him; among other things, he showed us several letters of the old Lord of Liecesters in Queen Elizabeth's time – under the very handwriting of Queen Elizabeth and Queen Mary Queen of Scotts and others, very venerable names. But Lord, how poorly methinks they wrote in those days, and in what plain uncut paper.

6 December. Up betimes, and by water to the Duke of Albemarle, who came to town from Oxford last night. He is mighty brisk, and very kind to me and asks my advice principally in everything. He surprizes me with the news that my Lord Sandwich goes Embassador to Spayne speedily – though I know not whence this arises, yet I am heartily glad of it. I spent the afternoon upon a song of Solyman's words to Roxolana that I have set; and so with my wife walked, and Mercer, to Mrs Pierces, where Captain Rolt and Mrs Knipp, Mr Coleman and his wife, and Laneare, Mrs Worship, and her singing daughter met; and by and by unexpectedly comes Mr Pierce from Oxford. Here the best company for musique I ever was in in my life, and wish I could live and die in it, both for music and the face of Mrs Pierce and my wife and Knipp, who is pretty enough, but the most excellent mad-humourd thing; and sings the noblest that ever I heard in my life, and Rolt with her, some things together most excellently – I spent the night in an ectasy almost; and having invited them to my house a day or two hence, we broke up.

The song Pepys had composed – he had probably written only the voice line – was a delightful setting of words from Davenant's The Siege of Rhodes *– 'Beauty retire, thou dost my pity move' etc. It became his favourite song. In the portrait by Hayls (opposite page 104) he is shown holding the manuscript.*

25 December. Christmas Day. To church in the morning, and there saw a wedding in the church, which I have not seen many a day, and the young people so merry one with another; and strange, to see what delight we married people have to see these poor fools decoyed into our condition, every man and wife gazing and smiling at them.

30 December. Up, and to the office. At noon home to dinner, and all the afternoon to my accounts again; and there find myself, to my great joy, a great deal worth above 4000*l*, for which the Lord be praised – and is principally occasioned by my getting 500*l* of Cocke for my profit in his bargains of prize goods, and from Mr Gawden's making me a present of 500*l* more when I paid him 8000*l* for Tanger. So to my office to write letters, then to my accounts again, and so to bed, being in great ease of mind.

1666

5 January. I, with my Lord Brouncker and Mrs Williams, by coach with four horses to London, to my Lord's house in Covent Garden. But Lord, what staring to see a nobleman's coach come to town – and porters everywhere bow to us, and such begging of beggars. And a delightful thing it is to see the town full of people again, as now it is, and shops begin to open, though in many places, seven or eight together, and more, all shut; but yet the town is full compared with what it used to be – I mean the City end, for Covent Gu[a]rden and Westminster are yet very empty of people, no Court nor gentry being there.

On 7 January the Pepyses return to their home in Seething Lane, and on the 9th the Navy Board resumes its sittings there.

10 January. To the Change, and there hear, to our grief, how the plague is encreased this week from 70 to 89.

12 January. To the office and there had an extraordinary meeting of Sir J. Mennes, Sir W. Batten, Sir W. Penn, and my Lord Brouncker and I, to hear my paper read about pursers, which they did all of them, with great good will and great approbation of my method and pains in all; only Sir W. Penn, who must except against everything and remedy nothing.

14 January. Lords Day. Long in bed – till raised by my new taylor, Mr Penny; comes and brings me my new velvet coat, very handsome but plain; and a day hence will bring me my camelott cloak. He gone, I close to my papers to set all in order, and to perform my vow to finish my journall and other things before I kiss any woman more, or drink any wine, which I must be forced to do tomorrow if I go to Greenwich, as I am invited by Mr Boreman to hear Mrs Knipp sing. And I would be glad to go, so as we may be merry. At noon eat the second of the two cygnets Mr Sheply sent us for a New Year's gift; and presently to my chamber again, and so to work hard all day about my Tanger accounts, which I am going again to make up – as also upon writing a letter to my father about Pall, whom it is time now, I find, to think of disposing of, while God Almighty hath given me something to give with her; and in my letter to my father I do offer to give her 450*l*, to make her own 50*l*, given her by my uncle, up 500*l*. I do also therein propose Mr Harman the upholster for a husband for her, to whom I have a great love, and did heretofore love his former wife, and a civil man he is, and careful in his way. Besides, I like his trade and place he lives in, being Cornehill.

Paulina did not marry Harman. Both he and another candidate for her hand (Ensum) were rejected this

Covent Garden, by W. Hollar c. 1640. Originally a 'Convent Garden' belonging to Westminster Abbey, it had been developed by the 4th Earl of Bedford (d. 1641). Inigo Jones designed St Paul's Church and the Piazza. Pepys's friend Lord Brouncker had a house there, but by the end of the century it had ceased to be fashionable.

· ·

year. In February 1668 she married John Jackson, a farmer of Ellington, Hunts. Their younger son, John, became Pepys's heir.

20 January. To the office, where I sent my boy home for some papers; where, he staying longer then I would have him and being vexed at the business and to be kept from my fellows in the office longer then was fit, I became angry and boxed my boy when he came, that I do hurt my thumb so much, that I was not able to stir all the day after and in great pain. At noon to dinner, and then to the office again late, and so to supper and to bed.

22 January. To the Crowne tavern behind the Exchange by appointment, and there met the first meeting of Gresham College since the Plague. Dr Goddard did fill us with talk in defence of his and his fellow physicians' going out of town in the plague-time; saying that their perticular patients were most gone out of town, and they left at liberty – and a great deal more, &c. But what, among other fine discourse, pleased me most, was Sir G. Ent about respiration; that it is not to this day known or concluded on among physicians, nor to be done either, how that action is managed by nature or for what use it is. Here late, till poor Dr Merritt was drunk; and so all home, and I to bed.

23 January. Up, and to the office and then to dinner. After dinner, to the office again all the afternoon, and much business with me. Good news, beyond all expectation, of the decrease of the plague; being now but 79. So home with comfort to bed. A most furious storme all night and morning.

'A delightful thing it is to see the town full of people again . . . and shops begin to open.' (5 January 1666.) Street cries, from drawings by Marcellus Laroon II 1688–9. (*From left to right*) Twelve pence a peck of oysters; the merry milk maid; a merry new song; ripe speragas; knives combs or inkhornes.

. . . .

24 January. Great Storme.   By agreement, my Lord Brouncker called me up; and though it was a very foul windy and rainy morning, yet down to the waterside we went, but no boat could go, the storm continued so. So my Lord, to stay till fairer weather, carried me into the Tower to Mr Hores, and there we stayed talking an hour; but at last we found no boat yet could go, so we to the office, where we met upon an occasion extraordinary, of examining abuses of our clerks in taking money for examining of tickets, but nothing done in it. Thence my Lord and I, the weather being a little fairer, by water to Detford to Sir G. Carteret's house, where W. How met us; and there we opened the chests and saw the poor sorry rubys which have caused all this ado to the undoing of W. How; though I am not much sorry for it, because of his pride and ill-nature. About 200 of these very small stones and a cod of muske (which it is strange I was not able to smell) is all we could find. So locked them up again, and my Lord and I, the wind being again very furious, so as we durst not go by water, walked to London quite round the bridge, no boat being able to stirre; and Lord, what a dirty walk we had, and so strong the wind, that in the fields we many times could not carry our bodies against it, but was driven backward. It was dangerous to walk the streets, the bricks and tiles falling from the houses, that the whole streets were covered with them – and whole chimneys, nay, whole houses in two or three places, blowed down. But above all, the pales on London Bridge on both sides were blown away, so that we were fain to stoop very low, for fear of blowing off of the bridge. We could see no boats in the Thames afloat but what were broke loose and carried through the bridge, it being ebbing water. And the greatest sight of all was, among other parcels of ships driven here and there in clusters together, one was quite overset, and lay with her masts all along in the water and keel above water. So walked home; my Lord away to his house and I to dinner.

The Navy Board now attends on the Duke of York at Hampton Court, where, with the King, he has just arrived from Oxford. The court has been out of London since 27 July of the previous year because of the Plague.

28 January. After changing a few words with Sir W. Coventry, who assures me of his respect and love to me and his concernment for my health in all this sickness – I went down into one of the courts and there met the King and Duke; and the Duke called me to him – and the King came to me of himself and told me: 'Mr Pepys', says he, 'I do give you thanks for your good service all this year, and I assure you I am very sensible of it.' And the Duke of Yorke did tell me with pleasure that he had read over my discourse about pursers and would have it ordered in my way, and so fell from one discourse to another.

29 January. I dined with [Sir W. Coventry] with a great deal of company and much merry discourse. Perticularly, [Mr Evelyn] intertained me with discourse of an Infirmery which he hath projected for the sick and wounded seamen against the next year, which I mightily approve of – and will endeavour to promote, it being a worthy thing.

This was a proposal for a hospital at Chatham. It came to nothing, for lack of funds. In 1708 the naval hospital at Greenwich was opened and served the navy until 1873.

4 February. Lords Day. And my wife and I the first time together at church since the Plague, and now only because of Mr Mills his coming home to preach his first sermon, expecting a great excuse for his leaving the parish before anybody went, and now staying till all are come home; but he made but a very poor and short excuse, and a bad sermon. It was a frost, and had snowed last night, which covered the graves in the churchyard, so I was the less afeared for going through.

7 February. It being fast day [for the Plague], I stayed at home all day long to set things to rights in my chamber, by taking out all my books and putting my chamber in the same condition it was before the Plague. But in the morning, doing of it and knocking up a nail, I did bruise my left thumb, so as broke a great deal of my flesh off, that it hung by a little. It was a sight frightened my wife – but I put some balsam of Mrs Turners to it, and though in great pain, yet went on with my business; and did it to my full content, setting everything in order, in hopes now that the worst of our fears are over as to the plague for the next year. Interrupted I was by two or three occasions this day, to my great vexation, having this the only day I have been able to set apart for this work since my coming to town. At night to supper, weary, and to bed – having had the plasterers and joiners also to do some jobbs.

14 February. St Valentine's Day. This morning called up by Mr Hill, who my wife thought had been come to be her valentine, she it seems having drawn him last night, but it proved not; however, calling him up to our bedside, my wife challenged him. I up and made myself ready, and so with him by coach to my Lord Sandwiches by appointment – to deliver Mr How's accounts to my Lord. My Lord being gone, I took Mr Hill to my Lord Chancellors new house that is building, and went with trouble to the top of it and there is there the noblest prospect that ever I saw in my life, Greenwich being nothing to it. And in everything is a beautiful house – and most strongly built in every respect – and as if, as it hath, it had the Chancellor for its maister. Thence with him to his painter, Mr Hales, who is drawing his picture – which will be mighty like him, and pleased me, so that I am resolved presently to have my wife's and mine done by him.

. . . .

Clarendon House, Piccadilly, 1682. Bond Street now occupies part of the site.

18 February. Lords Day. Lay long in bed, discoursing with my wife; among other things, about Pall's coming up, for she must be a little to be fashioned.

21 February. Up, and with Sir J. Mennes to Whitehall by his coach, by the way talking of my brother John, to get a spiritual promotion for him, which I now am to look after, forasmuch as he is shortly to be Maister in Arts, and writes me this week a Latin letter that he is to go into orders this Lent. There to the Duke's chamber and find our fellows discoursing there on our business; so I was sorry to come late, but no hurt was done thereby. Here the Duke, among other things, did bring out a book, of great antiquity, of some of the customs of the Navy about a hundred years since, which he did lend us to read and deliver him back again. Thence I to the Exchequer, and there did strike my tallies for a quarter for Tanger and carried them home with me. And thence to Trinity House, being invited to an Elder Brother's feast. And there met and sat by Mr Prin and had good discourse about the privileges of Parliament, which he says are few to the Commons' house, and those not examinable by them but only by the House of Lords. Thence with my Lord Bruncker to Gresham College, the first time after the sickness that I was there, and the second time any met. And hear a good lecture of Mr Hookes about the trade of felt-making, very pretty. And anon alone with me about art of drawing pictures by Prince Roberts rule and machine, and another of Dr Wren's; but he says nothing doth like squares, or, which is the best in the world, like a darke roome – which pleased me mightily.

25 February. Lords Day. My wife up between 3 and 4 of the clock in the morning to dress herself, and I about 5, and were all ready to take coach, she and I and Mercer, a little past 5; but to our trouble, the coach did not come till 6. Then, with our coach of four horses I hire on purpose, and Lashmore to ride by, we through the City, it being clear day, to Brandford, and so to Windsor (Captain Ferrer overtaking us at Kensington, being to go with us) and here drank; and so through, making no stay, to Cranborne about 11 a⁄clock, and found my Lord and the ladies at a sermon in the house – which being ended, we to them; and all the company glad to see us, and mighty merry to dinner. After dinner to talk to and again, and then to walk in the Parke, my Lord and I alone, talking.

26 February. When I consider the manner of my going hither, with a coach and four horses, and servants and a woman with us, and coming hither, being so much made of, and used with that state, and all in fine weather, and no fears nor cares upon me, I do think myself obliged to think myself happy, and do look upon myself at this time in the happiest occasion a man can be; and whereas we take pains in expectation of future comfort and ease, I have taught myself to reflect upon myself at present as happy and enjoy myself in that consideration, and not only please myself with thoughts of future wealth, and forget the pleasures we at present enjoy.

So took coach and to Windsor to the Guarter, and thither sent for Dr Childe – who came to us, and carried us to St Georges Chapel and there placed us among the Knights' stalls (and pretty the observation, that no man, but a woman, may sit in a Knight's place where any brasse plates are set). And hither comes cushions to us, and a young singing⁄boy to bring us a copy of the anthemne to be sung. And here, for our sakes, had this anthem and the great service sung extraordinary, only to entertain us. It is a noble place endeed, and a good quire of voices. After prayers, we to see the plate of the Chapel and the robes of Knights, and a man to show us the banners of the several Knights in being, which hang up over the stalls. And so to other discourse, very pretty, about that Order. Was shown where the late [King] is buried, and King Henry the 8, and my Lady Seymour. This being done, to the King's house and to observe the neatness and contrivance of the house and gates; it is the most romantique castle that is in the world. But Lord, the prospect that is in the balcone in the Queen's lodgings, and the tarrace and walk, are strange things to consider, being the best in the world, sure. Infinitely satisfied, I and my wife with all this; she being in all points mightily pleased too, which added to my pleasure. And so giving a great deal of money to this and that man and woman, we to our tavern and there dined, the Doctor with us; and so took coach and away to Eaton, the Doctor with me. At Eaton I left my wife in the coach, and he and I to the college and there find all mighty fine. The school good, and the custom pretty of boys cutting their names in the shuts of the window when they go to Cambrige; by which many a one hath lived to see himself Provost and Fellow, that had his name in the window standing. To the hall, and there find the boys' verses, *De peste*; it being their custom to make verses at Shrovetide. I read several, and very good they were, and better I think then ever I made when I was a boy – and in rolls as long and longer then the whole hall by much. Thence to the Porters, in the absence of the Butler, and did drink of the college beer, which is very good, and went into the back fields to see the scholars play. Thence took leave of the Doctor; and so

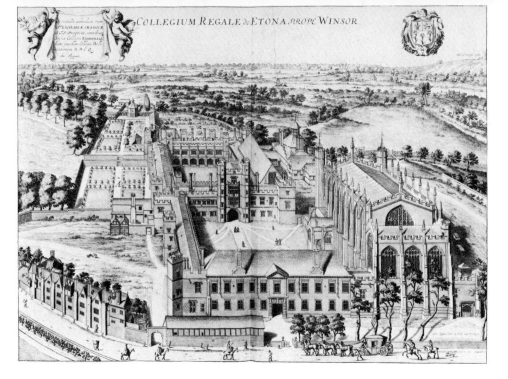

'At Eaton I left my wife in the coach, . . . and I to the college and there find all mighty fine.' (26 February 1666.) Eton College, from D. Loggan's *Cantabrigia Illustrata* 1690.

· · · · · · · · · · · · · · · · · · · ·

took coach, and finely, but sleepy, away home, and got thither about 8 at night; and after a little at my office, I to bed.

9 March. To Sir W. Batten's, and there, Mrs Knipp coming, we did spend the even together very merry, she and I singing; and God forgive me, I do still see that my nature is not to be quite conquered, but will esteem pleasure above all things; though, yet in the middle of it, it hath reluctancy after my business, which is neglected by my fallowing my pleasure. However, music and women I cannot but give way to, whatever my business is.

14 March. To Hales's to see my wife's picture, which I like mighty well; and there had the pleasure to see how suddenly he draws the heavens, laying a dark ground and then lightening it when and where he will.

17 March. Out to Hales's, where I am still infinitely pleased with my wife's picture. I paid him 14*l* for it, and 25*s* for the frame, and I think it not a whit too dear for so good a picture. It is not yet quite finished and dry, so as to be fit to bring home yet. This day I begun to sit, and he will make me, I think, a very fine picture. He promises it shall be as good as my wife's, and I sit to have it full of shadows, and do almost break my neck looking over my shoulder to make the posture for him to work by.

19 March. My Lord [Brouncker] and I to Mrs Williams's and there I saw her closet, where endeed a great many fine things there are – but the woman I hate. Here we dined, and Sir J. Minnes came to us – and after dinner we walked to the King's playhouse, all in dirt, they being altering of the stage to make it wider – but God knows when they will begin to act again. But my business here was to see the inside of the stage and all the tiring roomes and machines; and endeed it was a sight worthy seeing. But to see their clothes and the various sorts, and what a mixture of things there was, here a wooden leg, there a ruff, here a hobbyhorse, there a crowne, would make a man split himself to see with laughing – and perticularly Lacys wardrobe, and Shotrell's. But then again, to think how fine they show on the stage by candle-light, and how poor things they are to look now too near-hand, is not pleasant at all. The machines are fine, and the paintings very pretty.

24 March. After dinner I to Whitehall to a committee for Tanger, where the Duke of York was – and I acquainted myself well in what I had to do. After the committee up, I had occasion to fallow the Duke into his lodgings into a chamber where the Duchesse was sitting to have her picture drawn by Lilly, who was there at work. But I was well pleased to see that there was nothing near so much resemblance of her face in his work, which is now the second, if not the third time, as there was of my wife's at the very first time. Nor do I think at last it can be like, the lines not being in proportion to those of her face. So home and to the office, where late; and so to bed.

30 March. Home and eat one mouthful, and so to Hales's and there sat till almost quite dark upon working my gowne, which I hired to be drawn [in] it – an Indian gown, and I do see all the reason to expect a most excellent picture of it. Thus home, and to my private accounts in my chamber till past one in the morning; and so to bed – with my head full of thoughts for my evening of all my accounts tomorrow, the latter end of the month; in which God give me good issue, for I never was in such a confusion in my life, and that in great sums.

5 April. I to the office till late; and so home, and late putting notes to [my song] 'It is decreed, nor shall thy fate', &c., and then to bed.

15 April. Easter Day. To the Queen's chapel and there heard a good deal of their mass and some of their musique, which is not so contemptible, I think, as our people would make it, it pleasing me very well – and indeed, better then the anthemne I heard afterward at Whitehall at my coming back. I stayed till the King went down to receive the

. . . .

(*Opposite*) Samuel Pepys, by J. Hayls 1666. Pepys (in a hired Indian gown) holds a copy of his song 'Beauty Retire'. 'I sit to have it full of shadows, and do almost break my neck looking over my shoulder to make the posture for him to work by.' (17 March 1666.)

(*Overleaf above*) London Bridge, by C. de Jongh *c.* 1639 (detail). Three Crane Stairs at low water. The buildings on the bridge survived the Fire and were not removed until the later eighteenth century.

(*Overleaf below*) 'Home by water . . . the river beginning to be very full of ice, so as I was a little frighted.' (18 December 1665.) The Frozen Thames, by A. Hondius 1667 detail. Before the river was embanked in the nineteenth century, it was liable to freeze in the most severe winters. In 1676–7 and 1684 ice fairs were held on the Thames.

sacrament; and stood in his closett with a great many others and there saw him receive it – which I did never see the manner of before. But do see very little difference between the degree of the ceremonies used by our people in the administration thereof and that in the Roman church, saving that methought our chapel was not so fine, nor the manner of doing it so glorious, as it was in the Queenes chapel. Thence walked to Mr Pierce's and there dined, I alone with him and her and their children. Very good company, and good discourse, they being able to tell me all the business of the Court – the amours and the mad doings that are there – how for certain, Mrs Steward doth do everything now with the King that a mistress should do, and that the King hath many bastard children that are known and owned, besides the Duke of Monmouth. After a great deal of this discourse, I walked thence into the park, with her little boy James with me, who is the wittiest boy, and the best company in the world. And so back again through Whitehall both coming and going. And people did generally take him to be my boy.

18 April. By coach with Sir W. Batten and Sir Tho. Allen to Whitehall: and there, after attending the Duke as usual, and there concluding of many things preparative to the Prince and the Generalls going to sea on Monday next – Sir W. Batten and Sir Tho. Allen and I to Mr Lillys the painter's, and there saw the heads, some finished and all begun, of the flaggmen in the late great fight with the Duke of Yorke against the Dutch. The Duke hath them done to hang in his chamber, and very finely they are done endeed.

20 April. Up, and after an hour or two's talk with my poor wife, who gives me more and more content every day then other, I abroad by coach to Westminster; and there met with Mrs Martin, and she and I over the water to Stangate; and after a walk in the fields, to the King's Head and there spent an hour or two with pleasure with her, and eat a tansy and so parted. And I to the New Exchange, there to get a list of all the modern plays – which I entend to collect and to have them bound up together. Thence to Mr Hales; and there, though against his perticular mind, I had my landskip done out, and only a heaven made in the room of it; which though it doth not please me thoroughly now it is done, yet it will do better then as it was before.

21 April. Up betimes and to the office, there to prepare some things against the afternoon, for discourse about the business of the pursers and settling the pursers' matters of the fleet according to my proposition. By and by the office sat; and they being up, I continued at the office to finish my matters against the meeting before the Duke this afternoon; so home about 3 to clap a bit of meat in my mouth, and so away with Sir W. Batten to Whitehall – and there to the Duke; but he being to go abroad to take the ayre, he dismissed us presently, without doing anything till tomorrow morning. So my Lord Brouncker and I down to walk in the garden, it being a mighty hot and pleasant day; and there was the

(*Opposite*) The Fire of London, by T. Wyck *c.* 1667–70 (detail). The scene (painted from a point just west of Arundel House) shows the state of the Fire on the evening of 3 September. The heart of the conflagration is in the Billingsgate area, and St Paul's is already alight. The fire was to spread within a hundred yards of the point from which the view is taken.

King, who, among others, talked to us a little; and among other pretty things, he swore merrily that he believed the ketch that Sir W. Batten bought the last year at Colchester was of his own getting, it was so thick to its length.

25 April. Abroad to my ruler's of my books, having, God forgive me, a mind to see Nan there, which I did; and so back again, and then out again to see Mrs Bettons, who were looking out of the window as I came through Fanchurch Street – so that endeed I am not, as I ought to be, able to command myself in the pleasures of my eye. So home, and with my wife and Mercer spent our evening upon our new leads by our bedchamber, singing, while Mrs Mary Batelier looked out of the window to us; and we talked together and at last bade goodnight. The plague, blessed be God, is decreased [to] 16 this week.

28 April. Up and to the office. At noon dined at home. After dinner abroad with my wife to Hales's to see only our pictures and Mrs Pierce's, which I do not think so fine as I might have expected it. My wife to her father's to carry him some ruling work which I have advised her to let him do; it will get him some money. She also is to look out again for another little girl, the last we had being also gone home, the very same day she came. She was also to look after a necklace of pearl, which she is mighty busy about, I being contented to lay out 80*l* in one for her.

30 April. Up, and, being ready to finish my journalls for four days past, to the office, where busy all the morning. At noon dined alone, my wife gone abroad to conclude about her necklace of pearl. I after dinner to even all my accounts of this month; and, bless God, I find myself, notwithstanding great expenses of late – viz., 80*l* now to pay for a necklace, near 40*l* for a set of chairs and couch, near 40*l* for my three pictures – yet I do gather, and am now worth 5200*l*. My wife comes home by and by, and hath pitched upon a necklace with three rows, which is a very good one, and 80*l* is the price. In the evening with my [wife] and Mercer by coach to take the ayre as far as Bow, and eat and drank in the coach by the way, and with much pleasure and pleased with my company: at night home and up to the leads; but were, contrary to expectation, driven down again with a stink, by Sir W. Pen's emptying of a shitten pot in their house of office close by; which doth trouble me, for fear it do hereafter annoy me. So down to sing a little, and then to bed.

1 May. Up, and all the morning at the office. At noon my Cosen Tho. Pepys did come to me to consult about the business of his being a Justice of the Peace, which he is much against; and among other reasons, tells me as a confidence that he is not free to exercise punishment according to the act against Quakers and other people, for religion. Nor doth he understand Latin, and so is not capable of the place as formerly, now all warrants do run in Latin. Nor is he in Kent, though he be of Deptford parish, his house standing in Surry. However, I did bring him to encline toward it if he be pressed to take it. I do think it may be some repute to me to have my kinsman in commission there.

4 May. To the office a little, and then to dinner – and had a great fray with my wife about Brown's coming to teach her to paint and sitting with me at table, which I will not yield to. I do thoroughly believe she means to hurt in it, but very angry we were; and I resolved all into my having my will done, be the reason what it will – and so I will have it.

5 May. At the office all the morning. After dinner, upon a letter from the fleet from Sir W. Coventry, I did do a great deal of work for the sending away of the victuallers that are in the river &c. – too much to remember. Till 10 at night busy about letters and other necessary matters of the office. About 11, I home, it being a fine moonshine; and so my wife and Mercer came into the garden, and my business being done, we sang till about 12 at night with mighty pleasure to ourselfs and neighbours, by their casements opening. And so home to supper and to bed.

16 May. To Mr Hales and paid him for my picture and Mr Hills: for the first, 14*l* for the picture and 25*s* for the frame; and for the other, 7*l* for the picture, it being a copy of his only, and 5*s* for the frame – in all, 22*l*. 10*s*. I am very well satisfied in my pictures and so took them in another coach home along with me – and there with great pleasure my wife and I hung them up. And that being done, to dinner, where Mrs Barbara Shelden came to see us and dined with us and we kept her all the day with us, I going down to Deptford; and Lord, to see with what itching desire I did endeavour to see Bagwell's wife, but failed, for which I am glad; only, I observe the folly of my mind, that cannot refrain from pleasure at a season, above all others in my life, requisite for me to show my utmost care in.

19 May. Up, and to the office all the morning. At noon took Mr Deane (lately come to town) home with me to dinner. And then he fell to explain to me his manner of casting the draught of water which a ship will draw beforehand – which is a secret the King and all admire in him; and he is the first that hath come to any certainty beforehand of foretelling the draught of water of a ship before she be launched. He being gone, I to the office, where much business and many persons to speak with me. Late home and to bed, glad to be a little quiet.'

29 May. King's Birth and Restauracion Day. Waked with the ringing of the bells all over the town. So up before 5 a'clock, and to the office, where we met; and I all the morning with great trouble upon my spirit to think how I should come off in the afternoon when Sir W. Coventry did go to the Victualling Office to see the state of matters there. However, I had last night and this morning made myself a little able to report how matters were – and did readily go with them after dinner to the Victualling Office; and there beyond belief did acquit myself very well, to full content. Being broke up there, I with a merry heart home to my office; and thither my wife comes to me to tell me that if I would see the handsomest woman in England, I shall come home presently; and who should it be but the pretty lady of our parish that did heretofore sit on the other side of our church over against our gallery, that is since married. And so I home, and there found Creed also come to me; so there I spent most of the afternoon with them; and endeed, she is a pretty black woman – her name, Mrs Horesly. But Lord, to see how my nature could not refrain from the temptation, but I must invite them to go to Foxhall to Spring Garden, though I had freshly received minutes of a great deal of extraordinary business. However, I could not help it; but sent them before with Creed, and I did some of my business, and so after them and find them there in an arbour; and had met with Mrs Pierce and some company with her. So here I spent 20s upon them, and were pretty merry. Among other things, had a fellow that imitated all manner of birds and dogs and hogs with his voice, which was mighty pleasant. Stayed here till night; then set Mrs Pierce in at the New Exchange, and ourselfs took coach and so set Mrs Horsly home and then home ourselfs, but with great trouble in the streets by bonefires, it being the King's birthday and day of restoration; but Lord, to see the difference, how many there was on the other side, and so few our, the City side of Temple, would make one wonder the difference between the temper of one sort of people and the other – and the difference among all, between what they do now, and what it was the night when Monke came into the City – such a night as that I never think to see again, nor think it can be. After I came home, I was till one in the morning with Captain Cocke drawing up a contract with him, intended to be offered to the Duke tomorrow – which if it proceeds, he promises me 500l.

Pepys's father and sister Paulina have arrived at Seething Lane on the 30th. They stay until 23 June.

31 May. Waked very betimes in the morning by extraordinary thunder and rain, which did keep me sleeping and waking till very late; and it being a holiday, and my eye very sore, and myself having had very little sleep for a good while, till 9 a'clock – and so up, and so saw all my family up, and my father and sister (who is a pretty good-bodied woman and not over thicke, as I thought she would have been; but full of freckles and not handsome in face); and so I out by water among the ships, and to Deptford and Blackewall about business; and so home and to dinner with my father and sister and family, mighty pleasant all of us – and among other things, with a sparrow that our Mercer hath brought up now for three weeks, which is so tame, that [it] flies up and down and upon the table and eats and pecks and doth everything so pleasantly, that we are mightily pleased with it.

2 June. Up, and to the office, where certain news is brought us of a letter come to the King this morning from the Duke of Albemarle, dated yesterday at 11 a'clock as they were sailing to the Gunfleet, that they were in sight of the Duch fleete and were fitting themselfs to fight them – so that they are, ere this, certainly engaged; besides, several do averr they heard the guns all yesterday in the afternoon. This put us at the board into a tosse. Presently comes orders for our sending away to the fleet a recruite of 200 soldiers. So I rose from the table, and to the Victualling Office and thence upon the river among several vessels, to consider of the sending them away; and lastly down to Greenwich and there appointed two yachts to be ready for them – and did order the soldiers to march to Blackewall. Having set all things in order against the next flood, I went on shore with Captain Erwin at Greenwich and into the parke and there we could hear the guns from the fleete most plainly. Thence he and I to the King's Head and there bespoke a dish of steaks for our dinner about 4 a'clock. While that was doing, we walked to the waterside, and there seeing the King and Duke come down in their barge to Greenwich House, I to them and did give them an account what I was doing. They went up to the park to hear the guns of the fleet go off. Down to Blackewall and there saw the soldiers (who were by this time gotten most of them drunk) shipped off. But Lord, to see how the poor fellows kissed their wifes and sweethearts in that simple manner at their going off, and shouted and let off their guns, was strange sport.

3 June. Lords Day, Whitsunday. I to St Margaret's Westminster, and there saw at church my pretty Betty Michell. And thence to the Abbey, and so to Mrs Martin and there did what je voudrais avec her, both devante and backward, which is also muy bon plazer. I away to Whitehall and there met with this bad news: that Prince [Rupert] came to Dover but at 10 a-clock last night, and there heard nothing of a fight; that the King's orders that went on Friday for calling back the Prince, was sent but by the ordinary post on Wednesdy, and came to the Prince his hands but on the evening.

4 June. News is brought me of a couple of men come to speak with me from the fleet. So I down, and who should it be but Mr Daniel, all muffled up, and his face as black as the chimney and covered with dirt, pitch and tar, and powder, and muffled with dirty clouts and his right eye stopped with okum. He is come last night at 5 a-clock from the fleet, with a comrade of his that hath endangered another eye. They were set on shore at Harwich this morning at 2 a-clock in a ketch, with about twenty more wounded men from the *Royall Charles*. They being able to ride, took post about 3 this morning and was here between 11 and 12. I went presently into the coach with them, and carried them to Sumersett House Stairs and there took water (all the world gazing upon us and concluding it to be news from the fleet; and everybody's face appeared expecting of news) to the Privy Stairs and left them at Mr Coventry's lodging (he, though, not being there); and so I into the park to the King, and told him my Lord Generall was well the last night at 4 o'clock, and the Prince come with his fleet and joyned with his about 7. The King was mightily pleased with this news and so took me by the hand and talked a little of it – I giving him the best account I could; and then he bid me to fetch the two seamen to him – he walking into the house. So I went and fetched the seamen into the Vane Room to him, and there he heard the whole account.

The Four Days Fight (1–4 June), even more than most naval battles of this period, was a complicated engagement because of its duration. It was fought over a wide area of the North Sea between the mouth

The Four Days Fight, 1666, attributed to W. van de Welde the elder. The flagship of
the English White Squadron, commanded by the Duke of Albemarle, is in the centre.

of the Thames and the Dutch coast. For a time the English seemed to have the upper hand, but in the end it was a Dutch victory, though not a decisive one.

7 June. Up betimes, and to my office about business, and with the same expectation of congratulating ourselfs with the victory that I had yesterday. My Lord Brouncker and Sir T. Harvey, that came from Court, tell me quite contrary news, which astonishes me. That is to say, that we are beaten – lost many ships and good commanders – have not taken one ship of the enemy's; nor is it certain that we were left maisters of the field. But above all that the *Prince* run on shore upon the Galoper, and there stuck – was endeavoured to be fetched off by the Duch but could not, and so they burned her – and Sir G. Ascue is taken prisoner and carried into Holland. This news doth much trouble me, and the thoughts of the ill-consequences of it, and the pride and presumption that brought us to it.

10 June. Lords Day. The Queene, in ordinary talk before the ladies in her drawing room, did say to my Lady Castlemayne that she feared the King did take cold by staying so late abroad at her house. She answered, before them all, that he did not stay so late abroad with her, for he went betimes thence (though he doth not before 1, 2, or 3 in the morning), but must stay somewhere else. The King then coming in, and overhearing, did whisper in the eare aside and told her she was a bold impertinent woman, and bid her be gone out of the Court and not come again till he sent for her – which she did presently; and went to a lodging in the Pell Mell and kept there two or three days, and then sent to the King to know whether she might send for her things away out of her house; the King sent to her, she must first come and view them; and so she came, and the King went to her and all friends again. He tells me she did in her anger say she would be even with the King, and print his letters to her. So putting all together, we are, and are like to be, in a sad condition. We are endeavouring to raise money by borrowing it on the City; but I do not think the City will lend a farthing.

12 June. To Whitehall in hopes of a meeting of Tanger, but it could not be obtained. Walking here in the galleries, I find the Ladies of Honour dressed in their riding garbs, with coats and doublets with deep skirts, just for all the world like men, and buttoned their doublets up the breast, with perriwigs and with hats; so that, only for a long petticoat dragging under their men's coats, nobody could take them for women in any point whatever – which was an odde sight, and a sight did not please me.

Among the casualties in the recent naval battle was Sir Christopher Myngs, Vice-Admiral of the Red, who died on board his flagship the Victory. *He was a shoemaker's son, bred to the sea, and of all the English commanders the one most popular with his men. Pepys and Coventry now attend his funeral at Whitechapel.*

13 June. To Sir Chr. Mings's funerall, but find them gone to church. However, I into the church, and there met with Sir W. Coventry (who was there out of great generosity, and no person of quality there but he) and went with him into his coach; and being in it with him, there happened this extraordinary case – one of the most romantique that ever I hear of in my life, and could not have believed but that I did see it – which was this. About a dozen able, lusty, proper men came to the coach‑side with tears in their eyes, and one of them, that spoke for the rest, begun and says to Sir W. Coventry – 'We are here a dozen of us that have known and loved and served our dead commander, Sir Chr. Mings, and have now done the last office of laying him in the ground. We would be glad we had any other to offer after him, and in revenge of him – all we have is our lives. If you will please to get his Royal Highness to give us a fireshipp among us all, here is a dozen of us, out of all which choose you one to be commander, and the rest of us, whoever he is, will serve him, and, if possible, do that that shall show our memory of our dead commander and our revenge.' Sir W. Coventry was herewith much moved (as well as I, who could hardly abstain from weeping) and took their names; and so parted, telling me that he would move his Royal Highness as in a thing very extraordinary, and so we parted. The truth is, Sir Chr. Mings was a very stout man, and a man of great parts and most excellent tongue among ordinary men; and as Sir W. Coventry says, could have been the most useful man in the world at such a pinch of time as this. He was come into great renowne here at home, and more abroad, in the West Indys. He had brought his family into a way of being great. But dying at this time, his memory and name (his father being always, and at this day, a shoomaker, and his mother a hoymans daughter, of which he was used frequently to boast) will be quite forgot in a few months, as if he had never been, nor any of his name be the better by it – he having not had time to coll[ect] any estate; but is dead poor rather then rich.

16 June.   It seems the Dutch do mightily insult of their victory, and they have great reason. Sir Wm. Barkely was killed before his ship taken – and there he lies dead in a sugar chest for everybody to see, with his flagg standing up by him – and Sir George Ascue is carried up and down The Hague for people to see.

17 June. Lords Day.   My father and I walked to Grayse Inn Fields and there spent an hour or two, walking and talking of several businesses. First, as to his estate, he told me it produced about 80*l* per annum. But then there goes 30*l* per annum taxes and other things, certain charge – which I do promise to make good, as far as this 30*l* – at which the poor man was overjoyed and wept. As to Pall, he tells me he is mightily satisfied with Ensum; and so I promised to give her 500*l* presently, and to oblige myself to 100*l* more on the birth of her first child, he insuring her in 10*l* per annum for every 100*l*. And in the meantime, till she doth marry, I promise to allow her 10*l* per annum. Then as to John, I tell him I will promise him nothing, but will supply him as so much lent him – I declaring that I am not pleased with him yet. And that when his degree is over, I will send for him up hither, and if he be good for anything, doubt not to get him preferment.

20 June.   Up, but in some pain of the collique – hav[ing] of late taken too much cold by washing my feet and going in a thin silk waistcoat, without any other coat over it, and open‑breasted. But I hope it will go over. I did this morning (my father being to go away tomorrow) give my father some money to buy him a horse, and for other things, to himself and my mother and sister, among them, 20*l* – besides undertaking to pay for other things for them to about 3*l* – which the poor man takes with infinite kindness, and I do not think I can bestow it better.

23 June. My father and sister very betimes took their leave; and my wife, with all possible kindness, went with them to the coach – I being mightily pleased with their company thus long, and my father with his being here; and it rejoices my heart that I am in condition to do anything to comfort him, and could, were it not for my mother, have contented he should have stayed alway here with me – he is such innocent company.

24 June. Sir W. Coventry took his coach to Hide Parke, he and I alone. There we had much talk. First, he started a discourse of a talk he hears about the town, which, says he, is a very bad one, and fit to be suppressed if we knew how: which is the comparing of the success of the last year with that of this, saying that that was good and that bad. I was as sparing in speaking as I could, being jealous of him, and myself also, but wished it could be stopped; but said I doubted it could not, otherwise then by the fleet's being abroad again, and so finding other work for men's minds and discourse. Then to discourse of himself, saying that he heard that he was under the lash of people's discourse about the Prince's not having notice of the Dutch being out and for him to come back again, nor the Duke of Albemarle notice that the Prince was sent for back again. To which, he told me very perticularly how careful he was, the very same night that it was to resolve to send for the Prince back, to cause orders to be writ; and waked the Duke, who was then in bed, to sign them; and that they went by express that very night, being the Wednesday night before the Fight, which begun on the Friday; and that, for sending them by the post express and not by gentlemen on purpose, he made a sport of it, and said, 'I knew none to send it with but would at least have lost more time in fitting themselfs out then any diligence of theirs beyond that that the ordinary post would have recovered.' I told him that this was not so much the towne talk as the reason of dividing the fleete. To this, he told me he ought not to say much; but did assure me in general, that the proposition did first come from the fleete; and the resolution not being prosecuted with orders so soon as the Generall thought fit, the Generall did send Sir Edwd Spragge up on purpose for them; and that there was nothing in the whole business which was not done with the full consent and advice of the Duke of Albemarle.

28 June. The Dutch are now known to be out, and we may expect them every hour upon our coast. But our fleet is in pretty good readiness for them.

29 June. I away to Whitehall; and thence, the Council being up, walked to St James's and there had much discourse with Sir W. Coventry at his chamber – who I find quite weary of the war. Decries our having any war at all, or himself to have been any occasion of it. That he hopes this will make us shy of any war hereafter, or to prepare better for it. Believes that one overthrow on the Duch side would make them desire peace, and that one on ours will make us willing to accept of one. Thence home, and to the office – where I met with a letter from Dover which tells me (and it did come by express) that news is brought over by a gentleman from Callice that the Duch fleet, 130 sail, are come upon the

French coast – and that the country is bringing in pickeaxes and shovells and wheelbarrows into Callice. That there are 6,000 men, armed with head, back, and breast (Frenchmen), ready to go on board the Duch fleet, and will be fallowed by 12,000 more. That they pretend they are to come to Dover. And that thereupon the Governor of Dover Castle is getting the victuallers' provision out of the town into the castle, to secure it – but I do think this is a ridiculous conceit. But a little time will show.

1 July. Sunday. To the office, where busy; and then down to Deptford to the yard, thinking to have seen Bagwell's wife, whose husband is gone yesterday back to the fleet; but I did not see her, so missed what I went for; and so back and to the Tower several times about the business of the pressed men, and late at it, till 12 at night, shipping of them. But Lord, how some poor women did cry, and in my life I never did see such natural expression of passion as I did here – in some women's bewailing themselfs, and running to every parcel of men that were brought, one after another, to look for their husbands, and wept over every vessel that went off, thinking they might be there, and looking after the ship as far as ever they could by moonlight – that it grieved me to the heart to hear them. Besides, to see poor patient labouring men and housekeepers, leaving poor wifes and families, taken up on a sudden by strangers, was very hard; and that without press-money, but forced against all law to be gone. It is a great tyranny.

4 July. In the evening Sir W. Pen came to me, and we walked together and talked of the late fight. He says three things must [be] remedied, or else we shall be undone, by this fleet.

1. That we must fight in line, whereas we fight promiscuously, to our utter and demonstrable ruine – the Duch fighting otherwise – and we, whenever we beat them.

2. We must not desert ships of our own in distress as we did, for that makes a captain desperate, and will fling away his ship when there is no hopes left him of succour.

3. That ships, when they are a little shattered, must not take the liberty to come in of themselfs; but refit themselfs the best they can, and stay out – many of our ships coming in with very small disablings.

He told me that our very commanders, nay, our very flag-officers, do stand in need of exercizing among themselfs and discoursing the business of commanding a fleet – he telling me that even one of our flag-men in the fleet did not know which tacke lost the wind or which kept it in the last engagement.

6 July. To the Tower about shipping of some more pressed men – and that done, away to Broadstreete to Sir G. Carteret, who is at a pay of tickets all alone. And I believe not less then 1000 people in the streets. But it is a pretty thing to observe, that both there and everywhere else a man shall see many women nowadays of mean sort in the streets, but no men; men being so afeared of the press.

10 July. To the office, the yard being full of women (I believe above 300) coming to get money for their husbands and friends that are prisoners in Holland; and they lay clamouring and swearing, and cursing us, that my wife and I were afeared to send a venison pasty that we have for supper tonight to the cook's to be baked, for fear of their offering violence to it – but it went, and no hurt done. Then I took an opportunity, when they were all gone into the fore yard, and slipped into the office and there busy all the afternoon. But by and by the women got into the garden, and came all to my closet window and there tormented me; and I confess, their cries were so sad for money, and laying down the condition of their families and their husbands, and what they have done and suffered for the King, and how ill they are used by us, and how well the Duch are used here by the allowance of their masters, and what their husbands are offered to serve the Duch abroad, that I do most heartily pity them, and was ready to cry to hear them – but cannot help them; however, when the rest was gone, I did call one to me, that I heard complain only and pity her husband, and did give her some money; and she blessed me and went away.

15 July. Lords Day. Up, and to church, where our lecturer made a sorry silly sermon upon the great point of proving the truth of the Christian religion. To the park, and there, it being mighty hot, and I weary, lay down by the canaille upon the grasse and slept awhile, and was thinking of a lampoone which hath run in my head this week, to make upon the late fight at sea and the miscarriages there – but other businesses put it out of my head.

18 July. With Sir W. Pen home, calling at Lillys to have a time appointed when to be drawn among the other Commanders of Flags the last year's fight. And so full of work Lilly is, that he was fain to take his table-book out to see how his time is appointed; and appointed six days hence for him to come, between 7 and 8 in the morning.

21 July. Up, and to the office, where all the morning sitting. At noon walked in the garden with Comissioner Pett (newly come to town), who tells me how infinite the disorders are among the commanders and all officers of the fleet – no discipline – nothing but swearing and cursing, and everybody doing what they please; and the Generalls, understanding no better, suffer it, to the reproaching of this Board or whoever it will be. He himself hath been challenged twice to the field, or something as good, by Sir Edwd Spragg and Captain Seamour; he tells me the captains carry, for all the late orders, what men they please. Demand and consume what provisions they please. So that he fears, and I do no less, that God Almighty can[not] bless us while we keep in this disorder that we are in. He observing to me too, and the truth is, the gentlemen captains will undo us, for they are not to be kept in order, their friends about the King and Duke is so free, that it is not for any person but the Duke himself to have any command over them.

22 July. Lords Day. To Whitehall, where saw nobody almost, but walked up and down with Hugh May, who is a very ingenious man – among other things, discoursing of the present fashion of gardens, to make them plain – that we have the best walks of gravell in the world, France having none, nor Italy; and our green of our bowling alleys is better then any they have. So our business here being ayre, this is the best way, only with a little mixture of statues or pots, which may be handsome, and so filled with another pot of such or such, a flower or greene, as the season of the year will bear. And then for flowers, they are best seen in a little plat by themselfs; besides, their borders spoil the walks of any other garden. And then for fruit, the best way is to have walls built circularly, one within another, to the south, on purpose for fruit, and leave the walking-garden only for that use. Thence walked through the house, where most people mighty hush, and methinks melancholy. I saw not a smiling face through the whole Court.

23 July. Up and to my chamber, doing several things there of moment. And then comes Simpson the joyner, and he and I with great pains contriving presses to put my books up in; they now growing numerous, and lying one upon another on my chairs, I lose the use, to avoid the trouble of removing them when I would open a book.

28 July. At noon to dinner to the Popes Head, where my Lord Brouncker (and his mistress) dined, and Comissioner Pett, Dr Charleton, and myself entertained with a venison pasty by Sir W. Warren. Here, very pretty discourse of Dr Charleton concerning Nature's fashioning every creature's teeth according to the food she intends them. And that man's, it is plain, was not for flesh, but for fruit. And that he can at any time tell the food of a beast unknown, by the teeth. My Lord Brouncker made one or two objections to it; that creatures find their food proper for their teeth, rather then that the teeth was fitted for the food. But the Doctor, I think, did well observe that creatures do naturally, and from the first, before they have had experience to try, do love such a food rather than another. And that all children love fruit, and none brought to flesh but against their wills at first. Thence with my Lord to his coach house, and there put in six horses into his coach and he and I alone to Highgate – all the way, going and coming. I learning of him the principles of optickes, and what it is that makes an object seem less or bigger. And how much distance doth lessen an object. And that it is not the eye at all, or any rule in optiques, that can tell distance; but it is only an act of reason, comparing of one mark with another. Which did both please and inform me mightily. Being come thither, we went to my Lord Lauderdale's house to speak with him about getting a man at Lieth to join with one we imploy to buy some prize goods for the King. We find [him] and his lady and some Scotch people at supper – pretty odd company; though my Lord Brouncker tells me my Lord Lauderdale is a man of mighty good reason and judgment. But at supper there played one of their servants upon the viallin, some Scotch tunes only; but Lord, the strangest ayre that ever I heard in my life, and all of one cast. But strange to hear my Lord Lauderdale say himself, that he had rather hear a catt mew then the best musique in the world – and the better the music, the more sick it makes him. And that of all instruments, he hates the lute most; and next to that, the baggpipe.

On 25 July, in the engagement off the mouth of the Thames which came to be known as the 'St James's Day Fight', the English fleet, under Rupert and Albemarle, had the better of the Dutch, and avenged their defeat in the Four Days Fight of the previous month.

29 July. Lords Day. Up and all the morning in my chamber, making up my accounts in my book with my father and brother, and stating them. Towards noon, before sermon was done at church, comes news by letter to Sir W. Batten (to my hand) of the late fight – which I sent to his house, he at church: but Lord, with what impatience I stayed till sermon was done, to know the issue of the fight, with a thousand hopes and fears and thoughts about the consequences of either. At last sermon is done and he came home, and the bells immediately rung as soon as the church was done. By and by, a letter from Sir W. Coventry tells me that we have the victory.

30 July. I find my wife plainly dissatisfied with me, that I can spend so much time with Mercer, teaching her to sing, but it is because that the girl doth take music mighty readily, and she doth not; and music is the thing of the world that I love most, and all the pleasure almost that I can now take. So to bed in some little discontent, but no words from me.

1 August. To Mrs Martins, but she abroad; so I sauntered to or again to the Abbey, and then to the parish church, fearful of being seen to do so; and so after the parish church was ended, I to the Swan and there dined upon a rabbit; and after dinner to Mrs Martins and there find Mrs Burroughs, and by and by comes a pretty widow, one Mrs Eastwood, and one Mrs Fenton, a maid. And here merry, kissing and looking on their breasts and all the innocent pleasure in the world. But Lord, to see the dissembling of this widow; how upon the singing of a certain jigg by Doll, Mrs Martin's sister, she seemed to be sick, and fainted and God knows what, because the jigg which her husband (who died this last sickeness) loved. But by and by I made her as merry as is possible, and tossed and tumbled her as I pleased, and then carried her and her sober pretty kinswoman, Mrs Fenton, home to their lodging in the new market of my Lord Treasurers, and there left them. Mightily pleased with this afternoon's mirth – but in great pain to ride in a coach with them for fear of being seen. So home, and there much pleased with my wife's drawing today in her pictures; and so to supper and to bed, very pleasant.

5 August. Lords Day. Up, and down to the Old Swan; and there called Betty Michell and her husband and had two or three long salutes from her out of sight of su marido, which pleased me mightily. And so carried them by water to Westminster; and I to St James's and there had a meeting before the Duke of York, complaining of want of money; but nothing done to any purpose, for want we shall; so that now our advices to him signify nothing. Thence walked to the parish church to have one look upon Betty Michell; and so away homeward by water, and landed to go to the church, where I believe Mrs Horsly

St James's Day Fight, 25 July 1666, by W. Hollar. The aim of both fleets was to fight in line.

goes, by Merchant Taylor hall. And there I find in the pulpit Elborough, my old schoolfellow and a simple rogue; and yet I find preaching a very good sermon, and in as right a parson-like manner, and in good manner too, as I have heard anybody; and the church very full – which is a surprizing consideration. But I did not see her. So home, and had a good dinner; and after dinner, with my wife and Mercer and Jane by water all the afternoon up as high as Moreclacke, with great pleasure, and a fine day – reading over the second part of *The Siege of Rhodes* with great delight. We landed and walked at Barne Elmes; and then at the neat-houses I landed and bought a millon (and we did also land and eat and drink at Wandsworth); and so to the Old Swan, and there walked home – it being a mighty fine evening, cool evening; and there being come, my wife and I spent an hour in the garden, talking of our living in the country when I shall be turned out of the office, as I fear the Parliament may find faults enough with the office to remove us all. And I am joyed to think in how good a condition I am to retire thither.

7 August. After dinner to the office and did a great deal of business. In the evening comes Mr Reeves with a 12-foote glasse; and so I left the office and home, where I met Mr Batelier with my wife, in order to their going tomorrow by agreement to Bow to see a dancing meeting. But Lord, to see how soon I could conceive evil fears and thought concerning them. So Reeves and I and they up to the top of the house, and there we endeavoured to see the moon and Saturne and Jupiter; but the heaven proved cloudy, and so we lost our labour, having taken pains to get things together in order to the managing of our long glass. So down to supper and then to bed, Reeves lying at my house; but good discourse I had from him in his own trade concerning glasses. And so all of us late to bed.

I receive fresh intelligence that Deptford and Greenwich are now afresh exceedingly afflicted with the sickness, more then ever.

8 August. Discoursed with Mr Hooke a little, about the nature of musicall sounds made by strings, mighty prettily; and told me that having come to a certain number of vibracions proper to make any tone, he is able to tell how many strokes a fly makes with her wings (those flies that hum in their flying) by the note that it answers to in musique during their flying. That, I suppose, is a little too much raffined; but his discourse in general of sound was mighty fine.

'By water all the afternoon up as high as Moreclacke, with great pleasure, and fine day
... we landed and walked at Barne Elmes.' (5 August 1666.) From a broadsheet ballad.

13 August. I to Paul's churchyard to treat with a bookbinder to come and gild the backs of all my books to make them handsome, to stand in my new presses when they come.

14 August. Thanksgiving Day [for the late victory.] After dinner with my wife and Mercer to the Beare Garden, where I have not been I think of many years, and saw some good sport of the bull's tossing of the dogs – one into the very boxes. But it is a very rude and nasty pleasure. We had a great many hectors in the same box with us (and one, very fine, went into the pit and played his dog for a wager, which was a strange sport for a gentleman), where they drank wine, and drank Mercer's health first, which I pledged with my hat off. And who should be in the house but Mr Pierce the surgeon, who saw us and spoke to us. Thence home, well enough satisfied however with the variety of this afternoon's exercise; and so I to my chamber, till in the evening our company came to supper we had invited to a venison pasty – Mr Batelier and his sister Mary, Mrs Mercer, her daughter Anne, Mr Le Brun, and W. Hewers. And so we supped, and very merry. And then about 9 a'clock to Mrs Mercers gate, where [was] the [bonfire], and her son had provided abundance of serpents and rockets; and there mighty merry (my Lady Pen and Pegg going thither with us and Nan Wright) till about 12 at night, flinging our fireworks and burning one another and the people over the way. And at last, our businesses being most spent – we into Mrs Mercers, and there mighty merry, smutting one another with candlegresse and soot, till most of us were like devils; and that being done, then we broke up and to my house, and there I made them drink; and upstairs we went, and then fell into dancing (W. Batelier dancing well) and dressing, him and I like women; and Mercer put on a suit of Toms, like a boy, and mighty mirth we had, and Mercer danced a jigg, and Nan Wright and my wife and Pegg Pen put on periwigs. Thus we spent till 3 or 4 in the morning, mighty merry; and then parted and to bed.

15 August. Mighty sleepy; slept till past 8 of the clock, and was called up by a letter from Sir W. Coventry; which, among other things, tells me how we have burned 160 ships of the enemy within the Fly. I up, and with all possible haste, and in pain for fear of coming late, it being our day of attending the Duke of York, to St James's, where they are full of the perticulars – how they are generally good merchant ships, some of them laden, and supposed rich ships. We spent five fireships upon them. We landed on the Schelling (Sir Ph. Howard with some men, and Holmes I think with others, about a thousand in all), and burned a town – and so came away. We were led to this by, it seems, a renegado captain of the Hollanders, who found himself ill-used by De Ruyter for his good service, and so came over to us; and hath done us good service, so that now we trust him, and he himself did go on this expedition.

16 August. I to the office, where all the afternoon very busy and doing much business. But here I had a most eminent experience of the evil of being behindhand in business; I was the most backward to begin anything, and would fain have framed to myself an occasion of going abroad, and should I doubt have done it – but some business coming in, one after another, kept me there, and I fell to the ridding away of a great deal of business; and when my hand was in it, was so pleasing a sight to [see] my papers disposed of, and letters answered which troubled my book and table, that I could have continued there with delight all night long.

17 August. With Captain Erwin, discoursing about the East Indys, where he hath often been. And among other things, he tells me how the King of Syam seldom goes out without thirty or forty thousand people with him, and not a word spoke nor a hum or cough in the whole company to be heard. He tells me the punishment frequently there for malefactors is cutting off the crowne of their head, which they do very dexterously, leaving their brains bare, which kills them presently. He told me, what I remember he hath once done heretofore – that everybody is to lie flat down at the coming by of the King, and nobody to look upon him, upon pain of death. And that he and his fellows, being strangers, were invited to see the sport of taking of a wild eliphant. And they did only kneel and look toward the King. Their druggerman did desire them to fall down, for otherwise he should suffer for their contempt of the King. The sport being ended, a messenger comes from the King, which the druggerman thought had been to have taken away his life. But it was to enquire how the strangers liked the sport. The druggerman answered that they did cry it up to be the best that ever they saw, and that they never heard of any prince so great in everything as this King. The messenger being gone back, Erwin and his company asked their druggerman what he had said, which he told them. 'But why', say they, 'would you say that without our leave, it being not true?' 'It is no matter for that', says he, 'I must have said it, or have been hanged, for our King doth not live by meat nor drink, but by having great lyes told him.'

19 August. Lords Day. Up, and to my chamber, and there begun to draw out fair and methodically my accounts of Tanger. But by and by comes by agreement Mr Reeves, and after him Mr Spong; and all day with them, both before and after dinner till 10 a-clock at night, upon opticke enquiries – he bringing me a frame with closes on, to see how the rays of light do cut one another, and in a dark room with smoake, which is very pretty. He did also bring a lantern with pictures in glass to make strange things appear on a wall, very pretty. We did also at night see Jupiter and his girdle and satellites very fine with my 12-foot glass, but could not Saturne, he being very dark. Spong and I also had several fine discourses upon the globes this afternoon, perticularly why the fixed stars do not rise and set at the same hour all the year long, which he could not demonstrate, nor I neither, the reason of. So it being late, after supper they away home. But it vexed me to understand no more from Reeves and his glasses touching the nature and reason of the several refractions of the several figured glasses, he understanding the acting part but not one bit the theory, nor can make anybody understand it – which is a strange dullness methinks.

21 August. Home and there find Mr Batelier and his sister Mary, and we sat chatting a great while, talking of wiches and spirits; and he told me of his own knowledge, being with some others at Bourdeaux, making a bargain with another man at a taverne for some claretts, they did hire a fellow to thunder (which he had the art of doing upon a deale board) and to rain and hail; that is, make the noise of – so as did give them a pretence of undervaluing their merchants wines, by saying this thunder would spoil and turn them – which was so reasonable to the merchant that he did abate two pistolls per ton for the wine, in belief of that – whereas, going out, there was no such thing.

During the night of 2 September the Great Fire broke out. It was to rage for four days and nights, causing more damage than any similar calamity until the great blitz of 1940–2. Few lives were lost, but some four-fifths of the total area of the city was laid waste (see front endpaper). It began accidentally in a bakehouse in Pudding Lane, but was commonly believed to have been the work of papists and the foreign enemy. Pepys's account will remind many readers of their experiences in the air-raids of the Second World War.

2 September. Lords Day. Some of our maids sitting up late last night to get things ready against our feast today, Jane called us up, about 3 in the morning, to tell us of a great fire they saw in the City. So I rose, and slipped on my nightgown and went to her window, and thought it to be on the back side of Markelane at the furthest; but being unused to such fires as fallowed, I thought it far enough off, and so went to bed again and to sleep. About 7 rose again to dress myself, and there looked out at the window and saw the fire not so much as it was, and further off. So to my closet to set things to rights after yesterday's cleaning. By and by Jane comes and tells me that she hears that above 300 houses have been burned down tonight by the fire we saw, and that it was now burning down all Fishstreet by London Bridge. So I made myself ready presently, and walked to the Tower and there got up upon one of the high places, Sir J. Robinsons little son going up with me; and there I did see the houses at that end of the bridge all on fire, and an infinite great fire on this and the other side the end of the bridge – which, among other people, did trouble me for poor little Michell and our Sarah on the Bridge. So down, with my heart full of trouble, to the Lieutenant of the Tower, who tells me that it begun this morning in the King's bakers house in Pudding Lane, and that it hath burned down St Magnes Church and most part of Fishstreete already. So I down to the waterside and there got a boat and through bridge, and there saw a lamentable fire. Poor Michells house, as far as the Old Swan, already burned that way and the fire running further, that in a very little time it got as far as the Stillyard while I was there. Everybody endeavouring to remove their goods, and flinging into the river or bringing them into lighters that lay off. Poor people staying in their houses as long as till the very fire touched them, and then running into boats or clambering from one pair of stair by the waterside to another. And among other things, the poor pigeons I perceive were loath to leave their houses, but hovered about the windows and balconies till they were some of them burned, their wings, and fell down.

Having stayed, and in an hour's time seen the fire rage every way, and nobody to my sight endeavouring to quench it, but to remove their goods and leave all to the fire; and having seen it get as far as the Steeleyard, and the wind mighty high and driving it into the city, and everything, after so long a drougth, proving combustible, even the very stones of churches. I to Whitehall with a gentleman with me who desired to go off from the Tower to see the fire in my boat – to Whitehall, and there up to the King's closet in the chapel, where people came about me and I did give them an account dismayed them all; and word was carried in to the King, so I was called for and did tell the King and Duke of York what I saw, and that unless his Majesty did command houses to be pulled down, nothing could stop the fire. They seemed much troubled, and the King commanded me to go to my Lord Mayor from him and command him to spare no houses but to pull down before the fire every way. The Duke of York bid me tell him that if he would have any more soldiers, he shall. Here meeting with Captain Cocke, I in his coach, which he lent me, and Creed with me, to Pauls; and there walked along Watling Street as well as I could, every creature coming away loaden with goods to save – and here and there sick people carried away in beds. Extraordinary good goods carried in carts and on backs. At last met my Lord Mayor in Canning Streete, like a man spent, with a hankercher about his neck. To the King's message, he cried like a fainting woman, 'Lord, what can I do? I am spent! People will not obey me. I have been pull[ing] down houses. But the fire overtakes us faster then we can do it.' That he needed no more soldiers; and that for himself, he must go and refresh himself, having been up all night. So he left me, and I him, and walked home – seeing people all almost distracted and no manner of means used to quench the fire. The houses too, so very thick thereabouts, and full of matter for burning, as pitch and tar, in Thames Street – and warehouses of oyle and wines and brandy and other things. Here I saw Mr Isaccke Houblon, that handsome man – prettily dressed and dirty at his door at Dowgate, receiving some of his brothers things whose houses were on fire; and as he says, have been removed twice already, and he doubts (as it soon proved) that they must be in a little time removed from his house also – which was a sad consideration. And to see the churches all filling with goods, by people who themselfs should have been quietly there at this time.

As soon as dined, I and Moone away and walked through the City, the streets full of nothing but people and horses and carts loaden with goods, ready to run over one another, and removing goods from one burned house to another – they now removing out of Canning Street (which received goods in the morning) into Lumbard Streete and further. We parted at Pauls, he home and I to Pauls Wharf, where I had appointed a boat to

'The streets full of . . . people and horses and carts loaden with goods, ready to run over one another.' (2 September 1666.) The flights from the Fire, by a Dutch artist *c*. 1666.

· ·

attend me; and took in Mr Carcasse and his brother, whom I met in the street, and carried them below and above bridge, to and again, to see the fire, which was now got further, both below and above, and no likelihood of stopping it. Met with the King and Duke of York in their barge, and with them to Queen Hith and there called Sir Rd. Browne to them. Their order was only to pull down houses apace, and so below bridge at the waterside; but little was or could be done, the fire coming upon them so fast. Good hopes there was of stopping it at the Three Cranes above, and at Buttolphs Wharf below bridge, if care be used; but the wind carries it into the City, so as we know not by the waterside what it doth there. River full of lighter[s] and boats taking in goods, and good goods swimming in the water; and only, I observed that hardly one lighter or boat in three that had the goods of a house in, but there was a pair of virginalls in it. Having seen as much as I could now, I away to Whitehall by appointment, and there walked to St James's Park, and there met my wife and Creed and Wood and his wife and walked to my boat, and there upon the water again, and to the fire up and down, it still increasing and the wind great. So near the fire as we could for smoke; and all over the Thames, with one's face in the wind you were almost burned with a shower of firedrops – this is very true – so as houses were burned by these drops and flakes of fire, three or four, nay five or six houses, one from another. When we could endure no more upon the water, we to a little alehouse on the Bankside over against the Three Cranes, and there stayed till it was dark almost and saw the fire grow; and as it grow darker, appeared more and more, and in corners and upon steeples and between churches and houses, as far as we could see up the hill of the

City, in a most horrid malicious bloody flame, not like the fine flame of an ordinary fire. We stayed till, it being darkish, we saw the fire as only one entire arch of fire from this to the other side the bridge, and in a bow up the hill, for an arch of above a mile long. It made me weep to see it. The churches, houses, and all on fire and flaming at once, and a horrid noise the flames made, and the cracking of houses at their ruine. So home with a sad heart, and there find everybody discoursing and lamenting the fire; and poor Tom Hater came with some few of his goods saved out of his house, which is burned upon Fish Street Hill. I invited him to lie at my house, and did receive his goods; but was deceived in his lying there, the noise coming every moment of the growth of the fire, so as we were forced to begin to pack up our own goods and prepare for their removal. And did by mooneshine (it being brave, dry, and moonshine and warm weather) carry much of my goods into the garden, and Mr Hater and I did remove my money and iron chests into my cellar – as thinking that the safest place. And got my bags of gold into my office ready to carry away, and my chief papers of accounts also there, and my tallies into a box by themselfs. So great was our fear, as Sir W. Batten had carts come out of the country to fetch away his goods this night. We did put Mr Hater, poor man, to bed a little; but he got but very little rest, so much noise being in my house, taking down of goods.

3 September. About 4 a-clock in the morning, my Lady Batten sent me a cart to carry away all my money and plate and best things to Sir W. Riders at Bednall Greene; which I did, riding myself in my nightgown in the cart; and Lord, to see how the streets and the highways are crowded with people, running and riding and getting of carts at any rate to fetch away thing[s]. I find Sir W. Rider tired with being called up all night and receiving things from several friends. His house full of goods – and much of Sir W. Batten and Sir W. Penn's. I am eased at my heart to have my treasure so well secured. Then home, with much ado to find a way. Nor any sleep all this night to me nor my poor wife. But then, and all this day, she and I and all my people labouring to get away the rest of our things, and did get Mr Tooker to get me a lighter to take them in, and we did carry them (myself some) over Tower Hill, which was by this time full of people's goods, bringing their goods thither. At night, lay down a little upon a quilt of W. Hewer in the office (all my own things being packed up or gone); and after me, my poor wife did the like – we having fed upon the remains of yesterday's dinner, having no fire nor dishes, nor any opportunity of dressing anything.

4 September. Sir W. Batten, not knowing how to remove his [wine], did dig a pit in the garden and laid it in there; and I took the opportunity of laying all the papers of my office that I could not otherwise dispose of. And in the evening Sir W. Penn and I did dig another and put our wine in it, and I my parmezan cheese as well as my wine and some other things.

This afternoon, sitting melancholy with Sir W. Penn in our garden and thinking of the certain burning of this office without extraordinary means, I did propose for the sending up of all our workmen from Woolwich and Deptford yards (none whereof yet appeared), and to write to Sir W. Coventry to have the Duke of York's permission to pull down houses rather then lose this office, which would much hinder the King's business.

Within the engraving: *These Engins,(which are the best)to quinch great Fires; are*

JOHN KEELING Fecit

(*Left*) A seventeenth-century fire squirt, and (*right*) John Keeling's fire engine. In the absence of efficient pumps and flexible hose, fire-fighting equipment was hopelessly inadequate to cope with any large-scale outbreak.

So Sir W. Penn he went down this night, in order to the sending them up tomorrow morning.

This night Mrs Turner (who, poor woman, was removing her goods all this day – good goods, into the garden, and knew not how to dispose of them) – and her husband supped with my wife and I at night in the office, upon a shoulder of mutton from the cook's, without any napkin or anything, in a sad manner but were merry. Only, now and then walking into the garden and saw how horridly the sky looks, all on a fire in the night, was enough to put us out of our wits; and endeed it was extremely dreadfull – for it looks just as if it was at us, and the whole heaven on fire. I after supper walked in the dark down to Tower Street, and there saw it all on fire at the Trinity House on that side and the Dolphin tavern on this side, which was very near us – and the fire with extraordinary vehemence. Now begins the practice of blowing up of houses in Tower Street, those next the Tower, which at first did frighten people more then anything; but it stop[ped] the fire where it was done – it bringing down the houses to the ground in the same places they stood, and then it was easy to quench what little fire was in it, though it kindled nothing almost. W. Hewer this day went to see how his mother did, and comes late home, but telling us how he hath been forced to remove her to Islington, her house in Pye Corner being burned. So that it is got so far that way and all the Old Bayly, and was running down to Fleetestreete. And Pauls is burned, and all Cheapside. I wrote to my father this night; but the post-house being burned, the letter could not go.

5 September. I lay down in the office again upon W. Hewer's quilt, being mighty weary and sore in my feet with going till I was hardly able to stand. About 2 in the morning my wife calls me up and tells of new cryes of 'Fyre!' – it being come to Barkeing Church, which is the bottom of our lane. I up; and finding it so, resolved presently to take her away; and did, and took my gold (which was about 2,350*l*), W. Hewer, and Jane down by Poundy's boat to Woolwich. But Lord, what a sad sight it was by moonlight to see the whole City almost on fire – that you might see it plain at Woolwich, as if you were by it. There when I came, I find the gates shut, but no guard kept at all; which troubled me, because of discourses now begun that there is plot in it and that the French had done it. I got the gates open, and to Mr Shelden's, where I locked up my gold and charged my wife and W. Hewer never to leave the room without one of them in it night nor day. So back again, by the way seeing my goods well in the lighters at Deptford and watched well by people. Home, and whereas I expected to have seen our house on fire, it being now about 7 a'clock, it was not. But to the fyre, and there find greater hopes then I expected; for my confidence of finding our office on fire was such, that I durst not ask anybody how it was with us, till I came and saw it not burned. But going to the fire, I find, by the blowing up of houses and the great help given by the workmen out of the King's yards, sent up by Sir W. Penn, there is a good stop given to it, as well as Marke Lane end as ours – it having only burned the dyall of Barkeing Church, and part of the porch, and was there quenched. I up to the top of Barkeing steeple, and there saw the saddest sight of desolation that I ever saw. Everywhere great fires. Oyle cellars and brimstone and other things burning. I became afeared to stay there long; and therefore down again as fast as I could, the fire being spread as far as I could see it, and to Sir W. Penn's and there eat a piece of cold meat, having eaten nothing since Sunday but the remains of Sunday's dinner.

Here I met with Mr Young and Whistler; and having removed all my things, and received good hopes that the fire at our end is stopped, they and I walked into the town and find Fanchurch Street, Gracious Street, and Lumbard Street all in dust. The Exchange a sad sight, nothing standing there of all the statues or pillars but Sir Tho. Gresham's picture in the corner. Walked into Moorefields (our feet ready to burn, walking through the town among the hot coles) and find that full of people, and poor wretches carrying their goods there, and everybody keeping his goods together by themselfs (and a great blessing it is to them that it is fair weather for them to keep abroad night and day); drank there, and paid twopence for a plain penny loaf.

Thence homeward, having passed through Cheapside and Newgate Market, all burned. And took up (which I keep by me) a piece of glass of Mercer's Chapel in the street, where much more was, so melted and buckled with the heat of the fire, like parchment. I also did see a poor catt taken out of a hole in the chimney joyning to the wall of the Exchange, with the hair all burned off the body and yet alive. So home at night, and find there good hopes of saving our office – but great endeavours of watching all night and having men ready; and so we lodged them in the office, and had drink and bread and cheese for them. And I lay down and slept a good night about midnight – though when I rose, I hear that there had been a great alarme of French and Duch being risen – which proved nothing. But it is a strange thing to see how long this time did look since Sunday, having been alway full of variety of actions, and little sleep.

6 September. Up about 5 a-clock, and there met Mr Gawden at the gate of the office (I entending to go out, as I used every now and then to do, to see how the fire is) to call our men to Bishoppsgate, where no fire had yet been near, and there is now one broke out – which did give great grounds to people, and to me too, to think that there is some kind of plott in this (on which many by this time have been taken, and it hath been dangerous for any stranger to walk in the streets); but I went with the men and we did put it out in a little time, so that that was well again. It was pretty to see how hard the women did work in the cannells sweeping of water; but then they would scold for drink and be as drunk as devils. I saw good butts of sugar broke open in the street, and people go and take handfuls out and put into beer and drink it.

7 September. Up by 5 a-clock and, blessed be God, find all well, and by water to Paul's Wharfe. Walked thence and saw all the town burned, and a miserable sight of Pauls Church, with all the roofs fallen and the body of the quire fallen into St Fayths – Paul's School also, Ludgate, Fleet Street – my father's house, and the church, and a good part of the Temple the like. So to Creeds lodging near the New Exchange, and there find him laid down upon a bed, the house all unfurnished, there being fears of the fire's coming to them. There borrowed a shirt of him, and washed. To Sir W. Coventry at St James's, who lay without curtains, having removed all his goods – as the King at Whitehall and everybody had done and was doing.

This day our merchants first met at Gresham College, which by proclamation is to be their Exchange. Strange to hear what is bid for houses all up and down here – a friend of Sir W. Riders having 150*l* for what he used to let for 40*l* per annum. I home late to Sir W. Penn, who did give me a bed – but without curtains or hangings, all being down. So here I went the first time into a naked bed, only my drawers on – and did sleep pretty well; but still, both sleeping and waking, had a fear of fire in my heart, that I took little rest.

8 September. To Gresham College – where infinite of people; partly through novelty to see the new place, and partly to find out and hear what is become one man of another. I met with many people undone, and more that have extraordinary great losses. People speaking their thoughts variously about the beginning of the fire and the rebuilding of the City. Then to Sir W. Batten and took my brother with me, and there dined with a great company of neighbours, and much good discourse; among others, of the low spirits of some rich men in the City, in sparing any encouragement to the poor people that wrought for the saving their houses. Among others, Alderman Starling, a very rich man, without children, the fire at next door to him in our lane – after our men had saved his house, did give 2*s* 6*d* among thirty of them, and did quarrel with some that would remove the rubbish out of the way of the fire, saying that they came to steal.

Elizabeth's brother Balty St Michel and his wife now arrive to help the Pepyses to put their house and belongings to rights.

13 September. Up, and down to Tower Wharfe; and there with Balty and labourers from Deptford did get my goods housed well at home. So down to Deptford again to fetch the rest, and there eat a bit of dinner at the Globe, while the labourers went to dinner. Here I hear that this poor town doth bury still of the plague seven or eight in a day. So to Sir G. Carteret's to work; and there did, to my great content, ship off all the rest of my goods, saving my pictures and fine things, that I will bring home in wherrys when my house is fit to receive them. And so home and unloaden them by carts and hands before night, to my exceeding satisfaction; and so after supper to bed in my house, the first time I have lain there; and lay with my wife in my old closet upon the ground, and Balty and his wife in the best chamber, upon the ground also.

14 September. Up, and to work, having carpenters come to help in setting up bedsteads and hangings; and at that trade my people and I all the morning, till pressed by public business to leave them, against my will, in the afternoon; and yet I was troubled in being at home, to see all my goods lie up and down the house in a bad condition, and strange workmen going to and fro might take what they would almost. All the afternoon busy; and Sir W. Coventry came to me, and found me, as God would have it, in my office, and people about me setting my papers to rights; and there discoursed about getting an account ready against the Parliament, and thereby did create me infinite of business, and to be done on a sudden, which troubled me; but however, he being gone, I about it late and to good purpose; and so home, having this day also got my wine out of the ground again and set it in my cellar; but with great pain to keep the port[er]s that carried it in from observing the money chests there. So to bed as last night; only, my wife and I upon a bedstead with curtains in that which was Mercer's chamber, and Balty and his wife (who are here and do us good service) where we lay last night.

15 September. All the morning at the office, Harman being come, to my great satisfaction, to put up my beds and hangings; so I am at rest, and fallowed my business all day. Dined with Sir W. Batten. Mighty busy about this account, and while my people were busy, myself wrote near thirty letters and orders with my own hand. At it till 11 at night; and it is strange to see how clear my head was, being eased of all the matter of all those letters; whereas one would think that I should have been dozed – I never did observe so much of myself in my life. Home to bed and find, to my infinite joy, many rooms clean, and myself and wife lie in our own chamber again. But much terrified in the nights nowadays, with dreams of fire and falling down of houses.

17 September. Up betimes, and shaved myself after a week's growth; but Lord, how ugly I was yesterday and how fine today. By water, seeing the City all the way, a sad sight endeed, much fire being still in – to Sir W. Coventry, and there read over my yesterday's work; being a collection of the perticulars of the excess of charge created by a war – with good content.

7 October. Lords Day. With Sir J. Mennes to Whitehall, where met by W. Batten and Lord Brouncker, to attend the King and Duke of York at the cabinet; but nobody had determined what to speak of, but only in general to ask for money – so I was forced immediately to prepare in my mind a method of discoursing. And anon we were called in to the Green Room, where the King, Duke of York, Prince Rupert, Lord Chancellor, Lord Treasurer, Duke of Albemarle, G. Carteret, W. Coventry, Morrice. Nobody beginning, I did, and made a current and, I thought, a good speech, laying open the ill state of the Navy. I had no sooner done, but Prince Rupert rose up and told the King in a heat that whatever the gentleman had said, he had brought home his fleet in as good a condition as ever any fleet was brought home. I therefore did only answer that I was sorry for his Highness's offence, but that what I said was but the report we received from those entrusted in the fleet to inform us. He muttered, and repeated what he had said; and so after a long silence on all hands, nobody, not so much as the Duke of Albemarle, seconding the Prince, nor taking notice of what he said, we withdrew.

8 October. The King hath yesterday in council declared his resolution of setting a fashion for clothes, which he will never alter. It will be a vest, I know not well how. But it is to teach the nobility thrift, and will do good.

12–13 October. I met with notice of a meeting of the Commissioners for Tanger tomorrow, and so I must have my accounts ready for them; which caused me to confine myself to my chamber presently and set to the making up my accounts, which I find very clear, but with much difficulty, by reason of my not doing them sooner, things being out of my mind. It cost me till 4 a-clock in the morning; and which was pretty, to think I was above an hour, after I had made all right, in casting up of about twenty sums, being dozed with much work, and had for forty times together forgot to carry the 60 which I had in my mind in one denomination which exceeded 60 – and this did confound me for above an hour together. At last all even and done, and so to bed. Up at 7, and so to the office, after looking over my last night's work. To Whitehall, and there the Duke of York (who is gone over to all his pleasures again, and leaves off care of business, what with his woman, my Lady Denham, and his hunting three times a week) was just come in from hunting. So I stood and saw him dress himself and try on his vest, which is the King's new fashion, and will be in it for good and all on Monday next, the whole Court: it is a fashion the King says he will never change. He being ready, he and my Lord Chancellor and Duke of Albemarle and Prince Rupert, Lord Bellasses, Sir H. Cholmly, Povy, and myself met at a committee for Tanger. My Lord Bellasses propositions were read and discoursed of, about reducing the garrison to less charge. And endeed, I am mad in love with my Lord Chancellor, for he doth comprehend and speak as well, and with the greatest easiness and authority, that ever I saw man in my life. I did never observe how much easier a man doth speak, when he knows all the company to be below him, then in him; for though he spoke endeed excellent well, yet his manner and freedom of doing it, as if he played with it and was informing only all the rest of the company, was mighty pretty.

15 October. This day the King begins to put on his vest, and I did see several persons of the House of Lords, and Commons too, great courtiers, who are in it – being a long cassocke close to the body, of black cloth and pinked with white silk under it, and a coat over it, and the legs ruffled with black riband like a pigeon's leg – and upon the whole, I wish the King may keep it, for it is a very fine and handsome garment.

17 October. Up, and busy about public and private business all the morning at the office. At noon home to dinner, alone with my brother, with whom I had now the first private talk I have had, and find he hath preached but twice in his life. I did give him some advice to study pronunciation; but I do fear he will never make a good speaker – nor, I fear, any general good scholar – for I do not see that he minds optickes or mathematics of any sort, nor anything else that I can find – I know not what he may be at divinity and ordinary school-learning. However, he seems sober, and that pleases me.

The Court is all full of vests; only, my Lord St Albans not pinked, but plain black – and they say the King says the pinking upon white makes them look too much like magpyes, and therefore hath bespoke one of plain velvet.

31 October. After dinner to my closet, where I spent the whole afternoon till late at evening of all my accounts, public and private; and to my great satisfaction I do find that I do bring my accounts to a very near balance, notwithstanding all the hurries and troubles I have been put to by the late Fire, that I have not been able to even my accounts since July last before. And I bless God, I do find that I am worth more then ever I yet was, which is 6,200*l* – for which the Holy name of God be praised.

5 November. After dinner I and Sir Tho. Crew went aside to discourse of public matters, and do find by him that all the country gentlemen are publicly jealous of the courtiers in the Parliament, and that they do doubt everything that they propose. And that the true reason why the country gentleman is for a land tax and against a general excize, is because they are fearful that if the latter be granted, they shall never get it down again; whereas the land tax will be but for so much, and when the war ceases there will be no ground got by the Court to keep it up. He doth, from what he hath heard at the Committee for examining the burning of the City, conclude it as a thing certain, that it was done by plot – it being proved by many witnesses that endeavours were made in several places to encrease the fire, and that both in city and country it was bragged by several papists that upon such a day or in such a time we should find the hottest weather that ever was in England.

14 November. Dr Croone told me that at the meeting at Gresham College tonight (which it seems they now have every Wednesday again) there was a pretty experiment, of the blood of one dogg let out (till he died) into the body of another on one side, while all his own run out on the other side. The first died upon the place, and the other very well, and likely to do well. This did give occasion to many pretty wishes, as of the blood of a Quaker to be let into an Archbishop, and such like. But, as Dr Croone says, may if it takes be of mighty use to man's health, for the amending of bad blood by borrowing from a better body.

15 November. I took coach and to Mr Pierce's, where I find her as fine as possible, and himself going to the Ball at night at Court, it being the Queenes Birthday. And so I carried them in my coach; and having set them into the house, and gotten Mr Pierce to undertake the carrying in my wife, I to Unthankes, where she appointed to be, and there

Frances Stewart, Duchess of Richmond, by Lely (detail).

. . . .

told her; and back again about business to Whitehall while Pierce went and fetched her and carried her in. I, after I had met with Sir W. Coventry and given him some account of matters, I also to the Ball, and with much ado got up to the loft, where with much trouble I could see very well. And it was endeed a glorious sight to see Mrs Steward in black and white lace – and her head and shoulders dressed with dyamonds. And the like a great many great ladies more (only, the Queene none); and the King in his rich vest of some rich silk and silver trimming, as the Duke of York and all the dancers were, some of cloth of silver, and others of other sorts, exceeding rich. Presently after the King was come in, he took the Queene, and about fourteen more couple there was, and begun the bransles. After the bransles, then to a corant, and now and then a French dance; but that so rare that the corants grew tiresome, that I wished it done. Only, Mrs Steward danced mighty finely, and many French dances, especially one the King called the New Dance, which was very pretty. But upon the whole matter, the business of the dancing of itself was not extraordinary pleasing. But the clothes and sight of the persons was indeed very pleasing, and worth my coming, being never likely to see more gallantry while I live – if I should come twenty times.

17 November. Up, and to the office, where all the morning. At noon home to dinner, and in the afternoon shut myself in my chamber, and there till 12 at night finishing my great letter to the Duke of York; which doth lay the ill condition of the Navy so open to him, that it is impossible, if the King and he minds anything of their business, but it will operate upon them to set all matters right, and get money to carry on the war before it be too late, or else lay out for a peace upon any tearmes. It was a great convenience tonight, that what I had writ fowle in shorthand, I could read to W. Hewer and he take it fair in shorthand so as I can read it tomorrow to Sir W. Coventry, and then come home and he read to me, while I take it in longhand to present – which saves me much time. So to bed.

22 November. Up, and to the office, where we sat all the morning. And my Lord Brouncker did show me Holler's new print of the City, with a pretty representation of that part which is burnt, very fine endeed. And tells me that he was yesterday sworn the King's servant, and that the King hath commanded him to go on with his great map of the City which he was upon before the City was burned. At noon home to dinner, where my wife and I fell out, I being displeased with her cutting away a lace hankercher so wide about the neck, down to her breasts almost, out of a belief, but without reason, that it is the fashion. Here we did give one another the lie too much, but were presently friends; and then I to my office, where very late and did much business; and then home, and there find Mr Batelier – and did sup and play at cards awhile. But he tells me the news how the King of France hath, in defiance to the King of England, caused all his footmen to be put into vests, and that the noblemen of France will do the like; which, if true, is the greatest indignity ever done by one prince to another, and would incite a stone to be revenged. This noon Bagwell's wife was with me at the office, and I did what I would; and at night came Mrs Burroughs, and appointed to meet upon the next holiday and go abroad together.

25 November. Lords Day. I spoke with Mr May, who tells me that the design of building the City doth go on apace; and by his description, it will be mighty handsome, and to the satisfaction of people. But I pray God it come not out too late.

27 November. I spoke to Sir Tho. Crew to invite him and his brother John to dinner tomorrow at my house to meet Lord Hinchingbrooke; and so homeward, calling at the cook's who is to dress it to bespeak him; and then home, and there set things in order for a very fine dinner; and then to the office, where late, very busy and to good purpose; and then home, to bed, my people sitting up to get things in order against tomorrow.

· ·

(*Below left*) Cheapside by Mary-le-Bow, after the Fire. The houses are of the size and type specified by statute for the rebuilding of the principal streets. Among the street improvements are stone posts to protect pedestrians, stone house signs, and drain pipes (*Below right*) Ape and Apple, a painted stone house sign of 1670. In 1667 householders were required to use stone signs, but wooden hanging signs soon reappeared.

28 November. I by hackney coach to several places to get things ready against dinner, and then home and did the like there, to my great satisfaction; and at noon comes my Lord Hinchingbrooke, Sir Tho. Crew, Mr John Crew, Mr Carteret, and Brisband. I had six noble dishes for them, dressed by a man-cook, and commended, as endeed they deserved, for exceedingly well done. We eat with great pleasure, and I enjoyed myself in it with reflections upon the pleasures which I at best can expect, yet not to exceed this – eating in silver plates, and all things mighty rich and handsome about me. A great deal of fine discourse, sitting almost till dark at dinner; and then broke up with great pleasure, especially to myself, and they away; only, Mr Carteret and I to Gresham College, where they meet now weekly again. Thence home, and there comes my Lady Pen, Pegg, and Mrs Turner, and played at cards and supped with us, and were pretty merry – and Pegg with me in my closet a good while, and did suffer me a la besar mucho et tocar ses cosas upon her breast – wherein I had great pleasure, and so spent the evening; and then broke up, and I to bed, my mind mightily pleased with this day's entertainment.

7 December. By water to the Strand and so to the King's playhouse, where two acts were almost done when I came in; and there I sat with my cloak about my face and saw the remainder of *The Mayds Tragedy* – a good play, and well acted, especially by the younger Marshall, which is become a pretty good actor. And is the first play I have seen in either of the houses since before the great plague – they having acted now about fourteen days publicly. But I was in mighty pain lest I should be seen by anybody to be at a play.

8 December. Mr Pierce did also tell me as a great truth that Tom Killigrew should publicly tell the King that his matters were coming into a very ill state, but that yet there was a way to help all – which is, says he, 'There is a good honest able man that I could name, that if your Majesty would imploy and command to see all things well executed, all things would soon be mended; and this is one Charles Stuart – who now spends his time in imploying his lips and his prick about the Court, and hath no other imployment. But if you would give him this imployment, he were the fittest man in the world to perform it.' This he says is most true.

13 December. For these three or four days I perceive my overworking of my eyes by candlelight doth hurt them, as it did the last winter. That by day I am well and do get them right – but then after candlelight they begin to be sore and run – so that I entend to get some green spectacles.

17 December. Spent the evening in fitting my books, to have the number set upon each in order to my having an Alphabet of my whole, which will be of great ease to me.

19 December. Up and by water to Whitehall, and there with the Duke of York did our usual business. Thence, going away, met Mr Hingston the organist (my old acquaintance), and I took him to the Dogg tavern and got him to set me a bass to my 'It is decreed', which I think will go well; but he commends the song, not knowing the words, but says the ayre is good, and believes the words are plainly expressed. He is of my mind, against having of eighths unnecessarily in composition. This did all please me mightily. Then to talk of the King's family: he says many of the musique are ready to starve, they being five years behindhand for their wages. Nay, Evens, the famous man upon the harp, having not his equal in the world, did the other day die for mere want, and was fain to be buried at the almes of the parish – and carried to his grave in the dark at night, without one linke, but that Mr Hingston met it by chance and did give 12*d* to buy two or three links. He says all must come to ruin at this rate, and I believe him. [To Sir W. Batten's, where] I sat long, talking. Among other things, Sir R. Ford did make me understand how the House of Commons is a beast not to be understood – it being impossible to know beforehand the success almost of any small plain thing – there being so many to think and speak to any business, and they of so uncertain minds and interests and passions. He did tell me, and so did Sir W. Batten, how Sir Allen Brodericke and Sir Allen Apsly did come drunk the other day into the House, and did both speak for half an hour together, and could not be either laughed or pulled or bid to sit down and hold their peace – to the great contempt of the King's servants and cause – which I am aggrieved at with all my heart.

24 December. I this evening did buy me a pair of green spectacles, to see whether they will help my eyes or no. So to the Change, and went to the Upper Change, which is almost as good as the old one; only, shops are but on one side. Then home to the office and did business till my eyes begun to be bad; and so home to supper (my people busy making mince-pies) and so to bed.

25 December. Christmas Day. Lay pretty long in bed. And then rise, leaving my wife desirous to sleep, having sat up till 4 this morning seeing her maids make mince pies. I to church, where our parson Mills made a good sermon. Then home, and dined well on some good ribs of beef roasted and mince pies; only my wife, brother, and Barker, and plenty of good wine of my own; and my heart full of true joy and thanks to God Almighty for the goodness of my condition at this day.

31 December. Thus ends this year of public wonder and mischief to this nation – and therefore generally wished by all people to have an end. Myself and family well, having four maids and one clerk, Tom, in my house; and my brother now with me, to spend time in order to his preferment. Our healths all well; only, my eyes, with overworking them, are sore as soon as candlelight comes to them, and not else. Public matters in a most sad condition. Seamen discouraged for want of pay, and are become not to be governed. Nor, as matters are now, can any fleet go out next year. Our enemies, French and Duch, great, and grow more, by our poverty. The Parliament backward in raising, because jealous of the spending of the money. The City less and less likely to be built again, everybody settling elsewhere, and nobody encouraged to trade. A sad, vicious, negligent Court, and all sober men there fearful of the ruin of the whole kingdom this next year – from which, good God deliver us. One thing I reckon remarkable in my own condition is that I am come to abound in good plate, so as at all entertainments to be served wholly with silver plates, having two dozen and a half.

1667

1 January.   Lay long, being a bitter cold frosty day, the frost being now grown old and the Thames covered with ice. Up, and to the office, where all the morning busy. At noon to the Change a little, where Mr James Houblon and I walked a good while, speaking of our ill condition in not being able to set out a fleet (we doubt) this year, and the certain ill effects that must bring – which is lamentable. Home to dinner, where the best powdered goose that ever I eat.

7 January.   To the Duke's House and saw *Macbeth*; which though I saw it lately, yet appears a most excellent play in all respects, but especially in divertisement, though it be a deep tragedy; which is a strange perfection in a tragedy, it being most proper here and suitable. So home, it being the last play now I am to see till a fortnight hence, I being from the last night entered into my vows for the year coming on. So home from the office to write over fair my vows for this year, and then to supper and to bed – in great peace of mind, having now done it and brought myself into order again and a resolution of keeping it – and having entered my journall to this night. So to bed, my eyes failing me with writing.

11 January.   Up, being troubled at my being found abed a-days by all sorts of people – I having got a trick of sitting up later then I need, never supping, or very seldom, before 12 at night. Then to the office; there busy all the morning. At noon home to dinner; and then to the office with my people and very busy, and did despatch to my great satisfaction abundance of business, and do resolve by the grace of God to stick to it till I have cleared my hand of most things wherein I am in arrear in public and private matters. At night home to supper and to bed.

23 January.   I did observe the new buildings [at St James's]; and my Lord [Brouncker] seeing I had a desire to see them, they being the place for the priests and friers, he took me to my Lord Almner and he took us quite through the whole house and chapel and the new monastery. I saw the dortoire and the cells of the priests, and we went into one – a very pretty little room, very clean, hung with pictures, set with books. The priest was in his cell with his hair cloths to his skin, bare-legged, with a sandall only on, and his little bed without sheets, and no feather bed; but yet I thought saft enough. His cord about his middle. But in so good company, living with care, I thought it a very good life. A pretty library they have, and I was in the refectoire, where every man his napkin, knife, cup of earth, and basin of the same; and a place for one to sit and read while the rest are at meals. And into the kitchin I went, where a good neck of mutton at the fire, and other victuals boiling. I do not think they feed very hard. Their windows looking all into a fine garden

(*Left*) The Duke of York's Theatre, Dorset Gardens, off Fleet Street, 1673. The Duke's company moved here from Lincoln's Inn Fields in 1671 and opened with one of Pepys's favourite plays, Dryden's *Sir Martin Marall*. (*Right*) A scene from Elkanah Settle's *The Empress of Morocco*, performed at the Duke of York's Theatre in 1673.

. . . .

and the park. And mighty pretty rooms all. I wished myself one of the Capuchins – having seen what we could here, and all with mighty pleasure. So away with the Almoner in his coach, talking merrily about the difference in our religions.

1 February. Up, and to the office, where I was all the morning doing business. At noon home to dinner; and after dinner down by water, though it was a thick misty and raining day, and walked to Deptford from Redriffe and there to Bagwells by appointment – where the moher erat within expecting mi venida. And did sensa alguna difficulty monter los degres and lie, comme jo desired it, upon lo lectum; and there I did la cosa con much voluptas. By and by su marido came in, and there, without any notice taken by him, we discoursed of our business of getting him the new ship building by Mr Deane, which I shall do for him.

3 February. Lords Day. Up, and with Sir W. Batten and W. Penn by coach to Whitehall; and there to Sir W. Coventry's chamber and there stayed till he was ready – talking; and among other things, of Prince [Rupert's] being trepanned, which was in doing just as we passed through the Stone Gallery, we asking at the door of his lodgings and were told so. We are all full of wishes for the good success – though I dare say but few do really concern ourselfs for him in our hearts.

8 February. At noon Lord Brouncker, W. Batten, W. Penn and myself to the Sun in Leadenhall Street to dinner, where an exceeding good dinner and good discourse. We talked much of Cromwell, all saying he was a brave fellow and did owe his crowne he got to himself as much as any man that ever got one.

10 February. Lords Day. Up and with my wife to church, where Mr Mills made an unnecessary sermon upon originall sin, neither understood by himself nor the people. Home, where Michell and his wife, and also there came Mr Carter, my old acquaintance of Magdalen College, who hath not been here of many years. We had much talk of all our old acquaintance of the College, concerning their various fortunes; wherein, to my joy, I met not with any that have sped better then myself.

11 February. With Creed to Westminster Hall, and there up and down and hear that Prince Rupert is still better and better. My Lord [Belasyse] carried me and set me down at the New Exchange; where I stayed at Pottle's shop till B. Michell came, which she did about 5 a-clock and was surprised not to trover mi moher there. But I did make an excuse good enough, and so I took ella down and over the way to the cabinet-makers, and there bought a dressing box for her of 20*s*, but would require an hour's time to make fit. This I was glad of, thinking to have got ella to andar to a casa de biber; but ella would not, so I did not much press it but suffered ella to andar a la casa de uno de sos hermanos, and I passed my time walking up and down. By and by Betty comes, and here we stayed in the shop and above, seeing the workmen work; which was pretty, and some exceeding good work and very pleasant to see them do it – till it was late, quite dark. And the mistress of the shop took us into the kitchen and there talked and used us very prettily; and took her for my wife, which I owned and her big belly; and there very merry till my thing done, and then took coach and home, in the way tomando su mano and putting it where I used to do; which ella did suffer, but not avec tant de freedom as heretofore, I perceiving plainly she had alguns apprehensions de me, but I did offer natha more then what I had often done. But now comes our trouble; I did begin to fear that su marido might go to my house to enquire por ella, and there trovando mi moher at home, would not only think himself, but give my femme occasion to think strange things. This did trouble me mightily; so though ella would not seem to have me trouble myself about it, yet did agree to the stopping the coach at the street's end; and yo allais con ella home and there presently hear by him that he had newly sent su maid to my house to see for her mistress. This doth much perplex me, and I did go presently home (Betty whispering me, behind the tergo de her mari, that if I would say that we did come home by water, ella could make up la cosa well satis). And there in a sweat did walk in the entry antes my door, thinking what I should say a my femme; and as God would have it, while I was in this case (the worst in reference a my femme that ever I was in in my life), a little woman comes stumbling to the entry steps in the dark; whom asking whom she was, she enquired for my house; so knowing her voice and telling her su dona is come home, she went away. But Lord, in what a trouble was I when she was gone, to recollect whether this was not the second time of her coming; but at last concluding that she had not been here before, I did bless myself in my good fortune in getting home before her, and do verily believe she had loitered some time by the way, which was my great good fortune; and so I in a-door and there find all well.

12 February. With my Lord Brouncker by coach to his house, there to hear some Italian musique. But I perceive there is a proper accent in every country's discourse; and that doth reach in their setting of notes to words, which therefore cannot be natural to anybody else but them; so that I am not so much smitten with it as it may be I should be if I were acquainted with their accent.

13 February. A foul evening this was tonight, and mightily troubled to get a coach home; and, which is now my common practice, going over the ruins in the night, I rid with my sword drawn in the coach.

14 February. To my Lord Chancellor's, and there a meeting – the Duke of York, the Duke of Albemarle, and several other Lords of the Commission of Tanger; and there I did present a state of my accounts, and managed them well; and my Lord Chancellor did say, though he was in other things in an ill humour, that no man in England was of more method nor made himself better understood then myself. Thence away by coach with Sir H. Cholmly to the Temple and there walked in the dark in the walks; and he surprizes me with the certain news that the King did last night in council declare his being in treaty with the Dutch.

23 February. This day I am by the blessing of God 34 years old – in very good health and mind's content, and in condition of estate much beyond whatever my friends could expect of a child of theirs this day 34 year. The Lord's name be praised and may I be ever thankful for it. Up betimes to the office, in order to my letter to the Duke of York. And then the office met and spent the greatest part about this letter. At noon home to dinner and then to the office again, very close at it all the day till midnight, making an end and writing fair this great letter and other things, to my full content – it abundantly providing for the vindication of this office, whatever the success be of our wants of money.

25 February. Lay long in bed, talking with pleasure with my poor wife how she used to make coal fires and wash my foul clothes with her own hand for me, poor wretch, in our little room at my Lord Sandwiches; for which I ought for ever to love and admire her, and do, and persuade myself she would do the same thing again if God should reduce us to it. So up, and by coach abroad and at my goldsmith's did observe the King's new medall, where in little there is Mrs Stewards face, as well done as ever I saw anything in my whole life I think – and a pretty thing it is that he should choose her face to represent Britannia by.

So at the office late very busy, and much business with great joy despatched; and so home to supper and to bed.

27 February. [Mr Hunt] dined with us, and we had good discourse of the general ill state of things; and by the way he told me some ridiculous pieces of thrift of Sir G. Downing's, who is their countryman – in inviting some poor people at Christmas last, to charm the country people's mouths; but did give them nothing but beef porridge, pudding, and pork, and nothing said all dinner, but only his mother would say, 'It's good broth, son.' He would answer, 'Yes, it is good broth.' Then his lady confirm all and say, 'Yes, very good broth.' By and by she would begin and say, 'Good pork;' 'Yes,' says the mother, 'good pork.' Then he cries, 'Yes, very good pork.' And so they said of all things; to which nobody made any answer, they going there not out of love or esteem of them, but to eat his victuals, knowing him to be a niggardly fellow – and with this he is jeered now all over the country.

28 February. Up, and there comes to me Drumbleby with a flagelette made to suit with my former, and brings me one Greeting, a master to teach my wife. I agree by the whole with him; to teach her to take out any lesson of herself for 4*l*. I did within these six days see smoke still remaining of the late fire in the City; and it is strange to think how to this very day I cannot sleep a-night without great terrors of fire; and this very night could not sleep till almost 2 in the morning through thoughts of fire.

2 March. After dinner with my wife to the King's House, to see *The Mayden Queene*, a new play of Dryden's mightily commended for the regularity of it and the strain and wit;

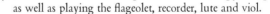

Flageolet player, 1682. A keen and accomplished musician, Pepys composed and sang as well as playing the flageolet, recorder, lute and viol.

Nell Gwyn, actress and the King's mistress, by Simon Verelst c. 1670.

· ·

and the truth is, there is a comical part done by Nell, which is Florimell, that I never can hope ever to see the like done again by man or woman. The King and Duke of York was at the play; but so great performance of a comical part was never, I believe, in the world before as Nell doth this, both as a mad girle and then, most and best of all, when she comes in like a young gallant; and hath the motions and carriage of a spark the most that ever I saw any man have.

6 March. Up, and with W. Penn to Whitehall by coach. Here the Duke of York did acquaint us (and the King did the like also, afterward coming in) with his resolution of altering the manner of the war this year; that is, that we shall keep what fleet we have abroad in several squadrons; so that now all is come out, but we are to keep it as close as we can, without hindering the work that is to be done in preparation to this. Great preparations there are to fortify Sheernesse and the yard at Portsmouth, and forces are drawing down to both those places, and elsewhere by the seaside; so that we have some fear of an invasion, and the Duke of York himself did declare his expectation of the enemy's blocking us up here in the river, and therefore directed that we should send away all the ships that we have to fit out hence.

9 March. I have got a great cold, so home late and drank some buttered ale, and so to bed

139

and to sleep. This cold did most certainly come by my staying a little too long bare-legged yesterday morning when I rose while I looked out fresh socks and thread stockings, yesterday's having in the night, lying near the window, been covered with snow within the window, which made me I durst not put them on.

12 March. This day a poor seaman, almost starved for want of food, lay in our yard a-dying; I sent him half-a-crown – and we ordered his ticket to be paid.

13 March. Late at my office, preparing a speech against tomorrow morning before the King at my Lord Treasurer's; and the truth is, it run in my head all night.

14 March. Up, and with W. Batten and W. Penn to my Lord Treasurer's, where we met with my Lord Brouncker an hour before the King came, and had time to talk a little of our business. By and by comes the King and Duke of York, and presently the officers of the Ordinance were called – then we, my Lord Brouncker, W. Batten, W. Penn, and myself, where we find only the King and Duke of York and my Lord Treasurer and Sir G. Carteret; where I only did speak, laying down the state of our wants; which the King and Duke of York seemed very well pleased with, and we did get what we asked, 500,000*l*, assigned upon the Eleven Months Tax. But it being a fine clear day, I did en gayeté de cœur propose going to Bow for ayre sake and dine there; which they imbraced, and so W. Batten and I (setting W. Penn down at Mark Lane end) straight to Bow to the Queen's Head and there bespoke our dinner, carrying meat with us from London. Here till the evening, so as it was dark almost before we got home.

20 March. I to Sir W. Batten to dinner, and had a good dinner of ling and herring pie, very good meat – best of that kind that ever I had. Thus having dined, I by coach to the Temple and there did buy a little book or two; and it is strange how Rycaut's discourse of Turky, which before the Fire I was asked but 8*s* for, there being all but twenty-two or thereabouts burnt, I did now offer 20*s*, and he demands 50*s*; and I think I shall give it him, though it be only as a monument of the Fire. So to Sir W. Penn's, where my wife was, and supped with a little, but yet little, mirth and a bad nasty supper; which makes me not love that family, they do all things so meanly, to make a little bad show upon their backs.

23 March. At the office all the morning, where Sir W. Penn came, being returned from Chatham from considering the means of fortifying the River Medway, by a chain at the stakes and ships laid there, with guns to keep the enemy from coming up to burn our ships – all our care now being to fortify ourselfs against their invading us.

27 March. I did go to the Swan; and there sent for Jervas my old periwig-maker and he did bring me a periwig; but it was full of nits, so as I was troubled to see it (it being his old fault) and did send him to make it clean. So I home, and there up to my wife in our chamber; and there received from my brother the news of my mother's dying on Monday, about 5 or 6 a-clock in the afternoon, and that the last time she spoke of her children was on Friday last and her last words was, 'God bless my poor Sam!' The reading hereof did set me a-weeping heartily; and so, weeping to myself a while and my wife also to herself – I then spoke to my wife, recollecting myself, and endeed having some thoughts how much better, both for her and us, it is then it might have been had she outlived my father and me or my happy present condition in the world, she being helpless, I was the sooner at ease in my mind; and then found it necessary to go abroad with my wife to look after the providing mourning to send into the country, some tomorrow and more against Sundy, for my family, being resolved to put myself and wife, and Barker and Jane, W. Hewers and Tom, in mourning; and my two under-maids, to give them hoods and scarfs and gloves. So to my tailor's and up and down; and then home and to my office a little; and then to supper and to bed – my heart sad and afflicted, though my judgment at ease.

5 April. This morning came to me the collectors for my pole mony; for which I paid for my title as Esquire and place of Clerk of Acts, and my head and wife's, and servants' and their wages, 40*l.* 17*s.* 00*d.* And though this be a great deal, yet it is a shame I should pay no more; that is, that I should not be assessed for my pay, as in the victualling business and Tanger, and for my money, which of my own accord I had determined to charge myself with 1000*l* money, till coming to the vestry and seeing nobody of our ablest merchants, as Sir Andrew Rickard, to do it, I thought it not decent for me to do it; nor would it be thought wisdom to do it unnecessarily, but vainglory.

11 April. I to Whitehall, thinking there to have seen the Duchesse of Newcastle's coming this night to Court to make a visit to the Queen, the King having been with her yesterday to make her a visit since her coming to town. The whole story of this lady is a romance, and all she doth is romantic. Her footmen in velvet coats, and herself in an antique dress, as they say; and was the other day at her own play, *The Humourous Lovers*; the most ridiculous thing that ever was wrote, but yet she and her Lord mightily pleased with it, and she at the end made her respect to the players from her box and did give them thanks.

12 April. Up; and when ready, I to my office to do a little business; and coming homeward again, saw my door and hatch open, left so by Luce our cookmaid; which so vexed me, that I did give her a kick in our entry and offered a blow at her, and was seen doing so by Sir W. Penn's footboy, which did vex me to the heart because I know he will be telling their family of it, though I did put on presently a very pleasant face to the boy and spoke kindly to him as one without passion, so as it may be he might not think I was angry; but yet I was troubled at it.

21 April. Lords Day. Up, and John, a hackney coachman whom of late I have much used, as being formerly Sir W. Penn's coachman, coming to me by my direction to see whether I would use him today or no, I took him to our back gate to look upon the ground which is to be let there, where I have a mind to buy enough to build a coach house and stable; for I have had it much in my thoughts lately that it is not too much for me now, in degree or cost, to keep a coach; but contrarily, that I am almost ashamed to be seen in a hackney. And so home and with my wife to church; and then to dinner, Mercer with us,

To Westminster, in the way meeting many milkmaids with their garlands (1 May 1667.) A May Day procession on Millbank Terrace (detail), after J. Griffier the elder *c.* 1706.

with design to go to Hackney to church in the afternoon. That which we went chiefly to see was the young ladies of the schools, whereof there is great store, very pretty; and also the organ, which is handsome and tunes the psalm and plays with the people; which is mighty pretty and makes me mighty earnest to have a pair at our church, I having almost a mind to give them a pair if they would settle a maintenance on them for it – I am mightily taken with them. So church done, we to coach and away to Kingsland and Islington and there eat and drank at the old house; and so back, it raining a little; which is mighty welcome, it having not rained in many weeks, so that they say it makes the fields just now mighty sweet; so with great pleasure home by night.

26 April. To Westminster Hall and took a turn with Mr Eveling, with whom walked two hours, till almost 1 of the clock – talking of the badness of the government, where nothing but wickedness, and wicked men and women command the King. That it is not in his nature to gainsay anything that relates to his pleasures. That much of it arises from the sickliness of our ministers of state, who cannot be about him as the idle companions are, and therefore give way to the young rogues; and then from the negligence of the clergy, that a bishop shall never be seen about him, as the King of France hath always. That the King would fain have some of the same gang to be Lord Treasurer; which would be yet worse, for now some delays are put to the getting gifts of the King, as that whore my Lady Byron, who had been, as he called it, the King's seventeenth whore abroad, did not leave him till she had got him to give her an order for 4000*l* worth of plate to be made for her; but by delays, thanks be to God, she died before she had it. He tells me the King of France hath his Maistresses, but laughs at the foolery of our King, that makes his bastards princes, and loses his revenue upon them – and makes his mistresses his maisters. And the King of France did never grant Lavaliere anything to bestow on others; and gives a little subsistence, but no more, to his bastards.

28 April. Lords Day. Home, and there to write down my journall, and so to supper and to read, and so to bed – mightily pleased with my reading Boyles book of Colours today; only, troubled that some part of it, endeed the greatest part, I am not able to understand for want of study. My wife this night troubled at my leaving her alone so much and keeping her within doors; which endeed I do not well nor wisely in.

Arundel House, by W. Hollar 1646, looking toward the river. London residence of the 6th Duke of Norfolk. The Royal Society met there for eight years after the Fire.

. . . .

29 April. To Whitehall to Sir G. Carteret to dinner. Here I hear that my Lord Treasurer [is] very bad of the stone, and hath been so some days.

30 April. Sir Jo. Winter to discourse with me about the Forest of Deane and then about my Lord Treasurer; and asking me whether, as he had heard, I had not been cut of the stone, I took him to my closet and there showed it him; of which he took the dimensions and had some discourse of it, and I believe will show my Lord Treasurer it.

1 May. To Westminster, in the way meeting many milkmaids with their garlands upon their pails, dancing with a fiddler before them, and saw pretty Nelly standing at her lodgings door in Drury Lane in her smock-sleeves and bodice, looking upon one – she seemed a mighty pretty creature.

16 May. To my Lord Treasurer's, where I find the porter crying, and suspected it was that my Lord is dead; and, poor Lord, we did find that he was dead just now; and the crying of that fellow did so trouble me, that considering that I was not likely to trouble him any more, nor have occasion to give any more anything, I did give him 3*s*; but it may be, poor man, he hath lost a considerable hope by the death of this Lord, whose house will be no more frequented as before – and perhaps I may never come thither again about any business. There is a good man gone; and I pray God that the Treasury may not be worse managed by the hand or hands it shall now be put into.

18 May. Up and all the morning at the office, and then to dinner; and after dinner to the office to dictate some letters; and by and by home and there find our Luce drunk, and when her mistress told her of it, would be gone; and so put up some of her things and did go away of her accord, nobody pressing her to it; and the truth is, though she be the dirtiest and homeliest servant that ever I kept, yet I was sorry to have her go, partly through my love to my servants and partly because she was a very drudging, working wench.

30 May. Up, and to the office, where all the morning. At noon dined at home. After dinner I walked to Arundell House, the way very dusty (the day of meeting the [Royal]

Society being changed from Wednesday to Thursday; which I knew not before because the Wednesday is a Council day and several of the Council are of the Society, and would come but for their attending the King at Council); where I find much company, endeed very much company, in expectation of the Duchesse of Newcastle, who had desired to be invited to the Society, and was, after much debate pro and con, it seems many being against it, and we do believe the town will be full of ballets of it. Anon comes the Duchesse, with her women attending her. [She] hath been a good comely woman; but her dress so antic and her deportment so unordinary, that I do not like her at all, nor did I hear her say anything that was worth hearing, but that she was full of admiration, all admiration. After they had shown her many experiments, and she cried still she was 'full of admiration', she departed, being led out and in by several lords that were there.

2 June. Lords Day. Up betimes, and down to chamber, without trimming myself or putting on clean linen, thinking only to keep to my chamber to do business today; but when I came there, I find that without being shaved I am not fully awake nor ready to settle to business, and so was fain to go up again and dress myself; which I did, and so down to my chamber and fell roundly to business.

4 June. To the office all the afternoon, where I despatched much business to my great content; and then home in the evening, and there to sing and pipe with my wife; and that being done, she fell all of a sudden to discourse about her clothes and my humours in not suffering her to wear them as she pleases, and grew to high words between us. But I fell to read a book (Boyle's *Hydrostatickes*) aloud in my chamber and let her talk till she was tired, and vexed that I would not hear her; and so become friends and to bed together, the first night after four or five that she hath lain from me by reason of a great cold she had got.

5 June. In the street Sir G. Carteret showed me a gentleman coming by in his coach, who hath been sent for up out of Lincolnshire; I think he says he is a Justice of Peace there, that the Council have laid by the heels here, and here lies in a messenger's hands for saying that a man and his wife are but one person and so ought to pay but 12d for both to the Pole bill.

8 June. Up and to the office, where all the news this morning is that the Duch are come with a fleet of eighty sail to Harwich, and that guns were heard plain by Sir W. Rider's people at Bednall Greene all yesterday noon.

9 June. Lords Day. Up and by water to Whitehall; and so walked to St James's. To Sir W. Coventry and there talked with him a great while. In comes my Lord Berkely, who is going down to Harwich to look after the militia there; and there is also the Duke of Monmouth, and with him a great many young hectors, but to little purpose, I fear, but to debauch the country women thereabouts.

. . . .

(*Opposite*) Charles II as President of the Royal Society, by M. Laroon 1684.
Commissioned by Christ's Hospital for £24 and a pair of leather gloves.

10 June. Up; and news brought us that the Dutch are come up as high as the Nore, and more pressing orders for fireships. W. Batten, W. Penn and I to St James, where the Duke of York gone this morning betimes to send away some men down to Chatham. So we three to Whitehall and met Sir W. Coventry, who presses all the possible for fireships; so we three to the office presently, and thither comes Sir Fr. Hollis, who is to command them all in some exploits he is to do with them on the enemy in the river. So we all down to Deptford and pitch upon ships and set men at work; but Lord, to see how backwardly things move at this pinch, notwithstanding that by the enemy's being now come up as high as almost the Hope. Sir J. Mennes (who was gone down to pay some ships there) hath sent up the money; and so we are possessed of money to [do] what we will with. Here I eat a bit; and then in the afternoon took boat and down to Greenwich, where I find the stairs full of people, there being a great riding there today for a man, the constable of the town, whose wife beat him. [So] to Gravesend, where I find the Duke of Albemarle just come, with a great many idle lords and gentlemen with their pistols and fooleries. I homeward, as long as it was light reading Mr Boyles book of *Hydrostatickes*, which is a most excellent book as ever I read; and I will take much pains to understand him through if I can, the doctrine being very useful. When it grew too dark to read, I lay down and took a nap, it being a most excellent fine evening; and about 1 a-clock got home, and after having wrote to Sir W. Coventry an account of what I had done and seen (which is entered in my letter-book), I to bed.

11 June. Up, and more letters still from Sir W. Coventry about more fireships; and so W. Batten and I to the office, where Brouncker came to us; who is just now going to Chatham upon a desire of Commissioner Pett's, who is in a very fearful stink for fear of the Dutch, and desires help for God and the King and kingdom's sake. So Brouncker goes down, and Sir J. Mennes also, from Gravesend. This morning Pett writes us word that Sherenesse is lost last night, after two or three hours' dispute – the enemy hath possessed himself of the place; which is very sad and puts us into great fears of Chatham.

12 June. Powell doth tell me that ill news is come to Court of the Dutch breaking the chaine at Chatham, which struck me to the heart, and to Whitehall to hear the truth of it; and there, going up the park stairs, I did hear some lackeys speaking of sad news come to Court, saying that hardly anybody in the court but doth look as if they cried. For the news is true, that the Dutch have broke the chain and burned our ships, and perticularly the *Royall Charles*; other perticulars I know not, but most sad to be sure.

The extent of the humiliation was soon revealed. The Dutch raiders towed away the Royal Charles *– the pride of the navy; sank or burnt three other great ships; raided Sheppey, and destroyed the fort at Sheerness. Pepys now makes what arrangements he can to secure his savings – fearing not so much the enemy as riotous mobs. His father has been staying with him since 22 May.*

. . . .

(*Opposite*) Dutch raid on English ships in the Medway, 1667, by P. van Soest (detail). On 12–14 June the Dutch under De Ruyter sailed into the Medway, and attacked the great ships laid up in the river. The *Royal Charles* (centre) was captured.

And the truth is, I do fear so much that the whole kingdom is undone, that I do this night resolve to study with my father and wife what to do with the little that I have in money by me, for I give all the rest that I have in the King's hands for Tanger for lost. The manner of my advising this night with my father was: I took him and my wife up to her chamber, and shut the door and there told them the sad state of the times; how we are like to be all undone – that I do fear some violence will be offered to this office, where all I have in the world is. And resolved upon sending it away – and with that resolution went to bed – full of fear and fright; hardly slept all night.

13 June. No sooner up but hear the sad news confirmed, of the *Royall Charles* being taken by them and now in fitting by them (which Pett should have carried up higher by our several orders, and deserves therefore to be hanged for not doing it) and burning several others, and that another fleet is come up into the Hope; upon which news the King and Duke of York have been below since 4 a⁄clock in the morning, to command the sinking of ships at Barking Creeke and other places, to stop their coming up higher; which put me into such a fear that I presently resolved of my father's and wife's going into the country; and at two hours' warning they did go by the coach this day – with about 1,300*l* in gold in their night bag; pray God give them good passage and good care to hide it when they come home, but my heart is full of fear. They gone, I continued in frights and fear what to do with the rest. W. Hewer hath been at the banquiers and hath got 500*l* out of Backewell's hands of his own money; but they are so called upon that they will be all broke, hundreds coming to them for money – and their answer is, 'It is payable at twenty days; when the days are out, we will pay you.' I must keep the silver by me, which sometimes I think to fling into the house of office – and then again, know not how I shall come by it if we be made to leave the office. Every minute some[one] or other calls for this order or that order; and so I forced to be at the office most of the day about the fireships which are to be suddenly fitted out. In the evening I sent for my cousin Sarah and her husband; who came, and I did deliver them my chest of writings about Brampton, and my brother Tom's papers and my journalls, which I value much – and did send my two silver flagons to Kate Joyce's: that so, being scattered what I have, something might be saved. I have also made a girdle, by which with some trouble I do carry about me 300*l* in gold about my body, that I may not be without something in case I should be surprized; for I think, in any nation but ours, people that appear (for we are not endeed so) so faulty as we would have their throats cut. Late at night comes Mr Hudson the cooper, my neighbour, and tells me that he came from Chatham this evening at 5 a⁄clock and saw this afternoon the *Royall James*, *Oake*, and *London* burnt by the enemy with their fireships. I made my will also this day, and did give all I had equally between my father and wife – and left copies of it in each of Mr Hater and W. Hewer's hands, who both witnessed the will; and so to supper and then to bed; and slept pretty well, but yet often waking.

14 June. Up and to the office, where by and by comes Mr Willson and, by direction of his, a man of Mr Gawden's who came from Chatham last night and saw the three ships burnt, they lying all dry, and boats going from the men⁄of⁄war and fire them. But that that he tells me of worst consequence is that he himself (I think he said) did hear many

Englishmen on board the Dutch ships, speaking to one another in English, and that they did cry and say, 'We did heretofore fight for tickets; now we fight for dollers!' and did ask how such and such a one did, and would commend themselfs to them – which is a sad consideration. It is said they did in open streets yesterday, at Westminster, cry, 'A Parliament! a Parliament!'; and do believe it will cost blood to answer for these miscarriages.

Mr Hater tells me at noon that some rude people have been, as he hears, at my Lord Chancellor's, where they have cut down the trees before his house and broke his windows; and a gibbet either set up before or painted upon his gate, and these words writ – 'Three sights to be seen; Dunkirke, Tanger, and a barren Queen.' At dinner we discoursed of Tom of the Wood, a fellow that lives like a hermit near Woolwich, who as they say, [did] foretell the burning of the City, and now says that a greater desolation is at hand.

17 June. Up and to my office, where busy all the morning. Perticularly, setting my people to work in transcribing pieces of letters public and private, which I do collect against a black day, to defend the office with and myself. Everybody cries out of the Office of the Ordinance for their neglects, both at Gravesend and Upner and everywhere else.

18 June. Word was brought me that Commissioner Pett is brought to the Tower and there laid up close prisoner – which puts me into a fright, lest they may do the same with us as they do with him. This puts me upon hastening what I am doing with my people, and collecting out of my papers our defence.

19 June. Hearing by Yorke the carrier that my wife was coming to town, I did make hast home to see her, that she might not find me abroad. [She] did give me so bad an account of her and my father's method in burying of our gold, that made me mad – and she herself is not pleased with it, she believing that my sister knows of it. My father and she did it on Sunday when they were gone to church, in open daylight in the midst of the garden, where for aught they knew, many eyes might see them; which put me into such trouble, that I was almost mad about it.

21 June. Sir H. Cholmly came to me this day, and tells me the Court is as mad as ever and that the night the Duch burned our ships, the King did sup with my Lady Castlemayne at the Duchess of Monmouth, and there were all mad in hunting of a poor moth. All the Court afeared of a Parliament; but he thinks nothing can save us but the King's giving up all to a Parliament.

22 June. In the evening came Captain Hart and Hayword to me about the six merchant ships now taken up for men-of-war, and in talk they told me about the taking of *Royall Charles*; that nothing but carelessness lost the ship, for they might have saved her the very tide that the Duch came up, if they would have but used means and had had but boats, and that the want of boats plainly lost all the other ships. That the Dutch did take her with a boat of nine men, who found not a man on board her (and her laying so near them was a main temptation to them to come on); and presently a man went up and struck her flag and jacke, and a trumpeter sounded upon her 'Joan's placket is torn'. That they did carry her down at a time, both for tides and wind, when the best pilot in Chatham would not have undertaken it, they heeling her on one side to make her draw little water, and so carried her away safe.

24 June. Sir H. Cholmly tells me great news; that this day in Council the King hath declared that he will call his Parliament in thirty days – which is the best news I have heard a great while, and will, if anything, save the kingdom. How the King came to be advised to this, I know not; but he tells me that it was against the Duke of York's mind flatly, who did rather advise the King to raise money as he pleased; and against the Chancellors, who told the King that Queen Elizabeth did do all her business in '88 without calling a Parliament, and so might he do for anything he saw; but blessed be God, it is done, and pray God it may hold, though some of us must surely go to the pot, for all must be flung up to them or nothing will be done.

28 June. I dined with my Lady [Carteret], and good company and good dinner. At table, my Lady and Sir Phill. Carteret have great and good discourse of the greatness of the present King of France; what great things he hath done, that a man may pass at any hour in the night all over that wild city, with a purse in his hand and no danger. That there is not a beggar to be seen in it, nor dirt lying in it. That he hath married two of Colberts daughters to two of the greatest princes of France, and given them portions. Bought the greatest dukedome in France and given it to Colbert, and ne'er a prince in France dare whisper against it. By coach home and there find my wife making of tea, a drink which Mr Pelling the pothecary tells her is good for her for her cold and defluxions.

30 June. Lords Day. [To Chatham and] here I was told that in all the late attempt there was but one man that they know killed on shore; and that was a man that had laid upon his belly, upon one of the hills on the other side of the river, to see the action; and a bullet came and took the ground away just under his belly, and ripped up his belly, and so was killed. Thence by barge, it raining hard, down to the chain; and in our way did see the sad wracks of the poor *Royall Oake*, *James*, and *London*, and several other of our ships by us sunk; and several of the enemy's, whereof three men-of-war, that they could not get off and so burned. We did also see several dead bodies lie by the sides of the water. So to the chain, and there saw it fast at the end on Upner side of the river; very fast, and borne up upon the several stages across the river – and where it is broke, nobody can tell me. I went on shore on Upner side to look upon the end of the chain; and caused the link to be measured, and it was 6 inch and a quarter in circumference. They have burned the crane house that was to haul it tought. It seems very remarkable to me, and of great honour to the Dutch, that those of them that did go on shore to Gillingham, though they went in fear of their lives and were some of them killed, and notwithstanding their provocation at Scelling, yet killed none of our people nor plundered their houses; but did take some things of easy carriage and left the rest, and not a house burned; and, which is to our eternal disgrace, that what my Lord Douglasse's men, who come after them, found there, they plundered and took all away. And the watermen that carried us did further tell us that our own soldiers are far more terrible to those people of the country towns then the Dutch themselfs.

6 July. Up and to the office, where some of us sat busy all the morning. At noon home to dinner, whither Creed came to dine with us and brings the first word I hear of the news of a peace, the King having letters come to him this noon, signifying that it is concluded on and that Mr [Henry] Coventry is upon his way, coming over for the King's ratification. The news was so good and sudden, that I went with great joy to W. Batten and then to W. Penn to tell it them and so home to dinner, mighty merry and light at my heart only on this ground, that a continuing of the war must undo us, and so, though peace may do the like, if we do not make good use of it to reform ourselfs and get up money, yet there is an opportunity for us to save ourselfs – at least, for my own perticular, we shall continue well till I can get my money into my hands, and then I will shift for myself. After dinner away, leaving Creed there, by coach to Westminster, where to the Swan and drank; and then to the Hall and there talked a little, with great joy of the peace; and then to Mrs Martins where I met with the good news que esta no es con child she having de estos upon her – the fear of which, which she did give me the other day, had troubled me much. My joy in this made me send for wine, and thither came her sister and Mrs Cragg and I stayed a good while there. But here happened the best instance of a woman's falseness in the world; that her sister Doll, who went for a bottle of wine, did come home all blubbering and swearing against one Captain Vandena, a Dutchman of the Rhenish wine house, that pulled her into a stable by the Dog tavern and there did tumble her and toss her; calling him all the rogues and toads in the world, when she knows that ella hath suffered me to do anything with her a hundred times.

8 July. Up and to my chamber; and by and by comes Greeting, and to my flagelette with him with a pretty deal of pleasure; and then to the office, where W. Batten, W. Penn and I met about putting men to work for the weighing of the ships in the river sunk. Then home again and there heard Mr Cæsar play some very good things on the lute, together with myself on the viall and Greeting on the viallin. Then with my wife abroad to Charing Cross, there to see the great boy and girle that are lately come out of Ireland; the latter, eight, the former but four years old, of most prodigious bigness for their age. I tried to weigh them in my arms, and find them twice as heavy as people almost twice their age; and yet I am apt to believe they are very young – their father a little sorry fellow, and their mother an old Irish woman. They have had four children of this bigness and four of ordinary growth, whereof two of each are dead.

12 July. Sir H. Cholmly tells me [Clarendon] did say the other day at his table – 'Treachery?' says he, 'I could wish we could prove there was anything of that in it, for that would imply some wit and thoughtfulness; but we are ruined merely by folly and neglect.'

Sir H. Cholmly, as a true English gentleman, doth decry the King's expenses of his privy purse; which in King James's time did not rise to above 5,000*l* a year and in King Charles's to 10,000*l*, do now cost us above 100,000*l* – besides the great charge of the monarchy; as, the Duke of York 100,000*l* of it, and other limbs of the royall family, and the guards, which for his part, says he, 'I would have all disbanded; for the King is not the better by them and would be as safe without them, for we have had no rebellions to make him fear anything.' But contrarily, he is now raising of a land army, which this Parliament and kingdom will never bear; besides, the commanders they put over them are such as will never be able to raise or command them. But the design is, and the Duke of York he says is hot for it, to have a land army, and so to make the government like that of France; but our princes have not brains, or at least care and forecast enough, to do that. It is strange how he and everybody doth nowadays reflect upon Oliver and commend him, so brave things he did and made all the neighbour princes fear him; while here a prince, come in with all the love and prayers and good liking of his people, and have given greater signs of loyalty and willingness to serve him with their estates then ever was done by any people, hath lost all so soon, that it is a miracle what way a man could devise to lose so much in so little time. So home and there find my wife in a dogged humour for my not dining at home, and I did give her a pull by the nose and some ill words, which she provoked me to by something she spoke, that we fell extraordinarily out; insomuch, that I going to the office to avoid further anger, she fallowed me in a devilish manner thither, and with much ado I got her into the garden out of hearing, to prevent shame; and so home, and by degrees I found it necessary to calme her, and did; and then to the office, where pretty late, and then to walk with her in the garden, and so to supper and pretty good friends; and so to bed – with my mind very quiet.

13 July. Up pretty betimes, it being mighty hot weather. Resolved upon going to Epsumm tomorrow, only for ayre, and got Mrs Turner to go with us.

14 July. Lords Day. Up, and my wife, a little before 4, and to make us ready; and by and by Mrs Turner came to us by agreement, and she and I stayed talking below while my wife dressed herself; which vexed me that she was so long about it, keeping us till past 5 a'clock before she was ready. She ready, and taking some bottles of wine and beer and some cold fowle with us into the coach, we took coach and four horses which I had provided last night, and so away – a very fine day; and so towards Epsum, talking all the way pleasantly. The country very fine; only, the way very dusty. We got to Epsum by 8 a'clock to the Well, where much company; and there we light and I drank the water; they did not, but do go about and walk a little among the women, but I did drink four pints and had some very good stools by it. Here I met with divers of our town; among others, with several of the tradesmen of our office, but did talk but little with them, it growing hot in the sun; and so we took coach again and to the towne to the King's Head, where our coachman carried us; and there had an ill room for us to go into, but the best in the house that was not taken up; here we called for drink and bespoke dinner. After dinner, we all lay down after (the day being wonderful hot) to sleep, and each of us took a good nap. By and by we took coach and to take the ayre, there being a fine breeze abroad; and I went and carried them to the Well and there filled some bottles of water to carry home with me. Then I carried them to see my Cosen [John] Pepys's house; and light and walked round about it, and they like it (as endeed it deserves) very well, and is a pretty place; and then I walked them to the wood hard by and there got them in in the thickets, till they had lost themselfs and I could not find the way into any of the walks in the wood, which endeed are very pleasant if I could have found them. At last got out of the wood again; and I, by leaping down the little bank coming out of the wood, did sprain my right foot, which brought me great present pain; but presently, with walking, it went away for the present, and so the women and W. Hewer and I walked upon the Downes, where a flock of sheep was, and the most pleasant and innocent sight that ever I saw in my life; we find a shepheard and his little boy reading, far from any houses or sight of people, the Bible to him. So I made the boy read to me, which he did with the forced tone that children do usually read, that was mighty pretty; and then I did give him something and went to the father and talked with him; and I find he had been a servant in my Cosen Pepys's house, and told me what was become of their old servants. He did content himself mightily in my liking his boy's reading and did bless God for him, the most like one of the old Patriarchs that ever I saw in my life, and it brought those thoughts of the old age of the world in my mind for two or three days after. We took notice of his woolen knit stockings of two colours mixed, and of his shoes shod with iron shoes, both at the toe and heels, and with great nails in the soles of his feet, which was mighty pretty; and taking notice of them, 'Why', says the poor man, 'the Downes, you see, are full of stones, and we are fain to shoe ourselfs thus; and these', says he, 'will make the stones fly till they sing before me.' I did give the poor man something, for which he was mighty thankful, and I tried to cast stones with his horne crooke. He values his dog mightily, that would turn a sheep any way which he would have him when he goes to fold them. Told me there was about 18 scoare sheep in his flock, and that he hath 4s a week the year round for keeping of them. So we parted thence, with mighty pleasure in the discourse we had with this poor man; and Mrs Turner, in the common fields here, did gather one of the prettiest nosegays that ever I saw in my life. So to our coach; and so over the common and through Epsum towne to our inne, in the way stopping a poor woman with her milkpail and in one of my gilt tumblers did drink our bellyfuls of milk, better then any creame; and so to our inne and there had a dish of creame, but it was sour and so had no pleasure in it; and so paid our reckoning and took coach, it being about 7 at night, and passed and saw the people walking with their wifes and children to take the ayre; and we set out for home, the sun by and by going down, and we in the cool of the evening all the way with much pleasure home, talking and pleasing ourselfs with the pleasure of this day's work; and Mrs Turner mightily pleased with my resolution, which I tell her is never to keep a country house, but to keep a coach and with my wife on the Saturday and to go sometimes for a day to this place and then quite to another place; and there is more variety, and as little charge and no trouble, as there is in a country house. Anon it grew dark, and as it grew dark we had the pleasure to see several glow wormes, which was mighty pretty.

17 July. At Sir W. Batten's and there he did give the company a bottle or two of his own last year's wine growing at Walthamstow, then which the whole company said they never drank better foreign wine in their lives. So I to my office and did business, and so home to supper and there find my sister Michell come from Lee to see us; but doth tattle so much of the late business of the Duch coming thither, that I was weary of it.

19 July. Up, and comes the flagelette maister and brings me two new great ivory pipes, which cost me 32*s*. And so to play. The Duch fleet are in great squadrons everywhere still about Harwich. And were lately at Portsmouth; and the last letters say at Plymouth, and now gone to Dartmouth to destroy our Straights fleet, lately got in thither; but God knows whether they can do it any hurt or no. But it was pretty news came the other day so fast, of the Dutch fleets being in so many places, that Sir W. Batten at table cried, 'By God!' says he, 'I think the Devil shits Dutchmen.'

25 July. [The Commons] did present it to the King as their desire, that as soon as peace was concluded, the land army might be laid down, and that this their request might be carried to the King by them of their House that were privy councillors; which was put to the vote, and carried *nemine contradicente*. So after this vote passed, they adjourned; but it is plain what the effects of this Parliament will be if they be suffered to sit, that they will fall foul upon the faults of the government; and I pray God they may be permitted to do it, for nothing else I fear will save the King and kingdom then the doing it betimes.

29 July. To Westminster Hall, where the Hall full of people to see the issue of the day, the King being to come to speak to the House today. One thing extraordinary was this day, a man, a Quaker, came naked through the Hall, only very civilly tied about the privities to avoid scandal, and with a chafing dish of fire and brimstone burning upon his head did pass through the Hall, crying, 'Repent! Repent!' So home, and there Cosen Roger and Creed to dinner with me, and very merry. But among other things, they told me of the strange bold sermon of Dr Creeton yesterday before the King; how he preach against the sins of the Court, and perticularly against adultery.

30 July. I to Creeds chamber and thence out to Whitehall with him, in our way meeting with Mr Cooling, my Lord Chamberlaines secretary on horseback, who stopped to speak to us; and he proved very drunk and did talk and would have talked all night with us, I not being able to break loose from him, he holding me so by the hand. But Lord, to see his present humour; how he swears at every word and talks of the King and my Lady Castleman in the plainest words in the world. And from him I gather that the King hath declared that he did not get the child of which she is conceived at this time, he having not as he says laid with her this half year; but she told him – 'God damn me! but you shall own it.' It seems he is jealous of Jermin and she loves him. And he, it seems, hath laid with her from time to time continually, for a good while; and once, as this Cooling says, the King had like to have taken him a-bed with her, but that he was fain to creep under the bed into her closet. And then took notice of my kindness to him on shipboard seven years ago, when the King was coming over, and how much he was obliged to me; but says, 'Pray look upon this acknowledgement of a kindness in me to be a miracle; for', says [he], 'it is against the law at Court for a man that borrows money of me, even to buy his place with, to own it the next Sunday'. And then told us his horse was a bribe, and his boots a bribe; and told us he was made up of bribes, as a Oxford scholar is set out with other men's goods when he goes out of town, and that he makes every sort of tradesman to bribe him; and invited me home to his house to taste of his bribe wine.

1 August. Up, and all the morning at the office. At noon my wife and I dined at Sir W. Pen's, only with Mrs Turner and her husband, on a damned venison-pasty that stunk like a devil.

10 August. To the office and there wrote as long as my eyes would give me leave, and then abroad and to the New Exchange to the bookseller's there, where I hear of several new books coming out – Mr [S]pratts history of the Royal Society and Mrs Phillips's poems. Sir Jo. Denhams poems are going to be all printed together; and among others, some new things, and among them he showed me a copy of verses of his upon Sir Jo. Minnes's going heretofore to Bulloigne to eat a pig. Cowly, he tells me, is dead; who it seems was a mighty civil, serious man, which I did not know before. Several good plays are also likely to be abroad soon – as, *Mustapha* and *Henry the 5th.*

12 August. To the print sellers over against the Exchange towards Covent Garden, and there bought a few more prints of cittys and so home with them; and my wife and maids being gone over the water to the whitsters with their clothes, this being the first time of her trying this way of washing her linen, I dined at Sir W. Batten's.

16 August. Up, and at the office all the morning; and so at noon to dinner. And after dinner, my wife and I to the Duke's playhouse, where we saw the new play acted yesterday, *The Feign Innocence of Sir Martin Marr-all*, a play made by my Lord Duke of Newcastle, but as everybody says corrected by Dryden. It is the most entire piece of mirth, a complete farce from one end to the other, that certainly was ever writ. I never laughed so in all my life; I laughed till my head [ached] all the evening and night with my laughing, and at very good wit therein, not fooling.

18 August. Lords Day. I walked toward Whitehall; but being weary, turned into St Dunstan's church, where I hear an able sermon of the minister of the place. And stood by a pretty, modest maid, whom I did labour to take by the hand and the body; but she would not, but got further and further from me, and at last I could perceive her to take pins out of her pocket to prick me if I should touch her again; which seeing, I did forbear, and was glad I did espy her design. And then I fell to gaze upon another pretty maid in a pew close to me, and she on me; and I did go about to take her by the hand, which she suffered a little and then withdrew. So the sermon ended and the church broke up, and my amours ended also; and so took coach and home, and there took up my wife and to Islington with her, our old road; but before we got to Islington, between that and Kingsland, there happened an odd adventure; one of our coach horses fell sick of the staggers, so as he was ready to fall down. The coachman was fain to light and hold him up and cut his tongue to make him bleed, and his tail – the horse continued shakeing every part of him, as if he had been in an ague a good while, and his blood settled in his tongue, and the coachman thought and believed he would presently drop down dead. Then he blew some tobacco in his nose; upon which the horse sneezed, and by and by grows well and draws us the rest of our way as well as ever he did; which was one of the strangest things of a horse I ever observed – but he says it is usual. It is the staggers.

'Took up my wife and to Islington with her . . . Stayed and eat and drank . . . at the old house.' (18 August 1667.) By Islington, W. Hollar 1665. The buildings in the centre are the London Spa (a house of entertainment), St Paul's and St Sepulchre's.

24 August. St Bartholomew's Day. This morning was proclaimed the peace between us and the States of the United Provinces, and also of the King of France and Denmarke, and in the afternoon the proclamations were printed and came out. And at night the bells rung, but no bonfires that I hear of anywhere, partly from the dearness of firing but principally from the little content most people have in the peace.

26 August. Up; and Greeting came and I reckoned with him for his teaching of my wife and me upon the flagielette to this day, and so paid him off, having as much as he can teach us. Then to the office, where we sat upon a perticular business all the morning, and my Lord Anglesey with us; who, and my Lord Brouncker, do bring us news how my Lord Chancellors seal is to be taken away from him today. The thing is so great and sudden to me, that it put me into a very great admiration what should be the meaning of it; and they do not own that they know what it should be.

27 August. This day Mr Pierce the surgeon was with me; and tells me how this business of my Lord Chancellors was certainly designed in my Lady Castlemaine's chamber, and that when he went from the King on Monday morning, she was in bed (though about 12 a-clock) and ran out in her smock into her aviary looking into Whitehall garden, and thither her woman brought her her nightgown, and stood joying herself at the old man's going away. And several of the gallants of Whitehall (of which there was many staying to see the Chancellor return) did talk to her in her birdcage; among others, Blanckford, telling her she was the bird of paradise.

2 September. This day is kept in the City as a public fast for the Fire this day twelve months. But I was not at church, being commanded with the rest to attend the Duke of York. When we had done, Sir W. Coventry called me down with him to his chamber and there told me that he is leaving the Duke of York's service, which I was amazed at; but he tells me that it is not with the least unkindness on the Duke of York's side, though he expects (and I told him he was in the right) it will be interpreted otherwise, because done just at this time. He tells me the true reason is that he being a man not willing to undertake more business then he can go through, and being desirous to have his whole time to spend upon the business of the Treasury and a little for his own ease, he did desire this of the Duke of York. He tells me that he was the man that did propose the removal of the Chancellor; and that he did still persist in it, and at this day publicly owns it and is glad of it; but that the Duke of York knows that he did first speak of it to the Duke of York, before he spoke to any mortal creature besides, which was fair dealing; and that the Duke of York was then of the same mind with him and did speak of it to the King, though since, for reasons best known to himself, he was afterward altered. I did then desire to know what was the great matter that grounded his desire of the Chancellor's removal; he told me many things not fit to be spoken, and yet not anything of his being unfaithful to the King; but, *instar omnium*, he told me that while he was so great at the Council-board and in the administration of matters, there was no room for anybody to propose any remedy to what was amiss or to compass anything, though never so good for the kingdom, unless approved of by the Chancellor, he managing all things with that greatness which now will be removed, that the King may have the benefit of others' advice.

From him I went to see a great match at tennis between Prince Rupert and one Captain Cooke against Bab. May and the elder Chichly, where the King was and Court, and it seems are the best players at tennis in the nation. But this puts me in mind of what I observed in the morning; that the King, playing at tennis, had a steele yard carried to him, and I was told it was to weigh him after he had done playing; and at noon Mr Asburnham told me that it is only the King's curiosity, which he usually hath, of weighing himself before and after his play, to see how much he loses in weight by playing; and this day he lost $4\frac{1}{2}$ lb. Thence home and took my wife out to Mile End Green and there drank; and so home, having a very fine evening. Then home, and I to Sir W. Batten and W. Penn and there discoursed of Sir W. Coventry's leaving the Duke of York and Mr Wren's succeeding him; they told me both seriously, that they had long cut me out for Secretary to the Duke of York if ever W. Coventry left him; which, agreeing with what I have heard from other hands heretofore, doth make me not only think that something of that kind hath been thought on, but doth comfort me to see that the world hath such an esteem of my qualities as to think me fit for any such thing – though I am glad with all my heart that I am not so, for it would never please me to be forced to the attendance that that would require, and leave my wife and family to themselfs, as I must do in such a case; thinking myself now in the best place that ever man was in to please his own mind in, and therefore I will take care to preserve it.

4 September. By coach to Whitehall to the Council-chamber. I stayed and heard Alderman Barker's case of his being abused by the Council of Ireland touching his lands there. All I observed there is the silliness of the King, playing with his dog all the while, or his codpiece, and not minding the business, and what he said was mighty weak; but my Lord Keeper I observe to be a mighty able man.

6 September. To Bartholomew Fair and there, it being very dirty and now night, we saw a poor fellow, whose legs were tied behind his back, dance upon his hands with his arse above his head, and also dance upon his crutches, without any legs upon the ground to help him; which he did with that pain, that I was sorry to see it, and did pity him and give him money after he had done. Then we to see a piece of clockework made by an Englishman; endeed, very good, wherein all the several states of man's age, to 100 year old, is shown very pretty and solemne, and several other things more cheerful; and so we ended and walked up and down to get a coach.

8 September. To Whitehall and saw the King and Queen at dinner; and observed (which I never did before) the formality, but it is but a formality, of putting a bit of bread wiped upon each dish into the mouth of every man that brings a dish – but it should be in the sauce. To Sir G. Carterets to dinner, where Mr Cofferer Ashburnham – who told a good story of a prisoner's being condemned at Salsbury for a small matter; while he was on the bench with his father-in-law, Judge Richardson, and while they were considering to transport him to save his life, the fellow flung a great stone at the Judge, that missed him but broke through the wainscoat. Upon this, he had his hand cut off and was hanged presently.

15 September. Lords Day. Up to my chamber, there to set some papers to rights. By and by to church, where I stood in continual fear of Mrs Markham's coming to church and offering to come into our pew; to prevent which, as soon as ever I heard the great door open, I did step back and clapped my breech to our pew door, that she might be forced to shove me to come in; but as God would have it, she did not come. Mr Mills preached; and after sermon, by invitation he and his wife came to dine with me. We to church, and then home, and there comes Mr Pelling with two men by promise, one Wallington and Piggott; the former whereof, being a very little fellow, did sing a most excellent bass, and yet a poor fellow, a working goldsmith, that goes without gloves to his hands. Here we sung several good things, but I am more and more confirmed that singing with many voices is not singing, but a sort of instrumentall music, the sense of the words being lost by not being heard, and especially as they set them with fuges of words, one after another; whereas singing properly, I think, should be but with one or two voices at most, and that counterpoint.

22 September. Lords Day. At my chamber all the morning making up some accounts to my great content. At noon comes Mr Sheres, whom I find a good engenious man, but doth talk a little too much of his travels. He left my Lord Sandwich well, but in pain to be at home for want of money, which comes very hardly.

27 September. Up and to the office, where very busy all the morning. While I was busy at the office, my wife sends for me to come to home, and what was it but to see the pretty girl [Deb Willet] which she is taking to wait upon her; and though she seems not altogether so great a beauty as she had before told me, yet endeed she is mighty pretty; and so pretty, that I find I shall be too much pleased with it, and therefore could be contented as to my judgment, though not to my passion, that she might not come, lest I may be found too much minding her, to the discontent of my wife. She is to come next week. She seems by her discourse to be grave beyond her bigness and age, and exceeding well-bred as to her deportment, having been a scholar in a school at Bow these seven or eight year. To the office again, my [mind] running on this pretty girl.

28 September. Up, having slept not so much tonight as I used to do, for my thoughts being so full of this pretty little girl that is coming to live with us, which pleases me mightily.

29 September. Lords Day. Up, and put off my summer's silk suit and put on a cloth one. Then to church and so home to dinner, my wife and I alone to a good dinner. All the afternoon talking in my chamber with my wife about my keeping a coach the next year, and doing something to my house which will cost money – that is, furnish our best

. . . .

'While I was busy at the office, my wife sends for me to come to home, and what was it but to see the pretty girl [Deb Willet] which she is taking to wait upon her.' (27 September 1667.) Drawing by E. Marmion 1640.

chamber with tapestry, and other rooms with pictures.

4 October. [Sir W. Batten] is so ill, that it is believed he cannot live till tomorrow; which troubles me and my wife mightily, partly out of kindness, he being a good neighbour, and partly because of the money he owes me upon our bargain of the late prize.

5 October. Much surprized with the news of the death of Sir W. Batten who died this morning, having been but two days sick. Sir W. Penn and I did despatch a letter this morning to Sir W. Coventry to recommend Collonell Middleton, who we think a most honest and understanding man, and fit for that place. I to my tailors and there took up my wife and Willet, who stayed there for me, and to the King's House; and there going in, met with Knipp and she took us up into the tireing rooms and to the women's shift, where Nell was dressing herself and was all unready; and is very pretty, prettier then I thought; and so walked all up and down the House above, and then below into the scene room, and there sat down and she gave us fruit; and here I read the qu's to Knepp while she answered me, through all her part of *Flora's Figarys*, which was acted today. But Lord, to see how they were both painted would make a man mad, and did make me loath them – and what base company of men comes among them, and how lewdly they talk, and how poor the men are in clothes, and yet what a show they make on the stage by candlelight, is very observable.

7 October. Up betimes, and did do several things towards the settling all matters, both of house and office, in order for my journey [to Brampton] this day; and so about 9 a-clock, I and my wife and Willett set out in a coach I have hired, with four horses, and W. Hewer and Murford rode by us on horseback; and so, my wife and she in their morning gowns, very handsome and pretty and to my great liking, we set out; and so out at Allgate and so to the Greenman; and very merry, my wife and girl and [I], talking and telling tales and singing; and before night did come to Bishop Stafford, to the Raynedeere – where Mrs Aynsworth (who lived heretofore at Cambridge and whom I knew better then they think for, doth live – it was the woman that, among other things, was great with my Cosen Barmston of Cottenham, and did use to sing to him and did teach me 'Full forty times over', a very lewd song) doth live, a woman they are very well acquainted with, and is here what she was at Cambridge, and all the goodfellows of the country come hither. We to supper and so to bed, my wife and I in one bed and the girl in another in the same room. And lay very well, but there was so much tearing company in the house, that we could not see my landlady, so I had no opportunity of renewing my old acquaintance with her. But here we slept very well.

8 October. To Audly End and all over the house and garden; and mighty merry we were. The house endeed doth appear very fine, but not so fine as it hath heretofore to me. Perticularly the ceilings are not so good as I alway took them to be, being nothing so well wrought as my Lord Chancellors are; and though the figure of the house without be very extraordinary good, yet the stayrecase is exceeding poor; and a great many pictures, and not one good one in the house but one of Harry the 8th done by Holben; and not one good suit of hangings in all the house, but all most ancient things, such as I would not give the hanging up of in my house; and the other furniture, beds and other things, accordingly. Only, the gallery is good; and above all things, the cellars, where we went down and drank of much good liquor, and endeed the cellars are fine; and here my wife and I did sing to my great content. Away to Cambridge, it being foul, rainy weather; and there did take up at the Rose, for the sake of Mrs Dorothy Drawwater, the vintener's daughter, which is mentioned in the play of *Sir Martin Marr-all*. Here we had a good chamber and bespoke a good supper; and then I took my wife and W. Hewer and Willett (it holding up a little) and showed them Trinity College and St Johns Library, and went to King's College chapel to see the outside of it only, and so to our inne; and with much pleasure did this, they walking in their pretty morning gowns, very handsome, and I proud to find myself in condition to do this; and so home to our lodging, and there by and by to supper with much good sport, talking with the drawers concerning matters of the town and persons whom I remember; and so after supper to cards and then to bed, lying, I in one bed and my wife and girl in another in the same room; and very merry talking together and mightily pleased both of us with the girl.

9 October.   Up, and got ready and eat our breakfast and then took coach; and the poor, as they did yesterday, did stand at the coach to have something given them, as they do to all great persons, and I did give them something; and the town musique did also come and

. . . .

(*Below left*) 'The town musique did also come and play; but Lord, what sad music they made.' (9 October 1667.) City waits, playing shawms and sackbut, attributed to Marcellus Laroon II. (*Below right*) Magdalene College, Cambridge, from D. Loggan's *Cantabrigia Illustrata* 1690. The plate is dedicated to Pepys.

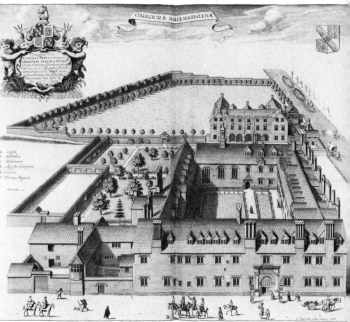

play; but Lord, what sad music they made – however, I was pleased with them, being all of us in very good humour; and so set forth and through the town, and observed at our college of Magdalen the posts new-painted, and understand that the Vice-Chancellor is there this year. And so away for Huntington, mightily pleased all along the road to remember old stories; and came to Brampton at about noon and there find my father and sister and brother all well; and here laid up our things, and up and down to see the garden with my father, and the house, and do altogether find it very pretty – especially the little parlour and the summerhouses in the garden. Only, the wall doth want greens upon it and the house is too low-roofed; but that is only because of my coming from a house with higher ceilings; but altogether is very pretty and I bless God that I am like to have such a pretty place to retire to. And I did walk with my father without doors and do find a very convenient way of laying out money there in building, which will make a very good seat; and the place deserves it, I think, very well. By and by to dinner, and after dinner I walked up to Hinchingbrooke, where my Lady expected me, and there spent all the afternoon with her; the same most excellent, good, discreet lady that ever she was. But a thousand questions my Lady asked me, till she could think of no more almost, but walked up and down the house with me; but I do find by her, that they are reduced to great straits for money, having been forced to sell her plate, 8 or 900l worth, and is now going to sell a suit of her best hangings, of which I could almost wish to buy a piece or two, if the pieces will be broke. But the house is most excellently furnished, and brave rooms and good pictures, so that it doth please me infinitely, beyond Audly End. Here we stayed till night, walking and talking and drinking, and with mighty satisfaction, my Lady with me alone most of the day, talking of my Lord's bad condition to be kept in Spain without money and at a great expense, which (as we will save the family) we must labour to remove. Night being come, we took leave with all possible kindness, and so home; and there Mr Sheply stayed with us and supped, and full of good country discourse; and when supper done, took his leave and we all to bed.

10 October. Waked in the morning with great pain I, of the collique, by cold taken yesterday, I believe with going up and down in my shirt; but with rubbing my belly, keeping of it warm, I did at last come to some ease, and rose; and up to walk up and down the garden with my father, to talk of all our concernments – about a husband for my sister, whereof there is at present no appearance. But we must endeavour to find her one now, for she grows old and ugly. Then for my brother; and resolve he shall stay here this winter, and then I will either send him to Cambridge for a year, till I get him some church promotion, or send him to sea as a chaplain, where he may study and earn his living. To dinner to Hinchingbrooke, where we had a good plain country dinner, but most kindly used; and stayed till it was almost night again; and then took leave, but with extraordinary kindness from my Lady, who looks upon me like one of her own family and interest. So thence, my wife and people [by] the highway, and I walked over the park

(*Opposite*) Whitehall from St James's Park, by Henrick Danckaerts (detail). The Coldstream Guards drill in front of the Horse Guards building, while Charles II strolls through the park with members of his court.

with Mr Sheply and through the grove, which is mighty pretty as is imaginable; and so over their drawbridge to Nun's Bridge and so to my father's, and there sat and drank and talked a little and then parted; and he being gone, and what company there was, my father and I with a dark lantern, it being now night, into the guarden with my wife and there went about our great work to dig up my gold. But Lord, what a tosse I was for some time in, that they could not justly tell where it was, that I begun heartily to sweat and be angry that they should not agree better upon the place, and at last to fear that it was gone; but by and by, poking with a spit, we found it, and then begun with a spudd to lift up the ground; but good God, to see how sillily they did it, not half a foot under ground and in the sight of the world from a hundred places if anybody by accident were near-hand, and within sight of a neighbour's window and their hearing also, being close by; only, my father says that he saw them all gone to church before he begun the work when he laid the money, but that doth not excuse it to me; but I was out of my wits almost, and the more from that upon my lifting up the earth with the spud, I did discern that I scattered the pieces of gold round about the ground among the grass and loose earth; and taking up the iron headpieces wherein they were put, I perceive the earth was got among the gold and wet, so that the bags were all rotten, that I could not tell what in the world to say to it, not knowing how to judge what was wanting; which, all put together, did make me mad; and at last was forced to take up the headpieces, dirt and all, and as many of the scattered pieces as I could with the dirt discern by the candlelight, and carry them up into my brother's chamber and there lock them up till I had eat a little supper; and then all people going to bed, W. Hewer and I did all alone, with several pales of water and basins, at last wash the dirt off of the pieces and parted the pieces and the dirt, and then begun to tell; and by a note which I had of the value of the whole (in my pocket) do find that there was short above a hundred pieces, which did make me mad; and considering that the neighbour's house was so near, that we could not suppose we could speak one to another in the garden at the place where the gold lay (especially by my father being deaf) but they must know what we had been doing on, I feared that they might in the night come and gather some pieces and prevent us the next morning; so W. Hewer and I out again about midnight (for it was now grown so late) and there by candlelight did make shift to gather forty-five pieces more – and so in and to cleanse them, and by this time it was past 2 in the morning; and so to bed, and there lay in some disquiet all night, telling of the clock till it was daylight.

11 October. And then rose and called W. Hewer, and he and I, with pails and a sive, did lock ourselfs into the garden and there gather all the earth about the place into pails, and then sive those pails in one of the summerhouses (just as they do for dyamonds in other parts of the world); and there to our great content did with much trouble by 9 a-clock, and by that time we emptied several pails and could not find one, we did make the last night's forty-five up to seventy; so that we are come to about twenty or thirty of what I

. . . .

(*Opposite*) Each year the Lord Mayor was sworn in at Guildhall on 28 October; the following day he went in procession (partly by water) to be sworn in at the Exchequer. By an unknown Dutch artist *c.* 1683 (detail).

think the true number should be, and perhaps within less; so that I am pretty well satisfied that my loss is not great and do bless God that it is so well; and do leave my father to make a second examination of the dirt – which he promises he will do; and poor man, is mightily troubled for this accident. And so got all my gold put up in bags; and so having the last night wrote to my Lady Sandwich to lend me John Bowles to go along with me my journy, not telling her the reason, but it was only to secure my gold, we to breakfast; and then about 10 a,clock took coach, my wife and I, and Willett and W. Hewer, and Murford and Bowles (whom my Lady lent me), and my brother John on horseback; and with these four I thought myself pretty safe. But before we went out, the Huntington music came to me and played, and it was better then that of Cambridge. Here I took leave of my father, and did give my sister 20s. She cried at my going; but whether it was at her unwillingness for my going or any unkindness of my wife's or no, I know not; but God forgive me, I take her to be so cunning and ill,natured that I have no great love for her; but only, is my sister and must be provided for. My gold, I put into a basket and set under one of the seats; and so my work every quarter of an hour was to look to see whether all was well, and did ride in great fear all the day; but it was a pleasant day and good company, and I mightily contented. Mr Sheply saw me beyond St Neotts and there parted, and we straight to Stevenage, through Baldock lanes, which are already very bad. And at Stevenage we came well before night, and all safe; and there with great care I got the gold up to the chamber, my wife carrying one bag and the girl another and W. Hewer the rest in the basket, and set it all under a bed in our chamber; and then sat down to talk and were very pleasant, satisfying myself, among other things from Jo. Bowles, in some terms of hunting and about deere, bucks, and does; and so anon to supper, and very merry we were and a good supper; and after supper to bed.

12 October. Up, and eat our breakfast and set out about 9 a,clock; and so to Barnett, where we stayed and baited (the weather very good all day and yesterday) and by 5 a,clock got home, where I find all well; and did bring my gold, to my heart's content, very safe home, having not this day carried it in a basket but in our hands: the girl took care of one and my wife another bag, and I the rest – I being afeared of the bottom of the coach, lest it should break; and therefore was at more ease in my mind then I was yesterday. At home do find that Sir W. Batten's buriall was today; carried from hence with a hundred or two of coaches to Walthamstow and there buried.

17 October. Up; and being sent for by my Lady Batten I to her and there she found fault with my not seeing her since her being a widow; which I excused as well as I could, though it is a fault, but it is my nature not to be forward in visits. But here she told me her condition (which is good enough, being sole executrix, to the disappointment of all her husband's children) and prayed my friendship about [her husband's] accounts, which I promised her. And here do see what creatures widows are in weeping for their husbands, and then presently leaving off; but I cannot wonder at it, the cares of the world taking place of all other passions. This afternoon my Lord Anglesy tells us that the House of Commons have this morning run into the enquiry in many things; as, the sale of Dunkirke, the dividing of the fleet the last year, the business of the prizes with my Lord

Sandwich, and many other things; so that now they begin to fall close upon it and God knows what will be the end of it, but a committee they have chosen to inquire into the miscarriages of the warr.

Pepys appeared before this committee on 22 October. It reported in February 1668 and Pepys had to answer its charges against the Navy Board before the whole House on the following 5 March.

21 October. My Cosen Pepys comes out of [the House of Commons] to me and walks in the Hall with me; and bids me prepare to answer to everything, for they do seem to lodge the business of Chatham upon the Commissioners of the Navy, and that they are resolved to lay the fault heavy somewhere and to punish it; and prays me to prepare to save myself and gives me hints what to prepare against – which I am obliged to him for – and do begin to mistrust lest some unhappy slip or other, after all my diligence and pains, may not be found (which I can foresee) that may prove as fatal to a man as the constant course of negligence and unfaithfulness of other men. Here we parted, and I home, where I find my wife and the two Mercers and Willett and W. Batelier have been dancing, but without a fidler; I had a little pleasure in talking with these, but my head and heart full of thoughts, between hope and fear and doubts what will become of us, and me perticularly, against a furious Parliament. Then broke up and to bed; and there slept pretty well till about 4 a⁄clock, and from that time could not, but my thoughts running on speeches to the Parliament to excuse myself from the blame which by other men's negligences will light, it may be, upon the office.

22 October. Slept but ill all the last part of the night, for fear of this day's success in Parliament; therefore up, and all of us all the morning close, till almost 2 a⁄clock, collecting all we had to say and had done from the beginning touching the safety of the River Medway and Chatham; and having done this and put it into order, we away, I not having time to eat my dinner; and so all in my Lord Brouncker's coach (that is to say, Brouncker, W. Penn, T. Harvy, and myself), talking of the other great matter with which they charge us, that is, of discharging men by ticket, in order to our defence in case that should be asked. We came to the Parliament door; and there, after a little waiting till the committee was sat, we were, the House being very full, called in. I had a chair brought for me to lean my books upon; and so did give them such an account, in a series, of the whole business that had passed the office touching the matter, and so answered all questions given me about it, that I did not perceive but they were fully satisfied with me and the business as to our office. None of my brethren said anything but myself; only two or three silly words my Lord Brouncker gave, in answer to one question about the number of men there in the King's yard at that time. At last the House dismissed us, and shortly after did adjourne the debate till Friday next; and my Cosen Pepys did come out and joy me in my acquitting myself so well, and so did several others, and my fellow officers all very briske to see themselfs so well acquitted – which makes me a little proud, but yet not secure but we may yet meet with a back⁄blow which we see not. So, with our hearts very light, Sir W. Penn and I in his coach home, it being now near 8 a⁄clock; and so to the office and did a little business by the post, and so home, hungry, and eat a good supper.

4 November. I took coach and went to Turlington the great spectacle-maker for advice; who dissuades me from useing old spectacles, but rather young ones. And doth tell me that nothing can wrong them more then for me to use reading glasses, which do magnify much.

7 November. Up, and at the office hard all the morning; and at noon resolve with Sir W. Penn to go see *The Tempest*, an old play of Shakespeares, acted here the first day. And so my wife and girl and W. Hewer by themselfs, and Sir W. Penn and I afterward by ourselfs, and forced to sit in the side balcone over against the musique room at the Dukes House, close by my Lady Dorsett and a great many great ones: the house mighty full, the King and Court there, and the most innocent play that ever I saw, and a curious piece of musique in an echo of half-sentences, the echo repeating the former half while the man goes on to the latter, which is mighty pretty. The play no great wit; but yet good, above ordinary plays. Thence home with W. Penn, and there all mightily pleased with the play; and so to supper and to bed, after having done at the office.

Clarendon, architect of the Restoration and leading minister since 1660, had been dismissed on 30 August. He had been unpopular ever since the war started and was now made a scapegoat for its disasters. On 6 November articles of impeachment were drawn up against him by the House of Commons. The Lords however refused to commit him on the ground that the charges did not amount to treason. On 29 November he took flight to France, where he died in 1674.

12 November. This morning, to my astonishment, I hear that yesterday my Lord Chancellor is voted to have matter against him for an impeachment of high treason, and that this day the impeachment is to be carried up to the House of Lords – which is very high and I am troubled at it – for God knows what will fallow, since they that do this must do more, to secure themselfs against any that will revenge this, if it ever come in their power.

15 November. To Westminster, and there I walked with several and do hear that there is to be a conference between the two Houses today; so I stayed, and it was only to tell the Commons that the Lords cannot agree to the confining or sequestering of the Earle of Clarendon from the Parliament, forasmuch as they do not specify any perticular crime which they lay upon him and call treason. Thence I away home (calling at my mercer and tailor's) and there find, as I expected, Mr Cæsar and little Pellam Humphrys, lately returned from France and is an absolute monsieur, as full of form and confidence and vanity, and disparages everything and everybody's skill but his own. The truth is, everybody says he is very able; but to hear how he laughs at all the King's music here, that they cannot keep time nor tune nor understand anything, and that Grebus the Frenchman, the King's Master of the Musique, how he understands nothing nor can play on any instrument and so cannot compose, and that he will give him a lift out of his place, and that he and the King are mighty great, and that he hath already spoke to the King of Grebus, would make a man piss.

21 November. To Arundell House, where the meeting of Gresham College was broke up; but there meeting Creed, I with him to the tavern in St Clements churchyard, where was Deane Wilkins, Dr Whistler, Dr Floyd, a divine, admitted, I perceive, this day, and other brave men. Among the rest, they discourse of a man that is a little frantic (that hath been a kind of minister, Dr Wilkins saying that he hath read for him in church) that is poor and a debauched man, that the College have hired for 20s to have some of the blood of a sheep let into his body; and it is to be done on Saturday next. They purpose to let in about twelve ounces, which they compute is what will be let in in a minutes time by a watch. They differ in the opinion they have of the effects of it; some think that it may have a good effect upon him as a frantic man, by cooling his blood; others, that it will not have any effect at all. But the man is a healthy man, and by this means will be able to give an account what alteration, if any, he doth find in himself, and so may be usefull. On this occasion Dr Whistler told a pretty story related by Muffett, a good author, of Dr Cayus that built Key's College: that being very old and lived only at that time upon woman's milk, he, while he fed upon the milk of a angry fretful woman, was so himself; and then being advised to take of a good-natured patient woman, he did become so, beyond the common temper of his age. Thus much nutriment, they observed, might do. Their discourse was very fine; and if I should be put out of my office, I do take great content in the liberty I shall be at of frequenting these gentlemen's companies.

29 November. Waked about 7 a-clock this morning with a noise I supposed I heard near our chamber, of knocking, which by and by increased, and I more awake, could distinguish it better; I then waked my wife and both of us wondered at it, and lay so a great while, while that encreased; and at last heard it plainer, knocking as if it were breaking down a window for people to get out – and then removing of stools and chairs, and plainly by and by going up and down our stairs. We lay both of us afeared; yet I would have rose, but my wife would not let me; besides, I could not do it without making noise; and we did both conclude that thiefs were in the house, but wondered what our people did, whom we thought either killed or afeared as we were. Thus, we lay till the clock struck 8, and high day. At last I removed my gown and slippers safely to the other side the bed over my wife, and there safely rose and put on my gown and breeches and then with a firebrand in my hand safely opened the door, and saw nor heard anything. Then (with fear, I confess) went to the maid's chamber door, and all quiet and safe. Called Jane up, and went down safely and opened my chamber, where all well. Then more freely about, and to the kitchen, where the cook-maid up and all safe. So up again, and when Jane came and we demanded whether she heard no noise, she said, 'Yes, and was afeared', but rose with the other maid and found nothing, but heard a noise in the great stack of chimneys that goes from Sir J. Mennes's through our house; and so we sent, and their chimneys have been swept this morning, and the noise was that and nothing else. It is one of the most extraordinary accidents in my life, and gives ground to think of Don Quixot's adventures how people may be surprized – and the more from an accident last night, that our young gibb cat did leap down our stairs from top to bottom at two leaps and frighted us, that we could not tell well whether it was the cat or a spirit, and do sometimes think this morning that the house might be haunted. Glad to have this so well over, and endeed really glad in my mind, for I was much afeared.

30 November. Up and to the office, where all the morning, and then by coach to Arundell House to the elections of officers for the next year; where I was near being chosen of the Council, but am glad I was not, for I could not have attended; though above all things, I could wish it, and do take it as a mighty respect to have been named there. The company great and elections long; and then to Cary House, a house now of entertainment, next my Lord Ashly's; and there, where I have heretofore heard Common Prayer in the time of Dr Mossum, we after two hours' stay, sitting at the table with our napkins open, had our dinners brought; but badly done. But here was good company, I choosing to sit next Dr Wilkins, Sir George Ent, and others whom I value. And there talked of several things; among others, Dr Wilkins, talking of the universall speech, of which he hath a book coming out, did first inform me how man was certainly made for society, he being of all creatures the least armed for defence; and of all creatures in the world, the young ones are not able to do anything to help themselfs, nor can find the dug without being put to it, but would die if the mother did not help it. And he says were it not for speech, man would be a very mean creature. Much of this good discourse we had. But here above all, I was pleased to see the person who had his blood taken out. He speaks well, and did this day give the Society a relation thereof in Latin, saying that he finds himself much better since, and as a new man. But he is cracked a little in his head, though he speaks very reasonably and very well. He had but 20*s* for his suffering it, and is to have the same again tried upon him – the first sound man that ever had it tried on him in England, and but one that we hear of in France, which was a porter hired by the virtuosi. And so home and supper and to bed – where frighted a good while, and my wife, again with noises; and my wife did rise twice, but I think it was Sir J. Mennes's people again, late cleaning their house, for it was past 1 a-clock in the morning before we could fall to sleep; and so slept – but I perceive well what the care of money and treasure in a man's house is to a man that fears to lose it.

3 December. Up by candlelight, the only time I think I have done so this winter; and a coach being got overnight, I to Sir W. Coventry, the first time I have seen him at his new house since he came to lodge there. At noon home to dinner and busy all the afternoon; and at night home and there met W. Batelier, who tells me the first great news, that my Lord Chancellor is fled this day. By and by to Sir W. Penn's, where Sir R. Ford. Sir Rd. Ford says, that this day [it] hath been made appear to them that the Keeper of Newgate hath made his house the only nursery of rogues and whores and pickpockets and thiefs in the world, where they were bred and entertained and the whole society met; and that for the sake of the Sheriffes they durst not this day commit him.

19 December. Up, and to the office, where Comissioner Middleton first took place at the Board as Surveyor of the Navy; and endeed I think will be an excellent officer I am sure, much beyond what his predecessor was. At noon, to avoid being forced to invite him to dinner, it being his first day and nobody inviting him, I did go to the Change with Sir W. Penn in his coach, who first went to Guildhall, whither I went with him – he to speak with Sheriffe Gawden, I only for company; and did here look up and down this place, where I have not been before since the Fire, and I saw the City are going apace on in the rebuilding of Guildhall.

'The City are going apace on in the rebuilding of Guildhall.' (19 December 1667.)
Guildhall, from the south *c.* 1690. Badly damaged in the Fire, Guildhall was rebuilt
by November 1671. The two wings were new. Much of the medieval building and the
statues on the porch had survived.

. . . .

22 December. Lords Day. Up, then to dress myself and down to my chamber to settle some
papers; and thither came to me Willet with an errand from her mistress, and this time I
first did give her a little kiss, she being a very pretty-humoured girl, and so one that I do
love mightily.

24 December. Up, and all the morning at the office; and at noon with my clerks to dinner
and then to the office again, busy at the office till 6 at night; and then by coach to St
James's, my design being to see the ceremonys, this night being the Eve of Christmas, at
the Queen's Chapel. But it being not begun, I to Westminster Hall and there stayed and
walked; and then to the Swan and there drank and talked, and did besar a little Frank;
and so to Whitehall and sent my coach round, and I through the park to chapel, where I
got in up almost to the rail and with a great deal of patience, stayed from 9 at night to 2 in
the morning in a very great crowd; and there expected, but found nothing extraordinary,
there being nothing but a high masse. The Queene was there and some ladies. But Lord,
what an odde thing it was for me to be in a crowd of people, here a footman, there a
beggar, here a fine lady, there a zealous poor Papist, and here a Protestant, two or three

together, come to see the show. I was afeared of my pocket being picked very much. Their music very good endeed, but their service I confess too frivolous, that there can be no zeal go along with it; and I do find by them themselfs, that they do run over their beads with one hand, and point and play and talk and make signs with the other, in the midst of their messe. But all things very rich and beautiful. And I see the Papists had the wit, most of them, to bring cushions to kneel on; which I wanted, and was mightily troubled to kneel. All being done, and I sorry for my coming, missing of what I expected; which was to have a child borne and dressed there and a great deal of do, but we broke up and nothing like it done; and there I left people receiving the sacrament, and the Queen gone, and ladies; only my Lady Castlemayne, who looks prettily in her nightclothes. And so took my coach, which waited, and away through Covent Garden to set down two gentlemen and a lady, who came thither to see also and did make mighty mirth in their talk of the folly of this religion; and so I stopped, having set them down, and drank some burnt wine at the Rose tavern door, while the constables came and two or three bell-men went by, it being a fine light moonshine morning; and so home round the City and stopped and dropped money at five or six places, which I was the willinger to do, it being Christmas Day; and so home and there find wife in bed, and Jane and the maids making pyes, and so I to bed and slept well.

28 December. To the King's House and there saw *The Mad Couple*, which is but an ordinary play; but only, Nells and Hearts mad parts are most excellently done, but especially hers.

Many fine faces here today. It pleased us mightily to see the natural affection of a poor woman, the mother of one of the children brought on the stage – the child crying, she by force got upon the stage, and took up her child and carried it away off of the stage from Hart.

29 December. Lords Day. At night comes Mrs Turner to see us; and there, among other talk, she tells me that Mr Will Pen, who is lately come over from Ireland, is a Quaker again, or some very melancholy thing; that he cares for no company, nor comes into any – which is a pleasant thing, after his being abroad so long – and his father such a hypocritical rogue, and at this time an atheist.

31 December. Thus ends the year, with great happiness to myself and family as to health and good condition in the world, blessed be God for it; only with great trouble to my mind in reference to the public, there being little hopes left but that the whole nation must in a very little time be lost, either by troubles at home, the Parliament being dissatisfied and the King led into unsettled counsels by some about him, himself considering little – and divisions growing between the King and Duke of York; or else by foreign invasion, to which we must submit, if any at this bad point of time should come upon us; which the King of France is well able to do. These thoughts, and some cares upon me concerning my standing in this office when the committee of Parliament [on miscarriages] shall come to examine our Navy matters, which they will now shortly do. I pray God they may do the kingdom service therein, as they will have sufficient opportunity of doing it.

1668

1 January. After dinner to the Duke of York's playhouse, and there saw *Sir Martin Marrall*, which I have seen so often; and yet am mightily pleased with it and think it mighty witty, and the fullest of proper matter for mirth that ever was writ. And I do clearly see that they do improve in their acting of it. Here a mighty company of citizens, prentices and others; and it makes me observe that when I begin first to be able to bestow a play on myself, I do not remember that I saw so many by half of the ordinary prentices and mean people in the pit, at 2*s* 6*d* apiece, as now; I going for several years no higher then the 12*d*, and then the 18*d* places, and though I strained hard to go in then when I did – so much the vanity and prodigality of the age is to be observed in this perticular. By and by I met with Mr Brisban; and having it in my mind this Christmas to go to see the manner of the gaming at the Groome Porter's [at Court], I did tell him of it and he did lead me thither; where after staying an hour, they begin to play at about 8 at night – where to see how differently one man took his losing from another, one cursing and swearing, and another only muttering and grumbling to himself, a third without any appearing discontent at all – to see how the dice will run good luck in one hand for half an hour together – and another have no good luck at all. To see how easily here, where they play nothing but guinnys, 100*l* is won or lost. To see two or three gentlemen come in there drunk, and putting their stock of gold together – one 22 pieces, the second 4, and the third 5 pieces; and these to play one with another, and forget how much each of them brought, but he that brought the 22 think that he brought no more then the rest. To see the different humours of gamesters to change their luck when it is bad – how ceremonious they are as to call for new dice, to shift their places, to alter their manner of throwing; and that with great industry, as if there was anything in it. To see how some old gamesters, that have no money now to spend as formerly, do come and sit and look on; as among others, Sir Lewes Dives, who was here and hath been a great gamester in his time. To hear their cursing and damning to no purpose. To see how persons of the best quality do here sit down and play with people of any, though meaner; and to see how people in ordinary clothes shall come hither and play away 100, or 2 or 300 guinnys, without any kind of difficulty. And lastly, to see the formality of the Groome Porter, who is their judge of all disputes in play and all quarrels that may arise therein; and how his under-officers are there to observe true play at each table and to give new dice, is a consideration I never could have thought had been in the world, had I not now seen it. And so I having enough for once, refusing to venture, though Brisband pressed me hard and tempted me with saying that no man was ever known to lose the first time, the devil being too cunning to discourage a gamester; and he offered me also to lend me ten pieces to venture, but I did refuse and so went away – and took coach and home about 9 or 10 at night.

6 January. Twelfe Day. To Mrs Pierce and took her and her cousin Corbet, Knipp, and little James, and brought them to the Duke's House; and the house being full, was forced to carry them to a box, which did cost me 20*s* besides oranges; which troubled me – though their company did please me. Thence, after the play, stayed till Harris was undressed (there being acted *The Tempest*) and so he withal, all by coaches home, where we find my house with good fires and candles ready, and our office the like, and the two Mercers, and Betty Turner, Pendleton, and W. Batelier; and so with much pleasure we into the [office] and there fell to dancing, having extraordinary music, two violins and a bass viallin and theorbo (four hands), the Duke of Buckingham's musique, the best in towne, sent me by Greeting; and there we set in to dancing. By and by to my house to a very good supper, and mighty merry and good music playing; and after supper to dancing and singing till about 12 at night; and then we had a good sack-posset for them and an excellent cake, cost me near 20*s* of our Jane's making, which was cut into twenty pieces, there being by this time so many of our company by the coming in of young Goodyer and some others of our neighbours, young men that could dance, hearing of our dancing and anon comes in Mrs Turner the mother and brings with her Mrs Hollworthy, which pleased me mightily; and so to dancing again and singing with extraordinary great pleasure, till about 2 in the morning; and then broke up, and Mrs Pierce and her family and Harris and Knip by coach home, as late as it was; and they gone, I took Mrs Turner and Hollworthy home to my house and there gave them wine and sweetmeats. They being gone, I paid the fiddler 3*l* among the four, and so away to bed, weary and mightily pleased; and have the happiness to reflect upon it as I do sometimes on other things, as going to a play or the like, to be the greatest real comforts that I am to expect in the world, and that it is that that we do really labour in the hopes of; and so I do really enjoy myself, and understand that if I do not do it now, I shall not hereafter, it may be, be able to pay for it or have health to take pleasure in it, and so fool myself with vain expectation of pleasure and go without it.

10 January. I have bought a great many books lately, to a great value; but I think to buy no more till Christmas next, and these that I have will so fill my two presses, that I must be forced to give away some to make room for them, it being my design to have no more at any time for my proper library then to fill them.

11 January. With my wife for half an hour walking by moonlight and, it being cold frosty weather, walking in the garden; and then home to supper, and so by the fireside to have my head combed, as I do now often do, by Deb, whom I love should be fiddling about me; and so to bed.

13 January. Stopped at Martins my bookseller, where I saw the French book which I did think to have had for my wife to translate, called *L'Escholle de Filles*; but when I came to look into it, it is the most bawdy, lewd book that ever I saw, rather worse then *Putana errante* – so that I was ashamed of reading in it.

16 January. To the office, where sat all the morning. At noon home to dinner with my gang of clerks, in whose society I am mightily pleased, and mightily with Mr Gibsons

This drawing by Nichols *c.* 1693, one of a pair of frontispieces to Pepys's catalogue,
shows Pepys's library in the house he later occupied in York Buildings, King Street, off
the Strand. The book presses were made of oak with glazed doors. Ultimately there
were twelve, all of which survive in the Pepys Library.

. . . .

talking; he telling me so many good stories relating to the warr and practices of
commanders, which I will find a time to recollect; and he will be an admirable help to my
writing a history of the Navy, if ever I do. So to the office, where busy all the afternoon and
evening, and then home. My work this night with my clerks till midnight at the office was
to examine my list of ships I am making for myself, and their dimensions, and to see how it
agrees or differs from other lists; and I do find so great a difference between them all that I
am at a loss which to take; and therefore think mine to be as much depended upon as any I
can make out of them all. So little care there hath been to this day to know or keep any
history of the Navy.

17 January. Up, and by coach to Whitehall to attend the Council there; and here I met all
the discourse of the duell yesterday between the Duke of Buckingham, Holmes, and one
Jenkins on one side, and my Lord of Shrewsbury, Sir Jo. Talbot, and one Bernard
Howard, on the other side; and all about my Lady Shrewsbury, who is a whore and is at
this time, and hath for a great while been a whore to the Duke of Buckingham; and so her
husband challenged him, and they met yesterday in a close near Barne Elmes and there
fought; and my Lord Shrewsbury is run through the body from the right breast through
the shoulder, and Sir Jo. Talbot all along up one of his arms, and Jenkins killed upon the

place, and the rest all in a little measure wounded. This will make the world think that the King hath good councillors about him, when the Duke of Buckingham, the greatest man about him, is a fellow of no more sobriety then to fight about a whore.

21 January. Up, and while at the office comes news from Kate Joyce that if I would see her hus[band] alive, I must come presently; so after the office was up, I to him, and W. Hewer with me and find him in his sick bed, very sensible in discourse, and thankful for my kindnesses to him; but his breath rattled in his throate and they did lay pigeons to his feet while I was in the house; and all despair of him, and with good reason. But the sorrow is that it seems on Thursday last he went sober and quiet out of doors in the morning to Islington, and behind one of the inns, the White Lion, did fling himself into a pond – was spied by a poor woman and got out by some people binding up hay in a barn there, and set on his head and got to life; and known by a woman coming that way, and so his wife and friends sent for. He confessed his doing the thing, being led by the Devil; and doth declare his reason to be his trouble that he found in having forgot to serve God as he ought since he came to this new imployment; and I believe that, and the sense of his great loss by the Fire, did bring him to it, and so everybody concludes. He stayed there all that night, and came home by coach next morning; and there grew sick, and worse and worse to this day. I stayed a while among the friends that were there; and they being now in fear that the goods and estate would be seized on, though he lived all this while, because of his endeavouring to drown himself, my cousin did endeavour to remove what she could of plate out of the house, and desired me to take my flagons; which I was glad of, and did take them away with me, in great fear all the way of being seized; though there was no reason for it, he not being dead; but yet so fearful I was. So home and there eat my dinner, and busy all the afternoon, and troubled at this business. In the evening, with Sir D. Gawden to Guildhall to advise with the Towne Clerke about the practice of the City and nation in this case, and he thinks it cannot be found self-murder; but if it be, it will fall, all the estate, to the King. So we parted, and I to my cousin's again; where I no sooner came but news was brought down from his chamber that he was departed. So at their entreaty I presently took coach and to Whitehall, and there find W. Coventry and he carried me to the King, the Duke of York being with him, and there told my story which I had told him; and the King without more ado granted that if it was found [self-murder] the estate should be to the widow and children.

A statutory commission – which Pepys refers to usually as the Commission of Accounts – had been appointed in December 1667 to enquire into war expenditure. Its meetings are about to begin, and Pepys is one of the principal witnesses it examines. He is also involved in the enquiries conducted by the Commons' Committee investigating the miscarriages of the war.

7 February. Up, and to the office to the getting of my books in order to carry to the Commissioners of Accounts this morning. This being done, I away, first to Westminster Hall and there met my Cosen Rogr. Pepys by his desire (the first time I have seen him since his coming to town, the Parliament meeting yesterday and adjurned to Monday next); and here he tells me that Mr Jackson, my sister's servant, is come to town and hath

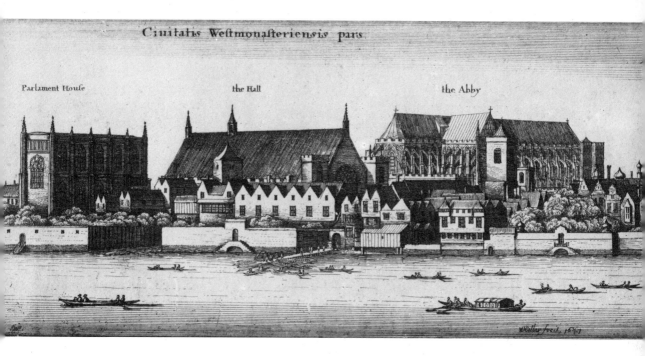

Westminster from the river, by W. Hollar 1644. Left to right are St Stephen's Chapel
(the Commons), Westminster Hall, and the Abbey with St Margaret's in front.

. . . .

this day suffered a recovery on his estate, in order to the making her a settlement. Thence I
to the Comissioners of Accounts and there presented my books, and was made to sit
down and used with much respect. I find these gentlemen to sit all day and only eat a bit of
bread at noon and a glass of wine; and are resolved to go through their business with great
severity and method. Thence I about 2 a⁄clock to Westminster Hall by appointment, and
there met my cousin Roger again and Mr Jackson, who is a plain young man, handsome
enough for her; one of no education nor discourse, but of few words, and one altogether
that I think will please me well enough. My cousin hath got me to give the od sixth, 100*l*,
presently, which I intended to keep to the birth of the first child: and let it go, I shall be
eased of that care; and so after little talk we parted.

8 February. Away to the Strand to my bookseller's, and there stayed an hour and bought
that idle, roguish book, *L'Escholle des Filles*; which I have bought in plain binding
(avoiding the buying of it better bound) because I resolve, as soon as I have read it, to burn
it, that it may not stand in the list of books, nor among them, to disgrace them if it should
be found.

9 February. Lords Day. Up, and at my chamber all the morning and the office, doing
business and also reading a little of *L'Escolle des Filles*, which is a mighty lewd book, but
yet not amiss for a sober man once to read over to inform himself in the villainy of the
world. At noon home to dinner, where by appointment Mr Pelling came, and with him

173

three friends: Wallington that sings the good bass, and one Rogers, and a gentleman, a young man, his name Tempest, who sings very well endeed and understands anything in the world at first sight. After dinner, we into our dining room and there to singing all the afternoon. We sang till almost night, and drank my good store of wine; and then they parted and I to my chamber, where I did read through *L'Escholle des Filles*; a lewd book, but what doth me no wrong to read for information sake (but it did hazer my prick para stand all the while, and una vez to decharger); and after I had done it, I burned it, that it might not be among my books to my shame; and so at night to supper and then to bed.

10 February. To Westminster Hall; and there met Roger Pepys and with him to his chamber and there read over and agreed upon the deed of settlement to our minds: my sister to have 600*l* presently and she to be joyntured in 60*l* per annum – wherein I am very well satisfied.

11 February. At the office all the morning, where comes a damned summons to attend the Committee of Miscarriages today; which makes me mad that I should by my place become the hackney of this office, in perpetual trouble and vexation, that need it least. At noon home to dinner, where little pleasure, my head being split almost with the variety of troubles upon me at this time and cares.

16 February. Lords Day. Up and to my chamber, where all the morning making a catalogue of my books; which did find me work, but with great pleasure, my chamber and books being now set in very good order and my chamber washed and cleaned, which it had not been in some months – my business and trouble having been so much.

17 February. Up and to the office, where all the morning till noon getting some things more ready against the afternoon for the Committee of Accounts – which did give me great trouble, to see how I am forced to dance after them in one place and to answer committees of Parliament in another. Thence to the Committee, where I did deliver the several things they expected from me with great respect and show of satisfaction, and my mind thereby eased of some care.

19 February. Up, and to the office, where all the morning drawing up an answer to the Report of the Committee for Miscarriages to the Parliament, touching our paying men by tickets – which I did do in a very good manner I think. Dined with my clerks at home, where much good discourse of our business of the Navy and the troubles now upon us, more then we expected. After dinner, my wife out with Deb to buy some things against my sister's wedding and I to the office to write fair my business I did in the morning.

23 February. This evening, my wife did with great pleasure show me her stock of jewells, encreased by the ring she had made lately as my Valentine's gift this year, a turky-stone set with diamonds; and with this and what she had, she reckons that she hath above 150*l* worth of jewells of one kind or other. And I am glad of it, for it is fit the wretch should have something to content herself with.

24 February. I was prettily served this day at the playhouse door; where giving six shillings into the fellow's hand for us three, the fellow by legerdemain did convey one away, and with so much grace face me down that I did give him but five, that though I knew the contrary, yet I was overpowered by his so grave and serious demanding the other shilling that I could not deny him, but was forced by myself to give it him.

27 February. All the morning at the office, and at noon home to dinner; and thence with my wife and Deb to the King's House to see *Virgin Martyr*, the first time it hath been acted a great while, and it's mighty pleasant; not that the play is worth much, but it is finely acted by Becke Marshall; but that which did please me beyond anything in the whole world was the wind musique when the Angell comes down, which is so sweet that it ravished me; and endeed, in a word, did wrap up my soul so that it made me really sick, just as I have formerly been when in love with my wife; that neither then, nor all the evening going home and at home, I was able to think of anything, but remained all night transported, so as I could not believe that ever any music hath that real command over the soul of a man as this did upon me; and makes me resolve to practise wind music and to make my wife do the like.

28 February. Up and to the office, where all the morning doing business; and after dinner with Sir W. Penn to Whitehall, where we and the rest of us presented a great letter of the state of our want of money to his Royal Highness. I did also present a demand of mine for consideration for my travelling charges of coach and boat hire during the war – which though his Royal Highness and the company did all like of, yet contrary to my expectation I find him so jealous now of doing anything extraordinary, that he desired the gentlemen that they would consider it and report their minds in it to him. This did unsettle my mind a great while, not expecting this stop. But that that troubles me most is that while we were thus together with the Duke of York, comes in Mr Wren from the House, where he tells us another storm hath been all this day almost against the Officers of the Navy upon this complaint: that though they have made good rules for payment of tickets, yet that they have not observed them themselfs; which was driven so high as to have it urged that we should presently be put out of our places – and so they have at last ordered that we be heard at the bar of the House upon this business on Thursdy next.

1 March. Lords Day. Up very betimes and by coach to Sir W. Coventry, and there, largely carrying with me all my notes and papers, did·run over our whole defence in the business of tickets, in order to the answering the House on Thursday next; and I do think, unless they be set without reason to ruin us, we shall make a good defence. Thence home; and there, my mind being a little lightened by my morning's work in the arguments I have now laid together in better method for our defence to the Parliament, I to talk with my wife; and in lieu of a coach this year, I have got my wife to be contented with her closet being made up this summer and going into the country this summer for a month or two to my father's. To Mr[s] Martin's, where I have not been also a good while, and with great difficulty, company being there, did get an opportunity to hazer what I would con her. And here I was mightily taken with a starling which she hath, that was the

King's, which he kept in his bedchamber, and doth whistle and talk the most and best that ever I heard anything in my life.

2 March. Up and betimes to the office, where I did much business and several came to me; and among others, I did prepare [Sir W.] Warren, and by and by Sir D. Gawden, about what presents I have had from them, that they may not publish them; or if they do, that in truth I receive none on the account of the Navy but Tanger. And this is true to the former, and in both, that I never asked anything of them. At noon home to dinner, where was Mercer, and very merry as I could be with my mind so full of business; and so with my wife, her and the girl, to the King's House to see *The Virgin Martyr* again; which doth mightily please me, but above all the musique at the coming down of the Angell – which at this hearing the second time doth so still command me as nothing ever did, and the other music is nothing to it. Thence with my wife to the Change; and so calling at the Cocke alehouse, we home, and there I settle to business and with my people preparing my great answer to the Parliament for the office about tickets, till past 12 at night; and then home to supper and to bed – keeping Mr Gibson all night with me. This day I have the news that my sister was married on Thursday last to Mr Jackson; so that work I hope is well over.

4 March. Fell to my work at the office, shutting the doors that we, I and my clerks, might not be interrupted; and so, only with room for a little dinner, we very busy all the day till night, that the officers met for me to give them the heads of what I intended to say; which I did, with great discontent to see them all rely on me that have no reason at all to trouble myself about it, nor have any thanks from them for my labour. This troubled me so much, as together with the shortness of the time and muchness of the business, did let me be at it till but about 10 at night; and then, quite weary and dull and vexed, I could go no further, but resolved to leave the rest to tomorrow morning; and so in full discontent and weariness did give over and went home with[out] supper, vexed and sickish, to bed – and there slept about three hours; but then waked, and never in so much trouble in all my life of mind, thinking of the task I have upon me, and upon what dissatisfactory grounds, and what the issue of it may be to me. With these thoughts I lay troubling myself till 6 a-clock, restless, and at last getting my wife to talk to me to comfort me; which she at last did, and made me resolve to quit my hands of this office and endure the trouble [of] it no longer then till I can clear myself of it.

5 March. So, with great trouble but yet with some ease from this discourse with my wife, I up and to my office, whither came my clerks; and so I did huddle up the best I could some more notes for my discourse today; and by 9 a-clock was ready and did go down to the Old Swan, and there by boat, with T. Hater and W. Hewer with me, to Westminster, where I found myself come time enough and my brethren all ready. But I full of thoughts and trouble touching the issue of this day; and to comfort myself did go to the Dogg and drink half a pint of mulled sack, and in the Hall did drink a dram of brandy at Mrs Howletts, and with the warmth of this did find myself in better order as to courage, truly. So we all up to the Lobby; and between 11 and 12 a-clock were called in, with the mace before us, into the House; where a mighty full House, and we stood at the Barr – viz.,

Brouncker, Sir J. Mennes, Sir T. Harvey and myself – W. Penn being in the house as a member. I perceive the whole House was full, and full of expectation of our defence what it would be, and with great præjudice. After the Speaker had told us the dissatisfaction of the House, and read the report of the Committee, I begin our defence most acceptably and smoothly, and continued at it without any hesitation or losse but with full scope and all my reason free about me, as if it had been at my own table, from that time till past 3 in the afternoon; and so ended without any interruption from the Speaker, but we withdrew. And there all my fellow officers and all the world that was within hearing, did congratulate me and cry up my speech as the best thing they ever heard, and my fellow officers overjoyed in it. We were called in again by and by to answer only one question, touching our paying tickets to ticket-mongers – and so out; and we were in hopes to have had a vote this day in our favour, and so the generality of the House was; but my speech being so long, many had gone out to dinner and come in again half drunk, and then there are two or three that are professed enemies to us and everybody else. I saw these did rise up and speak against the coming to a vote now, the House not being full, so that they put it off to tomorrow come sennit. However, it is plain we have got great ground; and everybody says I have got the most honour that any could have had opportunity of getting. And so, with our hearts mightily overjoyed at this success, we all to dinner to Lord Brouncker. And thence after dinner to the King's House and there saw part of *The Discontented Colonell* – but could take no great pleasure in it because of our coming in in the middle of it. After the play, home with W. Penn and there to my wife, whom W. Hewer had told of my success; and she overjoyed, and I also as to my perticular. And after talking awhile, I betimes to bed, having had no quiet rest a good while.

6 March. Up betimes, and with Sir D. Gawden to Sir W. Coventry's chamber, where the first word he said to me was, 'Good morrow Mr Pepys, that must be Speaker of the Parliament House' – and did protest I had got honour for ever in Parliament. He said that his brother, that sat by him, admires me; and another gentleman said that I could not get less than 1000l a year if I would put on a gown and plead at the Chancery Bar. But what pleases me most, he tells me that the Sollicitor Generall did protest that he thought I spoke the best of any man in England. Going to the parke, and by and by overtaking the King, the King and Duke of York came to me both, and he said, 'Mr Pepys, I am very glad of your success yesterday;' and fell to talk of my well speaking; and many of the Lords there, my Lord Berkely did cry me up for what they had heard of it; and others, Parliament[-men] there about the King, did say that they never heard such a speech in their lives delivered in that manner. Progers of the Bedchamber swore to me afterward before Brouncker in the afternoon, that he did tell the King that he thought I might teach the Sollicitor Generall. Everybody that saw me almost came to me, as Joseph Williamson and others, with such eulogys as cannot be expressed. From thence I went to Westminster Hall, where I met Mr G. Mountagu; who came to me and kissed me, and told me that he had often heretofore kissed my hands, but now he would kiss my lips, protesting that I was another Cicero, and said all the world said the same of me. Mr Ashburnham, and every creature I met there of the Parliament or that knew anything of the Parliament's actings, did salute me with this honour – Mr Godolphin, Mr Sands, who swore he would go twenty mile at any time to hear the like again, and that he never saw so many sit four hours together to hear any man in his life as there did to hear me. Mr Chichly, Sir Jo. Duncom, and everybody doth say that the kingdom will ring of my ability, and that I have done myself right for my whole life; and so Captain Cocke, and other of my friends, say that no man had ever such an opportunity of making his abilities known. And, that I may cite all at once, Mr Lieutenant of the Tower did tell me that Mr Vaughan did protest to him, and that in his hearing it, said so to the Duke of Albemarle and afterward to W. Coventry, that he had sat twenty-six years in Parliament and never heard such a speech there before – for which the Lord God make me thankful, and that I may make use of it not to pride and vainglory, but that now I have this esteem, I may do nothing that may lessen it.

12 March. To Gresham College, there to show myself, and was there greeted by Dr Wilkins, Whistler, and others, as the patron of the Navy Office and one that got great fame by my late speech to the Parliament. Here I saw a great trial of the goodness of a burning-glass, made of a new figure, not sphæricall (by one Smithys, I think they call him), that did burn a glove of my Lord Brouncker's from the heat of a very little fire – which a burning-glass of the old form, very much bigger, could not do – which was mighty pretty. Here I heard Sir Rob. Southwell give an account of some things committed to him by the Society at his going to Portugall, which he did deliver in a mighty handsome manner. Thence went away home, and there at my office as long as my eyes would endure; and then home to supper and to talk with Mr Pelling, who tells me what a fame I have in the City for my late performance.

13 March. Up betimes to my office, where to fit myself for attending the Parliament again; not to make any more speeches, which while my fame is good I will avoid for fear of losing of it, but only to answer to what objections shall be made against us. Thence walked to the Old Swan and drank at Michell's, whose house is going up apace; here I saw Betty, but could not besar la; and so to Westminster, there to the Hall, where my Lord Brouncker and the rest waiting till noon and not called for by the House, they being upon the business of money again; and at noon, all of us to Chatelin, the French house in Covent Garden, to dinner. Thence home; and there find one laying of my napkins against tomorrow in figures of all sorts, which is mighty pretty; and it seems it is his trade and gets much money by it, and doth now and then furnish tables with plate and linen for a feast at so much – which is mighty pretty, and a trade I could not have thought of. Thence I to Mrs Turner and did get her to go along with me to the French pewterers, and there did buy some new pewter against tomorrow. And thence to Whitehall to [get] a cook of her acquaintance, and so late to bed.

14 March. Up very betimes, and with Jane to Levetts, there to conclude upon our dinner; and thence to the pewterers to buy a pewter sestorne, which I have ever hitherto been without. And so up and down upon several occasions to set matters in order. I away home and there do find everything in mighty good order; only, my wife not dressed, which troubles me. Anon comes my company, viz., my Lord Hinchingbrooke and his Lady, Sir Ph. Carteret and his Lady, Godolphin and my Cosen Roger, and Creed, and mighty merry; and by and by to dinner, which was very good and plentiful (I should have said, and Mr George Mountagu, who came at a very little warning, which was exceeding kind of him): and there among other things, my Lord had Sir Samuel Morland's late invention for casting up of sums of pounds, shillings and pence; which is very pretty, but not very useful. Most of our discourse was of my Lord Sandwich and his family, as being all of us of that family; and with extraordinary pleasure all the afternoon thus together, eating and looking over my closet: and my Lady Hinchingbrooke I find a very sweet-natured and well-disposed lady, a lover of books and pictures and of good understanding. About 5 a-clock they went, and then my wife and I abroad by coach into Moorefields, only for a little ayre; and so home again, staying nowhere, and then up to her chamber, there to talk with pleasure of this day's passages and so to bed.

20 March. Up betimes and to my office, where we had a meeting extraordinary to consider of several things; among others, the sum of money fit to be demanded ready money to enable us to set out twenty-seven ships, everybody being now in pain for a fleet and everybody endeavouring to excuse themselfs for the not setting out of one, and our true excuse is lack of money.

22 March. Easter Day. I up and walked to the Temple; and there got a coach and to Whitehall, where spoke with several people, and find by all that Pen is to go to sea this year with this fleet. And they excuse the Prince's going by saying that it is not a command great enough for him.

24 March. To Whitehall, where great talk of the tumult at the other end of the town about Moorefields among the prentices, taking the liberty of these holidays to pull down bawdy-houses. And Lord, to see the apprehensions which this did give to all people at Court, that presently order was given for all the soldiers, horse and foot, to be in armes. And we heard a Justice of Peace this morning say to the King that he had been endeavouring to suppress this tumult, but could not; and that imprisoning some in the new prison at Clerkenwell, the rest did come and break open the prison and release them. And that they do give out that they are for pulling down of bawdy-houses, which is one of the great grievances of the nation. To which the King made a very poor, cold, insipid answer: 'Why, why do they go to them, then?', and that was all, and had no mind to go on with the discourse.

25 March. The Duke of York and all with him this morning were full of the talk of the prentices, who are not yet down, though the Guards and militia of the town have been in arms all this night and the night before; and the prentices have made fools of them, sometimes by running from them and flinging stones at them. But here it was said how these idle fellows have had the confidence to say that they did ill in contenting themselfs in pulling down the little bawdy houses and did not go and pull down the great bawdy house at Whitehall. And some of them have the last night had a word among them, and it was 'Reformation and Reducement!' This doth make the courtiers ill at ease to see this spirit among people, though they think this matter will not come to much; but it speaks people's mind. And then they do say that there are men of understanding among them, that have been of Cromwell's army; but how true that is I know not.

30 March. Up betimes and so to my office, there to do business – till about 10 a'clock; and then out with my wife and Deb and W. Hewers by coach to Common Garden coffee-house, where by appointment I was to meet Harris; which I did, and also Mr Cooper the great painter and Mr Hales; and thence presently to Mr Cooper's house to see some of his work; which is all in little, but so excellent, as though I must confess I do think the colouring of the flesh to be a little forced, yet the painting is so extraordinary, as I do never expect to see the like again. Here I did see Mrs Stewards picture as when a young maid, and now again done just before her having the smallpox; and it would make a man weep to see what she was then, and what she is like to be, by people's discourse, now. Here I saw my Lord Generalls picture, and my Lord Arlington and Ashlys, and several others. Being infinitely satisfied with this sight, and resolving that my wife shall be drawn by him when she comes out of the country, I away with Harris and Hales to the coffee-house (sending my people away) and there resolve for Hales to begin Harris's head for me – which I will be at the cost of. At noon by appointment to Cursiters Alley in Chancery Lane to meet Captain Cocke and some other creditors of the Navy and their counsel; and there dined. At dinner we had a great deal of good discourse about parliaments their number being uncertain and always at the will of the King to encrease, as he saw reason to erect a new burrow. But all concluded that the bane of Parliament hath been the leaving off the old custom of the places allowing wages to them that served them in Parliament, by which they chose men that understood their business and would attend it, and they could expect an account from, which now they cannot; and so the Parliament is become a company of men unable to give account for the interest of the place they serve for.

31 March. Took up my wife and Deb and to the parke; where being in a hackny and they undressed, I was ashamed to go into the Tour, but went round the park; and so with pleasure home, where Mr Pelling came and sat and talked late with us; and he being gone, I called Deb to take pen, ink, and paper and write down what things came into my head for my wife to do, in order to her going into the country; and the girl writing not so well as she would do, cried, and her mistress construed it to be sullenness and so was angry, and I seemed angry with her too; but going to bed, she undressed me, and there I did give her good advice and beso la, ella weeping still; and yo did take her, the first time in my life, sobra mi genu and did poner mi mano sub her jupes and toca su thigh, which did hazer me great pleasure; and so did no more, but besando-la went to my bed.

1 April. I to my office, where busy till noon, and then out to bespeak some things against my wife's going into the country tomorrow. And so home to dinner, my wife and I alone, she being mighty busy getting her things ready for her journey.

2 April. Up, after much pleasant talk with my wife and upon some alterations I will make in my house in her absence, and I do intend to lay out some money thereon. So she and I up, and she got her ready to be gone, [and] set out about 8 a'clock toward the carrier, there for to take coach for my father's (that is to say, my wife and Betty Turner, Deb and Jane); but I meeting my Lord Anglesy going to the office, was forced to light in Cheapside, and there took my leave of them (not besando Deb, which yo had a great mind to); left them to go to their coach, and I to the office, where all the morning busy. And so at noon with my other clerks (W. Hewer being a day's journey with my wife) to dinner. Thence with Lord Brouncker to the Royall Society, where they were just done; but there I was forced to subscribe to the building of a College, and did give 40*l*. Here to my great content I did try the use of the otacousticon, which was only a great glass bottle broke at the bottom, putting the neck to my eare; and there I did plainly hear the dashing of the oares of the boats in the Thames to Arundell gallery window; which without it I could not in the least do, and may I believe be improved to a great heighth – which I was mighty glad of. Thence with Lord Brouncker and several of them to the King's Head tavern by Chancery Lane, and there did drink and eat and talk; and above the rest, I did desire of Mr Hooke and my Lord an account of the reason of concords and discords in music – which they say is from the æquality of the vibrations; but I am not satisfied in it, but will at my leisure think of it more and see how far that doth go to explain it. So home, without more supper, to bed.

4 April. Up betimes, and by coach towards Whitehall; and took Aldersgate Street in my way and there called upon one Hayward that makes virginalls, and did there like of a little espinettes and will have him finish them for me; for I had a mind to a small harpsicon, but

(*Below left*) Lady playing a spinet, *c.* 1690. (*Below right*) Italian octave spinet, *c.* 1600. Pepys used his spinet mostly for composing.

New Palace Yard, Westminster, by W. Hollar 1647. Westminster Hall is on the left,
the Clock Tower on the right. The Gatehouse leads into King Street.

this takes up less room and will do my business as to finding out of chords – and I am very
well pleased that I have found it. Thence to Whitehall; and after long waiting did get a
small running Committee of Tanger, where I stayed but little; and little done but the
correcting two or three egregious faults in the charter for Tanger, after it had so long lain
before the council and been passed there and drawn up by the Atturny General, so slightly
are all things in this age done. After dinner, W. Penn and I did attend the Duke of York
and he did carry us to the King's lodgings; but he was asleep in his closet, so we stayed in
the Green Roome, where the Duke of York did tell us what rules he had of knowing the
weather, and did now tell us we should have rain before tomorrow (it having been a dry
season for some time); and so it did rain all night almost. And pretty rules he hath, and
told Brouncker and me some of them; which were such as no reason seems ready to be
given.

5 April. Lords Day. Up, and to my chamber and there to the writing fair some of my late
music notions; and so to church, where I have not been a good while. And thence home,
and dined at home with W. Hewers with me; and after dinner, he and I a great deal of
good talk touching this office: how it is spoilt by having so many persons in it, and so
much work that is not made the work of any one man but of all, and so is never done; and
that the best way to have it well done were to have the whole trust in one (as myself) to
set whom I pleased to work in the several businesses of the office, and me to be accountable
for the whole; and that would do it, as I would find instruments. But this is not to
be compassed; but something I am resolved to do about Sir J. Mennes before it be long.

I hear that eight of the ringleaders in the late tumults of the prentices at Easter are
condemned to die.

The Tower of London, by W. Hollar c. 1637–43.

. . . .

8 April. I to Drumbleby's and there did talk a great deal about pipes and did buy a recorder which I do intend to learn to play on, the sound of it being of all sounds in the world most pleasing to me.

22 April. I by water from the Privy Stairs to Westminster Hall; and taking water, the King and Duke of York were in the new buildings; and the Duke of York called to me whither I was going and I answered aloud, 'To wait on our maisters at Westminster;' at which he and all the company laughed; but I was sorry and troubled for it afterward, for fear any Parliament-man should have been there, and will be a caution to me for the time to come.

23 April. Up and to the office, where all the morning. And at noon comes Knepp and Mrs Pierce and her daughter, and one Mrs Foster, and dined with me – and mighty merry; and after dinner carried them to the Tower and showed them all to be seen there; and among other things, the crown and scepters and rich plate, which I myself never saw before and endeed is noble – and I mightily pleased with it. Thence by water to the Temple, and there to the Cocke alehouse and drank and eat a lobster and sang, and mighty merry. So, almost night, I carried Mrs Pierce home, and then Knipp and I to the Temple again and took boat, it being darkish, and to Foxhall, it being now night and a bonfire burning at Lambeth for the King's coronacion day. And there she and I drank; and yo did tocar her corps all over and besar sans fin her, but did not offer algo mas; and so back and led her home, it being now 10 at night, and so got a link; and walking towards home, just at my entrance into the ruines at St Dunstan's, I was met by two rogues with clubs, who came toward us; so I went back and walked home quite round by the Wall

183

and got well home; and to bed, weary but pleased at my day's pleasure – but yet displeased at my expense and time I lose.

30 April. Up, and at the office all the morning. At noon Sir J. Mennes and I to the Dolphin tavern, there to meet our neighbours, all of the parish, this being procession day, to dine – and did; and much very good discourse, they being most of them very able merchants, as any in the City. They talked with Mr Mills about the meaning of this day and the good uses of it; and how heretofore, and yet in several places, they do whip a boy at every place they stop at in their procession. This evening, coming home in the dusk, I saw and spoke to our Nell, Pain's daughter, and had I not been very cold, I should have taken her to Tower Hill para talk together et tocar her.

Thus ends this month; my wife in the country. Myself full of pleasure and expense; and some trouble for my friends, my Lord Sandwich by the Parliament, and more for my eyes, which are daily worse and worse, that I dare not write or read almost anything. The Parliament going in a few days to rise. Myself so long without accounting now, for seven or eight months I think or more, that I know not what condition almost I am in as to getting or spending for all that time – which troubles me, but I will soon do it. The kingdom in an ill state through poverty. A fleet going out, and no money to maintain it or set it out. Seamen yet unpaid, and mutinous when pressed to go out again. Our office able to do little, nobody trusting us nor we desiring any to trust us, and yet have not money to anything but only what perticularly belongs to this fleet going out, and that but lamely too. The Parliament several months upon an act for 300,000*l*, but cannot or will not agree upon it. And then the business of religion doth disquiet everybody, the Parliament being vehement against the nonconformists, while the King seems to be willing to countenance them: so we are all poor and in pieces, God help us; while the peace is like to go on between Spain and France, and then the French may be apprehended able to attack us. So God help us.

10 May. Lords Day. Up, and to my office, there to do business till church time, when Mr Sheply, lately come to town, came to see me; and we had some discourse of all matters, and perticularly of my Lord Sandwiches concernments; and here he did by the by, as he would seem, tell me that my Lady had it in her thoughts, if she had occasion, to borrow 100*l* of me – which I did not declare any opposition to, though I doubt it will be so much lost. It brings into my head some apprehensions what trouble I may hereafter be brought to when my Lord comes home, if he should ask me to come into bonds with him, as [I] fear he will have occasions to take up money. But I hope I shall have the wit to deny it.

20 May. Into Bishopsgate Street to bespeak places for myself and boy to go to Cambridge in the coach this week, and so to Brampton to see my wife. So home and to supper.

23 May. Up by 4 a-clock; and getting my things ready and recommending the care of my house to W. Hewer, I with the boy Tom, whom I take with me, to the Bull in Bishopsgate Street and there about 6 took coach, and so away to Bishops Stafford, and there dine and changed horses and coach at Mrs Aynsworth's; but I took no knowledge of her. Here I hear Mrs Aynsworth is going to live at London; but I believe will be mistaken in it, for it will be found better for her to be chief where she is then to have little to do at London, there being many finer then she there. After dinner, away again and came to Cambridge, after much bad way, about 9 at night; and there at the Rose I met my father's horses, with a man staying for me; but it is so late, and the waters so deep, that I durst not go tonight; but after supper to bed and lay very ill by reason of some drunken scholars making a noise all night, and vexed for fear that the horses should not be taken up from grass time enough for the morning.

24 May. Lords Day. I up at between 2 and 3 in the morning; and calling up my boy and father's boy, we set out by 3 a⁄clock, it being high day; and so through the waters with very good success, though very deep almost all the way, and got to Brampton, where most of them in bed; and so I weary up to my wife's chamber, whom I find in bed and pretended a little not well, and endeed she hath those upon her, but fell to talk and mightily pleased both of us; and up got the rest, Betty Turner and Willet and Jane, all whom I was glad to see, and very merry; and got me ready in my new stuff clothes that I sent down before me; and so my wife and they got ready too, while I to my father, poor man, and walked with him up and down the house, it raining a little – and the waters all over Portholme and the meadows so as no pleasure abroad. Here I saw my brothers [John and John Jackson] and sister Jackson, she growing fat, and since being married, I think looks comelier then before. But a mighty pert woman she is, and I think proud, he keeping her mighty handsome, and they say mighty fond – and are going shortly to live at Ellington of themselfs, and will keep malting and grazing of cattle. After dinner, my Lady Sandwich sending to see whether I was come, I presently took horse and find her

. . . .

'Talked an hour or two, with great pleasure and satisfaction to my Lady about my Lord's matters.' (24 May 1668.) Jemima, Countess of Sandwich, anon.

Hinchingbrooke, near Huntingdon; country residence of the Earl and Countess of Sandwich, 1730. 'The house is most excellently furnished, and brave rooms and good pictures, so that it doth please me infinitely.' (9 October 1667.)

. . . .

and her family at chapel; and thither I went in to them and sat out the sermon, where I heard Jervas Fullwood, now their chaplain, preach a very good and seraphic kind of sermon, too good for an ordinary congregation. After sermon, I with my Lady and my Lady Hinchingbrooke and Paulina and Lord Hinchingbrooke to the dining room, saluting none of them, and there sat and talked an hour or two, with great pleasure and satisfaction to my Lady about my Lord's matters; but I think not with that satisfaction to her or me that otherwise would, she knowing that she did design to borrow, and I remaining all the while in fear of being asked to lend her some money, as I was afterward (when I had taken leave of her) by Mr Sheply, 100*l*; which I will not deny my Lady, and am willing to be found when my Lord comes home to have done something of that kind for them. After supper, where very merry, we to bed, myself very weary, and to sleep all night.

25 May. Waked betimes, and lay long hazendo doz vezes con mi moher con grando pleasure to me and ella; and there fell to talking, and by and by rose, it being the first fair day, and yet not quite fair, that we have had some time; and so up and to walk with my father again in the garden, consulting what to do with him and this house when Pall and her husband goes away; and I think it will be to let it and he go live with her, though I am against letting the house for any long time – because of having it to retire to ourselfs. After dinner took horse, I promising to fetch her away about fourteen days hence. Away and got well to Cambridge about 7 to the Rose, the waters not being now so high as before. And here lighting, I took my boy and two brothers and walked to Magdalen College; and there into the butterys as a stranger and there drank my bellyfull of their beer, which pleased me as the best I ever drank; and hear by the butler's man, who was son to Goody Mulliner over against the college that we used to buy stewed prunes of, concerning the college and persons in it; and find very few, only Mr Hollins and Peachell I think, that were of my time. But I was mightily pleased to come in this condition to see and ask; and thence, giving the fellow something, away; walked to Chesterton to see our old walk; and there into the church, the bells ringing, and saw the place I used to sit in; and so to the ferry, and ferried over to the other side and walked with great pleasure, the river being mighty high by Barnwell Abbey; and so by Jesus College to the town, and so to our quarters and to supper; and then to bed, being very weary and sleepy, and mightily pleased with this night's walk.

26 May. Up by 4 a-clock; and by the time we were ready and had eat, we were called to the coach; where about 6 a-clock we set out, there being a man and two women of one company, ordinary people, and one lady alone that is tolerable handsome, but mighty well spoken whom I took great pleasure in talking to, and did get her to read aloud in a book she was reading in the coach, being [Charles I's] *Meditations*; and then the boy and I to sing, and so about noon came to Bishop's Stafford to another house then what we were at the other day, and better used; and here I paid for the reckoning 11s, we dining all together and pretty merry. And then set out again, sleeping most part of the way, and got to Bishopsgate Street before 8 a-clock.

27 May. Made the boy to read to me out of Dr Wilkins his *Real Character*, and perticularly about Noah's arke, wherein he doth give a very good account thereof, showing how few the number of the several species of beasts and fowls were that were to be in the arke, and that there was room enough for them and their food and dung; which doth please me mightily – and is much beyond whatever I heard of that subject. And so to bed.

3 June. Up, and to the office, where busy till 9 a-clock; and then to Whitehall to the Council chamber, where I did present the Duke of York with an account of the charge of the present fleet, to his satisfaction; and this being done, did ask his leave for my going out of town five or six days; which he did give me, saying that my diligence in the King's business was such, that I ought not to be denied when my own business called me anywhither.

Pepys and his wife therefore set off for the only holiday they had in the diary period. Pepys records it in note form, meaning to write it up more carefully later – but his eyestrain prevented him. They travel in a hired coach with Will Hewer, Deb Willet and Betty, daughter of Pepys's cousin Jane Turner, and are attended by Murford, an office messenger. They are away from 5 to 17 June – a somewhat longer leave than the 'five or six days' Pepys had asked for. They first spend two days at Brampton with Pepys's father, and then drive westwards towards Bristol, where they mean to give Deb a sight of her birthplace. On the way they pay visits to Oxford and Salisbury. By the 13th they have got as far as Bath.

13 June. Up at 4 a-clock being by appointment called up to the Cross Bath where we were carried after one another — myself and wife and Betty Turner, Willet, and W. Hewer. And, by and by, though we designed to have done before company came, much company came – very fine ladies – and the manner pretty enough, only methinks it cannot be clean to go so many bodies together into the same water. Good conversation among

'Methinks it cannot be clean to go so many bodies into the same water.'
(13 June 1668.) King's Bath, Bath, by W. Schellinks 1662.

. . . .

them that are acquainted here and stay together. Strange to see how hot the water is, and in some places, though this is the most temperate bath, the springs so hot as the feet not to endure. But strange to see what women and men herein that live all the season in these waters that cannot but be parboiled, and look like the creatures of the Bath. Carried back wrap in a sheet and in a chair home. I staying above two hours in the water, home to bed, sweating for an hour, and by and by comes music to play to me – extraordinary good as ever I heard at London [or] almost anywhere. Set out toward Bristow and came thither – the way bad (in coach hired to spare our own horses), but country good – about 2 a-clock, where set down at the Horse Shoe and there, being trimmed by a very handsome fellow, walked with my wife and people through the city, which is in every respect another London. No carts – it standing generally on vaults – only dog carts. Walked back to the Sun where I find Deb come back, and with her her uncle, a sober merchant – very good company and is so like one of our sober wealthy London merchants as pleased me mightily. Here dined and much good talk with him.

Then walked with him and my wife and company round the key, and he showed me the Custom House and made me understand many things of the place, and led us through Marsh Street where our girl was born. But Lord, the joy that was among the old poor people of the place to see Mrs Willets daughter – it seems her mother being a brave woman and mightily beloved. And so brought us a back way by surprize to his house, where a substantial good house and well furnished, and did give us good entertainment of strawberries, a whole venison pasty, cold, and plenty of brave wine – and above all Bristoll milk. Where comes in another poor woman, who hearing that Deb was here, did come running hither and with her eyes so full of tears and heart so full of joy that she could not speak when she came in that it made me weep too. I protest that I was not able to speak to her (which I would have done) to have diverted her tears. So thence took leave and he with us through the city, where in walking I find the city pay him great respect and he the like to the meanest which pleased me mightily. He showed us the place where the merchants meet here and a fine cross yet standing like Cheapside. And so to the Horse Shoe, where [paid] the reckoning [and took coach to Bath].

They start on their return journey on the 15th, travel via Avebury and Marlborough, stay overnight at Reading, and arrive home before dark on the 17th.

18 June. Up betimes and to the office, there to set my papers in order and books, my office having been new-whited and windows made clean. And so to sit, where all the morning; and did receive a hint or two from my Lord Anglesy, as if he thought much of my taking the ayre as I have done – but I care not a turd. But whatever the matter is, I think he hath some ill-will to me, or at least an opinion that I am more the servant of the Board then I am. At noon home to dinner, where my wife in a melancholy fusty humour, and crying; and doth not tell me plainly what it is, but I by little words find that she hath heard of my going to plays and carrying people abroad every day in her absence; and that I cannot help, but the storm will break out, I know, in a little time. After dinner, carried her by coach to St James's, where she sat in the coach till I to my Lady Peterborough. My business here was about her Lord's pension from Tanger. So, my wife not speaking a word going nor coming, nor willing to go to a play, though a new one, I to the office and did much business. At night home, where supped Mr Turner and his wife, and Betty and Mercer and Pelling, as merry as the ill melancholy humour that my wife was in would let us; which vexed me, but I took no notice of it, thinking that will be the best way, and let it wear away itself. After supper, parted and to bed; and my wife troubled all night, and about one a-clock goes out of the bed to the girl's bed; which did trouble me, she crying and sobbing, without telling the cause. By and by comes back to me, and still crying; I then rose and would have sat up all night, but she would have me come to bed again. And being pretty well pacified, we to sleep.

19 June. And about 9 rose; and then my wife fell into her blubbering again and at length had a request to make to me, which was that she might go into France and live there out of trouble: and then all came out, that I loved pleasure and denied her any, and a deal of do; and I find that there have been great fallings-out between my father and her, whom for ever hereafter I must keep asunder, for they cannot possibly agree. And I said nothing; but with very mild words and few suffered her humour to spend, till we begin to be very quiet and I think all will be over, and friends; and so I to the office, where all the morning doing business.

23 June. Up, and all the morning at the office. At noon home to dinner; and so to the office again all the afternoon, and then to Westminster to Dr Turberville about my eyes; whom I met with, and he did discourse I thought learnedly about them, and takes time, before he did prescribe me anything, to think of it.

27 June. With my wife to buy some linen, 13*l* worth, for sheets, &c., at the new shop over against the New Exchange, come out of London since the Fire; who says his and other tradesmen's retail trade is so great here, and better then it was in London, that they believe they shall not return, nor the City be ever so great for retail as heretofore.

29 June. Toward St James's; and I stop at Dr Turbervilles and there did receive a direction for some physic, and also a glass of something to drop into my eyes; who gives me hopes that I may do well. Thence to St James's and thence to Whitehall, where find the Duke of York in the Council chamber, where the Officers of the Navy were called in about Navy business, about calling in of more ships. Thence to the Chapel, it being St Peter's day, and did hear an anthem of Silas Taylors making – a dull old fashion thing of six and seven parts that nobody could understand; and the Duke of York, when he came out, told me that he was a better storekeeper then anthem maker – and that was bad enough too. Mr May showed me the King's new buildings at Whitehall, very fine; and among other things, his ceilings and his houses of office.

3 July. I to Eagle Court in the Strand and there to a ale house; met Mr Pierce the surgeon and Dr Clerke, Waldron, Turbeville my physician for the eyes, and Lowre, to dissect several eyes of sheep and oxen, with great pleasure – and to my great information; but strange that this Turbeville should be so great a man, and yet to this day had seen no eyes dissected, or but once, but desired this Dr Lowre to give him the opportunity to see him dissect some.

13 July. I to buy my espinette which I did now agree for; and did at Hawards meet with Mr Thacker and heard him play on the harpsicon, so as I never heard man before I think. This morning I was let blood, and did bleed about 14 ounces, towards curing my eyes.

16 July. To Arundell House to the Royal Society, and there saw an experiment of a dog's being tied through the back about the spinal artery, and thereby made void of all motion; and the artery being loosened again, the dog recovers.

24 July. Up, and by water to St James (having by the way shown Symson Sir W. Coventry's chimnypieces, in order to the making me one); and there, after the Duke of York was ready, he called me to his closet, and there I did long and largely show him the weakness of our office, and did give him advice to call us to account for our duties; which he did take mighty well, and desired me to draw up the what I would have him write to the office. I did lay open whole failings of the office, and how it was his duty to find them and to find fault with them, as Admiral, especially at this time – which he agreed to – and seemed much to rely on what I said.

11 August. At the office all the afternoon till night, being mightily pleased with a little trial I have made of the use of a tube spectacall of paper, tried with my right eye. This afternoon, my wife and Mercer and Deb went with Pelling to see the gipsys at Lambeth and have their fortunes told; but what they did, I did not enquire.

19 August. Up betimes; and all day and afternoon, without going out, busy upon my great letter to the Duke of York, which goes on to my content. W. Hewer and Gibson I imploy with me in it. This week my people wash over the water, and so I little company at home. In the evening, being busy above, a great cry I hear, and go down; and what should it be but Jane, in a fit of direct raveing which lasted half an hour; beyond four or five of our strength to keep her down. And when all came to all, a fit of jealousy about Tom, with whom she is in love. So at night, I and my wife and W. Hewer called them to us, and there I did examine all the thing. She in love, and he hath got her to promise him to marry, and he is now cold in it – so that I must rid my hands of them.

21 August. Up betimes and with my people again to work, and finished all before noon; and then I by water to Whitehall and there did tell the Duke of York that I had done; and he hath to my great content desired me to come to him at Sunday next in the afternoon to read it over, by which I have more time to consider and correct it. This day I did first see the Duke of York's room of pictures of some Maids of Honour, done by Lilly; good, but not like.

22 August. Going through Leadenhall, it being market day, I did see a woman ketched that had stolen a shoulder of mutton off of a butcher's stall, and carrying it wrapped up in a cloth in a basket. The jade was surprized, and did not deny it; and the woman so silly that took it as to let her go, only taking the meat.

23 August. Lords Day. After dinner to the office, Mr Gibson and I, to examine my letter to the Duke of York; which to my great joy, I did very well by my paper tube, without pain to my eyes. And I do mightily like what I have therein done; [and] did, according to the Duke of York's order, make haste to St James's; and about 4 a'clock got thither, and there the Duke of York was ready to expect me, and did hear it all over with extraordinary content and did give me many and hearty thanks, and in words the most expressive tell me his sense of my good endeavours, and that he would have a care of me on all occasions, and did with much inwardness tell me what was doing of design to make alterations in the Navy; and is most open to me, and with utmost confidence desires my further advice on all occasions. He resolves to have my letter transcribed and sent forthwith to the office.

29 August. Up, and all the morning at the office where the Duke of York's long letter was read, to their great trouble and their suspecting me to have been the writer of it.

1 September. To [Bartholomew] Fair and there saw several sights; among others, a mare that tells money and many things to admiration; and among others, came to me when she was bid to go to him of the company that most loved a pretty wench in a corner. And this did cost me 12*d* to the horse, which I had flung him before, and did give me occasion to besar a mighty belle fille that was in the house, that was exceeding plain but forte belle.

4 September. Up, and met at the office all the morning; and at noon, my wife and Deb and Mercer and W. Hewer to the Fair, and there at the old house did eat a pig, and was pretty merry; but saw no sights, my wife having a mind to see the play, *Bartholomew Fayre* with puppets; which we did, and it is an excellent play; the more I see it, the more I love the wit of it; only, the business of abusing the Puritans begins to grow stale, and of no use, they being the people that at last will be found the wisest.

12 September. To the office, where till noon; and I do see great whispering among my brethren about their replies to the Duke of York; which vexed me, though I knew no reason for it – for I have no manner of ground to fear them. At noon home to dinner; and after dinner, to work all the afternoon again; at home late and so to bed.

13 September. Lords Day. The like all this morning and afternoon, and finished it to my mind. So about 4 a-clock walked to the Temple, and there by coach to St James's and met, to my wish, the Duke of York and Mr Wren; and understand the Duke of York hath received answers from Brouncker, W. Penn and J. Mennes; and as soon as he saw me, he bid Mr Wren read them over with me. Mr Wren puts them into my hand to take home with me before himself had read them; which doth give me great opportunity of altering my answer, if there was cause. So took a hackney and home; and after supper made my wife to read them all over, wherein she is mighty useful to me. And I find them all evasions, and in many things false, and in few to the full purpose. Little said reflective on me, though W. Penn and J. Mennes do mean me in one or two places, and J. Mennes a little more plainly would lead the Duke of York to question the exactness of my keeping my records – but all to no purpose. My mind is mightily pleased by this, if I can but get them to have a copy taken of them for my future use; but I must return them tomorrow. So to bed.

16 September. I [to] Paul's, and there did go into St Fayth's church and also into the body of the west part of [St Paul's], and do see a hideous sight, of the walls of the church ready to fall, that I was in fear as long as I was in it. And here I saw the great vaults underneath the body of the church. No hurt, I hear, is done yet, since their going to pull down the church and steeple; but one man, on Monday this week, fell from the top to a piece of the roof of the east end that stands next the steeple, and there broke himself all to pieces. It is pretty here, to see how the last church was but a case brought over the old church; for you may see the very old pillars standing whole within the wall of this. When I came to St James's, I find the Duke of York gone with the King to see the muster of the Guards in Hyde Park; and their colonel, the Duke of Monmouth, to take his command this day of the King's Life Guard. So I took a hackney coach and saw it all; and endeed, it was mighty noble and their firing mighty fine, and the Duke of Monmouth in mighty rich clothes; but the well-ordering of the men I understand not. Here, among a thousand coaches that was there, I saw and spoke to Mrs Pierce; and by and by Mr Wren hunts me

'I [to] Paul's . . . and do see a hideous sight, of the walls of the church ready to fall.' (16 September 1668.) Old St Paul's, by W. Hollar 1658. The additions to the west front were by Inigo Jones. Work on Wren's design for the new cathedral began in 1673.

out and gives me my Lord Anglesy's answer to the Duke of York's letter, where I perceive he doth do what he can to hurt me, by bidding the Duke of York call for my books; but this will do me all the right in the world, and yet I am troubled at it. So away out of the park and home, and there Mr Gibson and I to dinner; and all the afternoon with him, writing over anew, and a little altering, my answer to the Duke of York, which I have not yet delivered and so have the opportunity of doing it after seeing all their answers, though this doth give me occasion to alter very little. This day, my father's letters tell me of the death of poor Fancy in the country, big with puppies, which troubles me, as being one of my oldest acquaintances and servants. Also, Goody Stankes is dead.

18 September. Up, and to St James's and there took a turn or two in the park; and then up to the Duke of York and there had opportunity of delivering my answer to his late letter; which he did not read but give to Mr Wren, as looking on it as a thing I needed not have done, but only that I might not give occasion to the rest to suspect my communication with the Duke of York against them.

28 September. To St James's, and there had good opportunity of speaking with the Duke of York, who desires me again, talking on that matter, to prepare something for him to do

St James's Palace, from the park, *c.* 1690.

. . . .

for the better managing of our office, telling me that my Lord Keeper and he talking about it yesterday, my Lord Keeper did advise him to do so, it being better to come from him then otherwise – which I have promised to do. Thence to my Lord Burlington's house, the first time I ever was there, it being the house built by Sir Jo. Denham, next to Clarendon House. And here I visited my Lord Hinchingbrooke and his Lady, Mr Sidny Mountagu being come last night, come to town unexpectedly from Mounts Bay, where he left my Lord well eight days since; so as we may now hourly expect to hear of his arrivall at Portsmouth. Sidny is mightily grown; and I am glad I am here to see him at his first coming, though it cost me dear, for here I come to be necessitated to supply them with 500*l* for my Lord: he sent him up with a declaration to his friends of the necessity of his being presently suppli[ed] with two thousand pounds. I also, standing by a candle that was brought for sealing of a letter, do set my periwigg a-fire; which made such an odd noise, nobody could tell what it was till they saw the flame, my back being to the candle. Thence to Westminster Hall and there walked a little, and to the Exchequer and so home by water. So I to Whitehall, and there all the evening on the Queen's side; and it being a most summerlike day and a fine warm evening, the Italians came in a barge under the leads before the Queen's drawing room, and so the Queen and ladies went out and heard it for almost an hour.

23 October. This day Pierce doth tell me, among other news, the late frolic and debauchery of Sir Ch. Sidly and Buckhurst, running up and down all the night with their arses bare through the streets, and at last fighting and being beat by the watch and clapped up all night; and how the King takes their parts and my Lord Chief Justice Keeling hath laid the constable by the heels to answer it next sessions – which is a horrid shame. How the King and these gentlemen did make the fiddlers of Thetford, this last progress, to sing them all the bawdy songs they could think of.

From 'Advice to Young Gentleman', a broadsheet ballad.

· ·

25 October. Lords Day. At night W. Batelier comes and sups with us; and after supper, to have my head combed by Deb, which occasioned the greatest sorrow to me that ever I knew in this world; for my wife, coming up suddenly, did find me imbracing the girl con my hand sub su coats; and endeed, I was with my main in her cunny. I was at a wonderful loss upon it, and the girl also; and I endeavoured to put it off, but my wife was struck mute and grew angry, and as her voice came to her, grew quite out of order; and I do say little, but to bed; and my wife said little also, but could not sleep all night; but about 2 in the morning waked me and cried, and fell to tell me as a great secret that she was a Roman Catholique and had received the Holy Sacrament; which troubled me but I took no notice of it, but she went on from one thing to another, till at last it appeared plainly her trouble was at what she saw; but yet I did not know how much she saw and therefore said nothing to her. But after her much crying and reproaching me with inconstancy and preferring a sorry girl before her, I did give her no provocations but did promise all fair usage to her, and love, and foreswore any hurt that I did with her – till at last she seemed to be at ease again.

26 October. And so toward morning, a little sleep; and so I, with some little repose and rest, rose, and up and by water to Whitehall, but with my mind mightily troubled for the poor girl, whom I fear I have undone by this, my [wife] telling me that she would turn her out of door. However, I was obliged to attend the Duke of York, thinking to have had a meeting of Tanger today, but had not; but he did take me and Mr Wren into his closet, and there did press me to prepare what I had to say upon the answers of my fellow officers to his great letter; which I promised to do against his coming to town again the next week. Thence by coach home and to dinner, finding my wife mightily discontented and the girl sad, and no words from my wife to her. So after dinner, they out with me about two or three things; and so home again, I all the evening busy and my wife full of trouble in her looks; and anon to bed – where about midnight, she wakes me and there falls foul on me again, affirming that she saw me hug and kiss the girl; the latter I denied, and truly; the other I confessed and no more. And upon her pressing me, did offer to give her under my hand that I would never see Mrs Pierce more, nor Knepp, but did promise her perticular demonstrations of my true love to her, owning some indiscretion in what I did, but that there was no harm in it. She at last on these promises was quiet, and very kind we were, and so to sleep.

28 October. At night to supper and to bed, my wife and I at good peace, but yet with some little grudgeings of trouble in her, and more in me, about the poor girl.

1 November. Lords Day. Up, and with W. Hewers at my chamber all this morning, going further in my great business for the Duke of York; and so at noon to dinner, and then W. Hewer to write fair what he had writ, and my wife to read to me all the afternoon; till anon Mr Gibson came, and he and I to perfect it to my full mind. And so to supper and to bed – my mind yet at disquiet that I cannot be informed how poor Deb stands with her mistress, but I fear she will put her away; and the truth is, though it be much against my mind and to my trouble, yet I think it will be fit that she be gone, for my wife's peace and mine; for she cannot but be offended at the sight of her, my wife having conceived this jealousy of me with reason. And therefore, for that, and other reasons of expense, it will be best for me to let her go – but I shall love and pity her. This noon Mr Povey sent his coach for my wife and I to see; which we like mightily, and will endeavour to have him get us just such another.

2 November. Up, and a cold morning, by water through bridge without a cloak; and there to Mr Wren at his chamber at Whitehall, and there he and I did read over my paper that I have with so much labour drawn up about the several answers of the Officers of this office to the Duke of York's reflections, and did debate a little what advice to give the Duke of York when he comes to town upon it.

This day I went by Mr Povey's direction to a coachmaker near him for a coach just like his, but it was sold this very morning.

3 November. Up and all the morning at the office. At noon to dinner; and then to the office and there busy till 12 at night, without much pain to my eyes; but I did not use them to read or write, and so did hold out very well. So home, and there to supper; and I observed my wife to eye my eyes whether I did ever look upon Deb; which I could not, but do now and then (and to my grief did see the poor wretch look on me and see me look on her, and then let drop a tear or two; which doth make my heart relent at this minute that I am writing this, with great trouble of mind, for she is endeed my sacrifice, poor girl); and my wife did tell me in bed, by the by, of my looking on other people, and that the only way is to put things out of sight.

5 November. With Mr Povy spent all the afternoon going up and down among the coachmakers in Cow Lane, and did see several, and at last did pitch upon a little chariott, whose body was framed but not covered, at the widow's that made Mr Lowther's fine coach. And we are mightily pleased with it, it being light, and will be very gent and sober – to be covered with leather, but yet will hold four. Being much satisfied with this, I carried him to Whitehall, and so by coach home.

6 November. Up, and presently my wife up with me, which she professedly now doth every day to dress me, that I may not see Willett; and doth eye me whether I cast my eye upon her or no. And doth keep me from going into the room where she is among the upholsters at work in our blue chamber.

7 November. Up, and at the office all the morning; and so to it again after dinner and there busy late, choosing to imploy myself rather then go home to trouble with my wife, whom, however, I am forced to comply with; and endeed I do pity her, as having cause enough for her grief. So to bed, and there slept ill because of my wife.

8 November. Lords Day. Up, and at my chamber all the morning, setting papers to rights with my boy. And so to dinner at noon, the girl with us; but my wife troubled thereat to see her, and doth tell me so; which troubles me, for I love the girl. At my chamber again to work all the afternoon till night, when Pelling comes, who wonders to find my wife so dull and melancholy; but God knows, she hath too much cause. However, as pleasant as we can, we supped together; and so made the boy read to me, the poor girl not appearing at supper, but hides herself in her chamber – so that I could wish in that respect that she was out of the house, for our peace is broke to all of us while she is here. And so to bed – where my wife mighty unquiet all night, so as my bed is become burdensome to me.

9 November. Up, and I did by a little note which I flung to Deb, advise her that I did continue to deny that ever I kissed her, and so she might govern herself. The truth [is], that I did adventure upon God's pardoning me this lie, knowing how heavy a thing it would be for me to be the ruin of the poor girl; and next, knowing that if my wife should know all, it were impossible ever for her to be at peace with me again – and so our whole lives would be uncomfortable.

10 November. Up, and my wife still every day as ill as she is all night; will rise to see me outdoors, telling me plainly that she dares not let me see the girl; and so I out to the office, where all the morning; and so home to dinner, where I find my wife mightily troubled again, more then ever, and she tells me that it is from her examining the girl and getting a confession now from her of all, even to the very tocando su thing with my hand – which doth mightily trouble me, as not being able to foresee the consequences of it as to our future peace together. So my wife would not go down to dinner, reproaching me with my unkindness and perjury, I having denied my ever kissing her – as also with all her old kindnesses to me, and my ill-using of her from the beginning, and the many temptations she hath refused out of faithfulness to me; whereof several she was perticular in, and especially from my Lord Sandwich by the sollicitation of Captain Ferrer; and then afterward, the courtship of my Lord Hinchingbrooke, even to the trouble of his Lady. All which I did acknowledge and was troubled for, and wept; and at last pretty good friends again, and so I to my office and there late, and so home to supper with her; and so to bed, where after half-an-hour's slumber, she wakes me and cries out that she should never sleep more, and so kept raving till past midnight, that made me cry and weep heartily all the while for her, and troubled for what she reproached me with as before; and at last, with new vows, and perticularly that I would myself bid the girl be gone and show my dislike to her – which I shall endeavour to perform, but with much trouble.

11 November. To supper and to bed; where after lying a little while, my wife starts up, and with expressions of affright and madness, as one frantic, would rise; and I would not let her, but burst out in tears myself; and so continued almost half the night, the moon shining so that it was light; and after much sorrow and reproaches and little ravings (though I am apt to think they were counterfeit from her), and my promise again to discharge the girl myself, all was quiet again and so to sleep.

12 November. I to my wife and to sit with her a little; and then called her and Willet to my chamber, and there did with tears in my eyes, which I could not help, discharge her and advise her to be gone as soon as she could, and never to see me or let me see her more while she was in the house; which she took with tears too, but I believe understands me to be her friend; and I am apt to believe, by what my wife hath of late told me, is a cunning girl, if not a slut. With Mr Gibson late at my chamber, making an end of my draft of a letter for the Duke of York, in answer to the answers of this office; which I have now done to my mind, so as, if the Duke of York likes it, will I think put an end to a great deal of the faults of this office, as well as my trouble for them. So to bed, and did lie now a little better then formerly, with but little and yet with some trouble.

13 November. I home, and there to talk, with great pleasure, all the evening with my wife, who tells me that Deb hath been abroad today, and is come home and says she hath got a place to go to, so as she will be gone tomorrow morning. This troubled me; and the truth is, I have a great mind for to have the maidenhead of this girl, which I should not doubt to have if yo could get time para be con her – but she will be gone and I know not whither.

14 November. Up, and had a mighty mind to have seen or given a note to Deb or to have given her a little money; to which purpose I wrapped up 40*s* in a paper, thinking to give her; but my wife rose presently, and would not let me be out of her sight; and went down before me into the kitchen, and came up and told me that she was in the kitchen, and therefore would have me go round the other way; which she repeating, and I vexed at it, answered her a little angrily; upon which she instantly flew out into a rage, calling me dog and rogue, and that I had a rotten heart; all which, knowing that I deserved it, I bore with; and word being brought presently up that she was gone away by coach with her things, my wife was friends; and so all quiet, and I to the office with my heart sad, and find that I cannot forget the girl, and vexed I know not where to look for her. It will be I fear a little time before I shall be able to wear Deb out of my mind.

I must here remember that I have laid with my moher as a husband more times since this falling-out then in I believe twelve months before – and with more pleasure to her then I think in all the time of our marriage before.

16 November. I away to Holborne about Whetstones Park, where I never was in my life before, where I understand by my wife's discourse that Deb is gone; and there, not hearing of any such man as Allbon, with whom my wife said she now was, I to the Strand and there, by sending of Drumbleby's boy, my flagelette-maker, to Eagle Court, where my wife also by discourse lately let fall that he did lately live, I found that this Dr Allbon is a kind of poor broken fellow that dare not show his head nor be known where he is gone.

18 November. Lay long in bed, talking with my wife, she being unwilling to have me go abroad, being and declaring herself jealous of my going out, for fear of my going to Deb; which I do deny – for which God forgive me, for I was no sooner out about noon but I did go by coach directly to Somerset House and there enquired among the porters there for Dr Allbun; and the first I spoke with told me he knew him, and that he was newly gone into Lincoln's Inn Fields, but whither he could not tell me, but that one of his fellows, not then in the way, did carry a chest of drawers thither with him, and that when he comes he would ask him. This put me in some hopes; and I to Whitehall and thence to Mr Povy's, but he at dinner; and therefore I away and walked up and down the Strand between the two turnstiles, hoping to see her out of a window; and then imployed a porter, one Osbeston, to find out this Doctors lodgings thereabouts; who by appointment comes to me to Hercules Pillars, where I dined alone, but tells me that he cannot find out any such but will enquire further. Thence back to Whitehall to the Treasury a while, and thence to the Strand; and towards night did meet with the porter that carried the chest of drawers with this Doctor, but he would not tell me where he lived, being his good maister he told me; but if I would have a message to him, he would deliver it. At last, I told him my business was not with him, but a little gent[le]woman, one Mrs Willet, that is with him; and sent him to see how she did, from her friend in London, and no other token. He goes while I walk in Somerset House; at last he comes back and tells me she is well, and that I may see her if I will – but no more. So I could not be commanded by my reason, but I must go this very night; and so by coach, it being now dark, I to her, close by my tailor's; and there she came into the coach to me, and yo did besar her and tocar her thing, but ella was against it and laboured with much earnestness, such as I believed to be real. I did nevertheless give her the best counsel I could, to have a care of her honour and to fear God and suffer no man para haver to do con her as yo have done – which she promised. Yo did give her 20s and directions para laisser sealed in paper at any time the name of the place of her being, at Herringman's my bookseller in the Change – by which I might go para her. And so home, and there told my wife a fair tale, God knows, how I spent the whole day; with which the poor wretch was satisfied, or at least seemed so; and so to supper and to bed, she having been mighty busy all day in getting of her house in order against tomorrow, to hang up our new hangings and furnishing our best chamber.

19 November. Up, and at the office all the morning, with my heart full of joy to think in what a safe condition all my matters now stand between my wife and Deb and me; and at noon, running upstairs to see the upholsters, who are at work upon hanging my best room and setting up my new bed, I find my wife sitting sad in the dining room; which inquiring into the reason of, she begun to call me all the false, rotten-hearted rogues in the world, letting me understand that I was with Deb yesterday; which, thinking impossible for her ever to understand, I did a while deny; but at last did, for the ease of my mind and hers, and for ever to discharge my heart of this wicked business, I did confess all; and above stairs in our bedchamber there I did endure the sorrow of her threats and vows and curses all the afternoon. And which was worst, she swore by all that was good that she would slit the nose of this girl, and be gone herself this very night from me; and did there demand 3 or 400*l* of me to buy my peace, that she might be gone without making any noise, or else protested that she would make all the world know of it. So, with most perfect confusion of face and heart, and sorrow and shame, in the greatest agony in the world, I did pass this afternoon, fearing that it will never have an end; but at last I did call for W. Hewers, who I was forced to make privy now to all; and the poor fellow did cry like a child [and] obtained what I could not, that she would be pacified, upon condition that I would give it under my hand never to see or speak with Deb while I live, as I did before of Pierce and Knepp; and which I did also, God knows, promise for Deb too, but I have the confidence to deny it, to the perjuring of myself. So before it was late, there was, beyond my hopes as well as desert, a tolerable peace; and so to supper, and pretty kind words, and to bed, and there yo did hazer con ella to her content; and so with some rest spent the night in bed, being most absolutely resolved, if ever I can maister this bout, never to give her occasion while I live of more trouble of this or any other kind, there being no curse in the world so great as this of the difference between myself and her; and therefore I do by the grace of God promise never to offend her more, and did this night begin to pray to God upon my knees alone in my chamber; which God knows I cannot yet do heartily, but I hope God will give me the grace more and more every day to fear Him, and to be true to my poor wife. This night the upholsters did finish the hanging of my best chamber, but my sorrow and trouble is so great about this business, that put me out of all joy.

20 November. This morning up, with mighty kind words between my poor wife and I; and so to Whitehall by water, W. Hewer with me, who is to go with me everywhere until my wife be in condition to go out along with me herself; for she doth plainly declare that she dares not trust me out alone, and therefore made it a piece of our league that I should always take somebody with me, or her herself; which I am mighty willing to, being, by the grace of God resolved never to do her wrong more. But when I came home, hoping for a further degree of peace and quiet, I find my wife upon her bed in a horrible rage afresh, calling me all the bitter names; and rising, did fall to revile me in the bitterest manner in the world, and could not refrain to strike me and pull my hair; which I resolved to bear with, and had good reason to bear it. So I by silence and weeping did prevail with her a little to be quiet, and she would not eat her dinner without me; but yet by and by into a raging fit she fell again worse then before, that she would slit the girl's nose; and at last W. Hewer came in and came up, who did allay her fury, I flinging myself in a sad desperate condition upon the bed in the blue room, and there lay while they spoke together; and at last it came to this, that if I would call Deb 'whore' under my hand, and write to her that I hated her and would never see her more, she would believe me and trust in me – which I did agree to; only, as to the name of 'whore' I would have excused, and therefore wrote to her sparing the word; which my wife thereupon tore it, and would not be satisfied till, W. Hewer winking upon me, I did write so, with the name of a whore, as that I did fear she might too probably have been prevailed upon to have been a whore by her carriage to me, and therefore, as such, I did resolve never to see her more. This pleased my wife, and she gives it W. Hewer to carry to her, with a sharp message from her. So from that minute my wife begun to be kind to me, and we to kiss and be friends, and so continued all the evening and fell to talk of other matters with great comfort, and after supper to bed. I did this night promise to my wife never to go to bed without calling upon God upon my knees by prayer; and I begun this night, and hope I shall never forget to do the like all my life – for I do find that it is much the best for my soul and body to live pleasing to God and my poor wife – and will ease me of much care, as well as much expense.

21 November. Up, with great joy to my wife and me, and to the office, where W. Hewer did most honestly bring me back that part of my letter under my hand to Deb wherein I called her 'whore', assuring me that he did not show it her – and that he did only give her to understand that wherein I did declare my desire never to see her, and did give her the best Christian counsel he could; which was mighty well done of him.

23 November. I met with Mr Povy, who I discoursed with about public business; who tells me that this discourse which I told him of, of the Duke of Monmouth being made Prince of Wales, hath nothing in it; though he thinks there are all the endeavours used in the world to overthrow the Duke of York. He doth think that the Duke of Buckingham hath a mind rather to overthrow all the kingdom and bring in a Commonwealth, wherein

. . . .

Will Hewer, by Sir Godfrey Kneller *c.* 1685. Pepys's clerk and lifelong friend.

he may think to be General of their army, or to make himself King; which he believes he may be led to by some advice he hath had with conjurors which he doth affect.

28 November. Up, and all the morning at the office; where, while I was sitting, one comes and tells me that my coach is come – so I was forced to go out; and to Sir Rd. Ford's, where I spoke to him, and he is very willing to have it brought in and stand there; and so I ordered it, to my great content, it being mighty pretty; only, the horses do not please me, and therefore resolve to have better.

29 November. Lords Day. Lay long in bed with pleasure [with my wife], with whom I have now a great deal of content; and my mind is in other things also mightily more at ease, and I do mind my business better than ever and am more at peace; and trust in God I shall ever be so, though I cannot yet get my mind off from thinking now and then of Deb. But I do, ever since my promise a while since to my wife, pray to God by myself in my chamber every night, and will endeavour to get my wife to do the like with me ere long; but am in much fear of what she hath lately frighted me with about her being a Catholique – and dare not therefore move her to go to church, for fear she should deny me. But this morning, of her own accord, she spoke of going to church the next Sunday; which pleases me mightily. This morning my coachman's clothes comes home, and I like my livery mightily.

5 December. Up, after a little talk with my wife which troubled me, she being ever since our late difference mighty watchful of sleep and dreams, and will not be persuaded but I do dream of Deb, and doth tell me that I speak in my dream and that this night I did cry 'Huzzy!' and it must be she – and now and then I start otherwise then I used to do, she says; which I know not, for I do not know that I dream of her more then usual, though I cannot deny that my thoughts waking do run now and then, against my will and judgment, upon her.

Now the great dispute is whether this Parliament or another; and my great design, if I continue in the Navy, is to get myself to be a Parliament-man.

7 December. Walked to my Lord Sandwiches and walked with him to Whitehall, and took a quarter of an hour's walk in the garden with him, which I had not done so much time with him since his coming in to England; and talking of his own condition, and perticularly of the world's talk of his going to Tangier – I find, if his conditions can be made profitable and safe as to money, he would go, but not else.

This afternoon, passing through Queen's Street, I saw pass by our coach on foot, Deb; which God forgive me, did put me into some new thoughts of her and for her, but durst not show them; and I think my wife did not see her, but I did get my thoughts free of her as soon as I could.

9 December. Up and to the office but did little there, my mind being still uneasy, though more and more satisfied that there is no occasion for it. But abroad with my wife to the Temple, where I met with Auditor Wood's clerk and did some business with him; and so to see Mr Spong, and found him out by Southampton Market and there carried my wife, and up to his chamber, in a by-place but with a good prospect to the fields; and there I had most infinite pleasure not only with his ingenuity in general, but in perticular with his showing me the use of the paralelogram, by which he drow in a quarter of an hour before me, in little from a great, a most neat map of England; that is, all the outlines – which gives me infinite pleasure and foresight of pleasure I shall have with it, and therefore desire to have that which I have bespoke made. Many other pretty things he showed us, and did give me a glass bubble to try the strength of liquors with.

11 December. With W. Hewer by coach to Smithfield, but met not Mr Pickering, he being not come; and so he and I to a cook's shop in Aldersgate Street and dined well for 19½d upon roast beef; and so having dined, we back to Smithfield and there met Pickering, and up and down all the afternoon about horses, and did see the knaveries and tricks of jockys. Here I met W. Joyce, who troubled me with his impertinencies a great while, and the like Mr Knepp, who it seems is a kind of a jocky and would fain have been doing something for me; but I avoided him, and the more for fear of being troubled thereby with his wife, whom I desire but dare not see – for my vow to my wife. At last went away and did nothing; only, concluded upon giving 50l for a fine pair of black horses we saw this day sennit.

20 December. Lords Day. Up and with my wife to church, and then home; and there found W. Joyce come to dine with me, as troublesome a talking coxcomb as ever he was – and yet once in a year I like him well enough. In the afternoon, my wife and W. Hewer and I to Whitehall, where they set me down and stayed till I had been with the Duke of York, with the rest of us of the office, and did a little business; and then the Duke of York in good humour did fall to tell us many fine stories of the wars in Flanders, and how the Spaniards are the [best] disciplined foot in the world – will refuse no extraordinary service if commanded, but scorn to be paid for it, as in other countries, though at the same time they will beg in the streets. Not a soldier will carry you a cloak-bag for money for the world, though he will beg a penny, and will do the thing if commanded by his commander. That in the citadel of Antwerp, a soldier hath not a liberty of begging till he hath served three years. They will cry out against their King and commanders and generals, none like them in the world, and yet will not hear a stranger say a word of them but he will cut his throat. That upon a time, some of the commanders of their army exclaiming against their generals, and perticularly the Marquis de Caranene, the confessor of the Marquis coming by and hearing them, he stops and gravely tells them that the three great trades of the world are, the lawyer[s], who govern the world; the churchmen, who enjoy the world; and a sort of fools whom they call souldiers, who make it their work to defend the world.

21 December. To the Temple, there to call Talbt. Pepys; and took him up, and first went into Holborne and there saw the woman that is to be seen with a beard; she is a little plain woman, a Dane, her name, Ursula Dyan, about forty years old, her voice like a little girl's, with a beard as much as any man I ever saw, as black almost, and grizzly. They offered

[to] show my wife further satisfaction if she desired it, refusing it to men that desired it there. But there is no doubt but by her voice she is a woman; it begun to grow at about seven years old – and was shaved not above seven months ago, and is now so big as any man almost that ever I saw, I say, bushy and thick. It was a strange sight to me, I confess, and what pleased me mightily. Thence to the Duke's playhouse and saw *Mackbeth*; the King and Court there, and we sat just under them and my Lady Castlemayne. And my wife, by my troth, appeared I think as pretty as any of them, I never thought so much before; and so did Talbot and W. Hewer, as they said, I heard, to one another.

23 December. Home to dinner; and then with my wife alone abroad with our new horses, the beautifullest almost that ever I saw, and the first time they ever carried her at all, and me but once. But we are mighty proud of them. To her tailor's and so to the Change and laid out three or four pound in lace for her and me; and so home.

25 December. Christmas Day. Up, and continued on my waistcoat, the first day this winter. And I to church, where Alderman Backewell coming in late, I beckoned to his lady to come up to us; who did, with another lady; and after sermon I led her down through the church to her husband and coach – a noble, fine woman, and a good one – and one my wife shall be acquainted with. So home and to dinner alone with my wife, who, poor wretch, sat undressed all day till 10 at night, altering and lacing of a black petticoat – while I by her, making the boy read to me the life of Julius Caesar and Des Cartes book of music – the latter of which I understand not, nor think he did well that writ it, though a most learned man. Then after supper made the boy play upon his lute, which I have not done twice before sence he came to me; and so, my mind in mighty content, we to bed.

26 December. Lay long, with pleasure prating with my wife; and then up, and I a little to the office, and my head busy setting some papers and accounts to rights; which being long neglected because of my eyes, will take me up much time and care to do, but it must be done. So home at noon to dinner; and then abroad with my wife to a play at the Duke of York's House; the house full of ordinary citizens; the play was *Women pleased*, which we had never seen before; and though but indifferent, yet there is a good design for a good play. So home, and there to talk and my wife to read to me, and so to bed.

27 December. Lords Day. Walked to Whitehall and there saw the King at chapel; but stayed not to hear anything, but went to walk in the park with W. Hewer, who was with me; and there, among others, met with Sir G. Downing and walked with him an hour, talking of business and how the late war was managed. He told me that he had so good spies, that he hath had the keys taken out of De Witts pocket when he was a-bed, and his closet opened and papers brought to him and left in his hands for an [hour], and carried back and laid in the place again and the keys put into his pocket again. He says he hath alway had their most private debates, that have been but between two or three of the chief of them, brought to him in an hour after, and an hour after that hath sent word thereof to the King – but nobody here regarded them.

1669

1 January. Up, and with W. Hewer to the New Exchange, and there he and I to the cabinet shops to look out, and did agree for a cabinett to give my wife for a New Year's gift; and I did buy one, cost me 11*l*, which is very pretty, of walnutt tree, and will come home tomorrow. So back to the Old Exchange and there met my uncle Wight; and there walked and met with the Houblons and talked with them, gentlemen whom I honour mightily. And so to my uncles and met my wife, and there, with W. Hewer, we dined with his family and had a very good dinner, and pretty merry; and after dinner my wife and I with our coach to the King's playhouse and there in a box saw *The Mayden Queene*. Knepp looked upon us, but I durst not show her any countenance and, as well as I could carry myself, I found my wife uneasy there, poor wretch. Therefore I shall avoid that house as much I can. So back to my aunts and there supped and talked, and stayed pretty late, it being dry and moonshine; and so walked home, and to bed in very good humour.

4 January. Lay long talking with my wife, and did of my own accord come to an allowance of her of 30*l* a year for all expenses, clothes and everything; which she was mightily pleased with, it being more then ever she asked or expected; and so rose with much content, and up and with W. Hewer to Whitehall, there to speak with Mr Wren; which I did, about several things of the office entered in my memorandum-books; and so about noon, going homeward with W. Hewer, he and I went in and saw the great tall woman that is to be seen, which is but twenty-one years old and I do easily stand under her arms. Then going further, The[ophila] Turner called me out of her coach, where her mother &c was, and invited me by all means to dine with them at my Cosen Roger's mistress, the Widdow Dickenson; so I went to them afterward and dined with them, and mighty handsomely treated; and she a wonderful merry, good-humoured, fat but plain woman, but I believe a very good woman – and mighty civil to me. So home and there with pleasure to read and talk; and so to supper and put into writing, in merry terms, our agreement about the 30*l* a year; and so to bed. This was done under both our hands merrily, and put into W. Hewer's to keep.

8 January. To Whitehall, where I alone did manage the business of the *Leopard* against the whole Committee of the East India Company, with Mr Blackburne with them – and to the silencing of them all, to my great content.

10 January. Lords Day. Accidentally, talking of our maids before we rose, I said a little word that did give occasion to my wife to fall out, and she did most vexatiously almost all the morning, but ended most perfect good friends; but the thoughts of the unquiet which her ripping up of old faults will give me did make me melancholy all day long.

12 January. This evening I observed my wife mighty dull; and I myself was not mighty fond, because of some hard words she did give me at noon, out of a jealousy at my being abroad this morning; when, God knows, it was upon the business of the office unexpectedly; but I to bed, not thinking but she would come after me; but waking by and by out of a slumber, which I usually fall into presently after my coming into the bed, I found she did not prepare to come to bed, but got fresh candles and more wood for her fire, it being mighty cold too. At this being troubled, I after a while prayed her to come to bed, all my people being gone to bed; so after an hour or two, she silent, and I now and then praying her to come to bed, she fell out into a fury, that I was a rogue and false to her; but yet I could perceive that she was to seek what to say; only, she invented, I believe, a business that I was seen in a hackney coach with the glasses up with Deb, but could not tell the time, nor was sure I was he. I did, as I might truly, deny it, and was mightily troubled; but all would not serve. At last, about 1 a'clock, she came to my side of the bed and drow my curtaine open, and with the tongs, red hot at the ends, made as if she did design to pinch me with them; at which in dismay I rose up, and with a few words she laid them down and did by little and little, very sillily, let the discourse fall; and about 2, but with much seeming difficulty, came to bed and there lay well all night, and long in bed talking together with much pleasure; it being, I know, nothing but her doubt of my going out yesterday without telling her of my going which did vex her, poor wretch, last night: and I cannot blame her jealousy, though it doth vex me to the heart.

15 January. Down with Lord Brouncker to Sir R. Murray into the King's little elaboratory under his closet, a pretty place, and there saw a great many chymicall glasses and things, but understood none of them.

21 January. My wife and I to the Change; and so home, where my wife mighty dogged; and vexed to see it, being mightily troubled of late at her being out of humour, for fear of her discovering any new matter of offence against me; though I am conscious of none, but do hate to be unquiet at home. So late up, silent and not supping, but hearing her utter some words of discontent to me with silence; and so to bed weeping to myself for grief – which she discerning, came to bed and mighty kind; and so, with great joy on both sides, to sleep.

22 January. Up and with W. Hewer to Whitehall, and there attended the Duke of York; and thence to the Exchange, in the way calling at several places on occasions relating to my feast tomorrow, on which my mind is now set – as, how to get a new looking glass for my dining room, and some pewter and good wine against tomorrow. And so home, where I had the looking glass set up; cost me 6*l.* 7*s.* 6*d.* And here at the Change I met with Mr Dancre, the famous lanskip painter – with whom I was on Wednesday; and he took measure of my panels in my dining room, where in the four I intend to have the four houses of the King – Whitehall, Hampton Court, Greenwich and Windsor. He gone, I to dinner with my people, and so to my office to despatch a little business; and then home to look after things against tomorrow. And among other things, was mightily pleased with the fellow that came to lay the cloth and fold the napkins – which I like so well, as that I am resolved to give him 40s. to teach my wife to do it. So to supper, with much kindness between me and my wife, which nowadays is all my care; and so to bed.

23 January. Up, and again to look after the setting things right against dinner, which I did to very good content; and so to the office, where all the morning till noon, when word brought me to the Board that my Lord Sandwich was come; so I presently arose, leaving the Board ready to rise, and there I found my Lord Sandwich, Peterburgh, and Sir Ch. Herberd; and presently after them come my Lord Hinchingbrooke, Mr Sidny, and Sir Wm. Godolphin; and after greeting them, and some time spent in talk, dinner was brought up, one dish after another, but a dish at a time; but all so good, but above all things, the variety of wines, and excellent of their kind, I had for them, and all in so good order, that they were mightily pleased, and myself full of content at it; and endeed it was, of a dinner of about six or eight dishes, as noble as any man need to have I think – at least, all was done in the noblest manner that ever I had any, and I have rarely seen in my life better anywhere else – even at the Court. After dinner, my Lords to cards, and the rest of us sitting about them and talking, and looking on my books and pictures and my wife's drawings, which they commend mightily; and mighty merry all day long, with exceeding great content, and so till 7 at night; and so took their leaves. So to my wife's chamber, and there supped and got her cut my hair and look my shirt, for I have itched mightily these six or seven days; and when all came to all, she finds that I am louzy, having found in my head and body above twenty lice, little and great; which I wonder at, being more then I have had I believe almost these twenty years. I did think I might have got them from the little boy, but they did presently look him, and found none – how they came, I know not; but presently did shift myself, and so shall be rid of them, and cut my hayre close to my head.

24 January. I to talk with Tom Killigrew, who told me and others, talking about the playhouses, that he is fain to keep a woman on purpose, at 20s a week, to satisfy eight or ten of the young men of his House, whom till he did so he could never keep to their business, and now he doth. By and by the King comes out, and so I took coach and fallowed his coaches to my Lord Keepers at Essex House, where I never was before since I saw my old Lord Essex lie in state when he was dead – a large but ugly house. Here all the Officers of the Navy attended, and by and by were called in to the King and Cabinet, where my Lord, who was ill, did lie upon the bed, as my old Lord Treasurer or Chancellor heretofore used to. And the business was to know in what time all the King's ships might be repaired fit for service; the Surveyor answered, 'In two years and not sooner.' I did give them hopes that with supplies of money suitable, we might have them all fit for sea some part of the summer after this. Then they demanded in what time we could set out forty ships: it was answered, as they might be chosen of the newest and most ready, we could, with money, get forty ready against May. The King seemed mighty full that we should have money to do all that we desired, and satisfied that without it nothing could be done; and so, without determining anything, we were dismissed; and I doubt all will end in some little fleet this year, and those of hired merchantmen; which would endeed be cheaper to the King, and have many conveniences attending it, more then to fit out the King's own.

25 January. Up and to the Committee of Tanger, where little done. And thence I home by my own coach, and busy after dinner at my office, all the afternoon till late at night, that my eyes were tired. So home, and my wife showed me many excellent prints of Nantueil's and others, which W. Batelier hath at my desire brought me out of France of the King's and Colberts and others, most excellent, to my great content. But he hath also brought over a great many gloves perfumed, of several sorts; but all too big by half for her, and yet she will have two or three dozen of them, which vexed me and made me angry; so she at last, to please me, did come to take what alone I thought fit; which pleased me. So after a little supper, to bed – my eyes being very bad.

26 January. Up and to the office, where busy sitting all the morning. Then to the office again, and then to Whitehall, leaving my wife at Unthankes; and I to the Secretary's chamber, where I was by perticular order this day summoned to attend, as I find Sir D. Gawden also was, and here was the King and the Cabinet met; and being called in among the rest, I find my Lord Privy Seale, whom I never before knew to be in so much play as to be of the Cabinet. The business is that the Algerins have broke the peace with us, by taking out some Spaniards and goods out of an English ship which had the Duke of York's pass – of which advice came this day; and the King is resolved to stop Sir Tho. Allen's fleet from coming home till he hath amends made him for this affront, and therefore sent for us to advise about victuals to be sent to that fleet, and some more ships – wherein I answered them to what they demanded of me, which was but some few mean things; but I see that on all these occasions they seem to rely most upon me. And so this being done, I took coach and took up my wife, and straight home and there late at the office busy; and then home, and there I find W. Batelier hath also sent the books which I bade him bring me out of France, to my great content; and so I was well pleased with them and shall take a time to look them over, as also one or two printed music books of songs; but my eyes are now too much out of tune to look upon them with any pleasure.

31 January. Lords Day. Lay long, talking with pleasure, and so up, and I to church and there did hear the Doctor that is lately turned divine, I have forgot his name, I met him a while since at Sir D. Gawden's at dinner, Dr Waterhouse; he preaches in devout manner of way, not elegant nor very persuasive, but seems to mean well and that he would preach holily, and was mighty passionate against people that make a scoff of religion. And the truth is, I did observe Mrs Hallworthy smile often, and many others of the parish, who I perceive have known him and were in mighty expectation of hearing him preach, but could not forbear smiling; and she perticularly upon me, and I on her.

And thus ended this month, with many different days of sadness and mirth, from differences between me and my wife, from her remembrance of my late unkindness to her with Willet, she not being able to forget it, but now and then hath her passionate remembrance of it, as often as prompted to it by any occasion; but this night we are at present very kind. And so ends this month.

1 February. To Mr Streeters the famous history painter, whom I have often heard of but did never see him before; and there I found him and Dr Wren and several virtuosos looking

The Sheldonian Theatre, Oxford, from D. Loggan's *Oxonia Illustrata* 1675. Designed by Wren, and completed in 1670.

. . . .

upon the paintings which he is making the new Theatre at Oxford; and endeed, they look as they would be very fine, and the rest thinks better then those of Rubens in the Banqueting House at Whitehall, but I do not so fully think so – but they will certainly be very noble, and I am mightily pleased to have the fortune to see this man and his work, which is very famous – and he a very civil little man and lame, but lives very handsomely. So thence to my Lord Bellasses and met him within; my business only to see a chimneypiece of Dancre's doing in distemper with egg to keep off the glaring of the light, which I must have done for my room; and endeed it is pretty, but I must confess I do think it is not altogether so beautiful as the oyle pictures; but I will have some of one and some of another. Thence set him down at Little Turnstile, and so I home; and there eat a little dinner, and away with my wife by coach to the King's playhouse, thinking to have seen *The Heyresse*, first acted on Saturday last; but when we came thither, we find no play there – Kinaston, that did act a part therein in abuse to Sir Charles Sidly, being last night exceedingly dry-beaten with sticks by two or three that assaulted him.

2 February. Up and to the office, where all the morning; and home to dinner at noon, where I find Mr Sheres; and there made a short dinner and carried him with us to the King's playhouse, where *The Heyresse*, notwithstanding Kinaston's being beaten, is acted; and they say the King is very angry with Sir Ch. Sidly for his being beaten; but he doth deny it. But his part is done by Beeston, who is fain to read it out of a book all the while, and thereby spoils the part and almost the play, it being one of the best parts in it; but it was pleasant to see Beeston come in with others, supposing it to be dark and yet he is forced to read his part by the light of the candles. And this I observing to a gentleman that sat by me, he was mightily pleased therewith and spread it up and down; but that that pleased me most in the play is the first song that Knepp sings (she singing three or four); and endeed, it was very finely sung, so as to make the whole house clap her. To the office about my letters; and then home to supper and to bed, my wife being in mighty ill humour all night; and in the morning, I found it to be from her observing Knepp to wink and smile on me, and she says I smiled on her; and poor wretch, I did perceive that she did, and doth on all such occasions, mind my eyes. I did with much difficulty pacify her, and were friends, she desiring that hereafter at that house we might always sit either above in a box or, if there be room, close up to the lower boxes.

[*3 February.*] So up, and to the office till noon and then home to a little dinner; and thither again till night, mighty busy, to my great content doing a great deal of business; and so home to supper and to bed – I finding this day that I may be able to do a great deal of business by dictateing, if I do not read myself or write, without spoiling my eyes, I being very well in my eyes after a great day's work.

7 February. Lords Day. My wife mighty peevish in the morning about my lying unquietly a-nights, and she will have it that it is a late practice, from my evil thoughts in my dreams; and I do often find that in my dreams she doth lay her hand upon my cockerel to observe what she can. And mightily she is troubled about it, but all blew over.

8 February. My wife in a wonderful ill humour, and after dinner I stayed with her alone, being not able to endure this life, and fell to some angry words together; but by and by were mighty good friends, she telling me plainly it was about Jane – whom she cannot believe but I am base with; which I made a matter of mirth at, but at last did call up Jane and confirmed her mistress's directions for her being gone at Easter: which I find the wench willing to be, but directly prayed that Tom might go with her; which I promised, and was but what I designed; and she being thus spoke with and gone, my wife and I good friends and mighty kind, I having promised, and I will perform it, never to give her for the time to come ground of new trouble; and so I to the office with a very light heart, and there close at my business all the afternoon.

10 February. To Whitehall, where I stayed till the Duke of York came from hunting, which he did by and by; and when dressed, did come out to dinner, and there I waited; and he did tell me that tomorrow was to be the great day that the business of the Navy would be discoursed of before the King and his Caball; and that he must stand on his guard. Here he dined, and did mightily magnify his sawce which he did then eat with everything, and said it was the best universal sauce in the world – it being taught him by the Spanish Imbassador – made of some parsley and a dry toast, beat in a mortar together with vinegar, salt, and a little pepper. He eats it with flesh or fowl or fish. And then he did now mightily commend some new sort of wine lately found out, called Navarr wine; which I tasted, and is I think good wine; but I did like better the notion of the sawce and by and by did taste it, and liked it mightily.

12 February. Up and my wife with me to Whitehall, and Tom, and there she sets us down; and there to wait on the Duke of York, with the rest of us; where the Duke of York did tell us that the King would have us prepare a draft of the present administracion of the Navy, and what it was in the late times – in order to his being able to distinguish between the good and the bad; which I shall do, but to do it well will give me a great deal of trouble. Thence I homeward; and calling my wife, called at my cousin Turner's and there met our new Cosen Pepys (Mrs Dickenson) and Bab and Betty [Pepys], come yesterday to town, poor girls; whom we have reason to love, and mighty glad we are to see them; and there stayed and talked a little, being also mightily pleased to see Betty Turner, who is now in town, and her brother[s] Charles and Will, being come from school to see their father; and there talked a while and so home, and there Pelling hath got me W. Pen's book against the Trinity; I got my wife to read it to me, and I find it so well writ, as I think it too good for him ever to have writ it – and it is a serious sort of book, and not fit for everybody to read. And so to supper and to bed.

18 February. Up, and to the office; and at noon home, expecting to have this day seen Babb and Betty Pepys here, but they came not; and so after dinner, my wife and I to the Duke of York's House to a play, and there saw *The Mad Lover*, which doth not please me so well as it used to do; only Baterton's part still pleases me. But here, who should we have come to us but Bab and Betty and Talbot, the first play they were yet at; and going to see us, and hearing by my boy, whom I sent to them, that we were here, they came to us hither and happened all of us to sit by my cousin Turner and The[ophila]. And we carried them home first, and then took Bab and Betty to our house, where they lay and supped, and pretty merry; and very fine with their new clothes, and good comely girls they are enough, and very glad I am of their being with us; though I could very well have been contented to have been without that charge. So they to bed and we to bed.

19 February. Up, and after seeing the girls, who lodged in our bed with their mayd Martha (who hath been their father's maid these twenty years and more), I with Lord Brouncker to Whitehall, where all of us waited on the Duke of York. All the afternoon I at the office while the young people went to see Bedlam; and at night home to them to supper, and pretty merry; only, troubled with a great cold at this time – and my eyes very bad, ever since Monday night last that the light of the candles spoiled me. So to bed.

23 February. Up, and to the office, where all the morning. And then home and put a mouthful of victuals in my mouth; and by a hackney coach fallowed my wife and the girls, who are gone by 11 a clock, thinking to have seen a new play at the Duke of York's House; but I do find them staying at my tailor's, the play not being today, and therefore I now took them to Westminster Abbey and there did show them all the tombs very finely, having one with us alone (there being other company this day to see the tombs, it being Shrove Tuesday); and here we did see, by perticular favour, the body of Queen Katherine of Valois, and had her upper part of her body in my hands. And I did kiss her mouth, reflecting upon it that I did kiss a Queen, and that this was my birthday, 36 year old, that I did first kiss a Queen. Thence to the Duke of York's playhouse, and there finding the play begun, we homeward to the glasshouse and there showed my cousins the making of glass, and had several things made with great content; and among others, I had one or two singing glasses made, which make an echo to the voice, the first that ever I saw; but so thin that the very breath broke one or two of them. So home, and thence to Mr Batelier's, where we supped, and had a good supper; and here was Mr Gumbleton, and after supper some fiddles and so to dance; but my eyes were so out of order that I had little pleasure this night at all, though I was glad to see the rest merry. And so about midnight home and to bed.

24 February. Lay long in bed, both being sleepy and my eyes bad, and myself having a great cold, so as I was hardly able to speak; but however, by and by up and to the office; and at noon home with my people to dinner; and then I to the office again and there till the evening, doing of much business; and at night my wife sends for me to W. Hewer's lodging, where I find two most [fine] chambers of his, so finely furnished and all so rich and neat, that I was mightily pleased with him and them; and here only my wife and I and the two girls, and had a mighty neat dish of custards and tarts, and good drink and talk; and so away home to bed, with infinite content at this his treat, for it was mighty pretty and everything mighty rich.

2 March. Up and at the office till noon, when home; and there I find my company come – viz., Madam Turner, Dike, The[ophila] and Betty Turner, and Mr Bellwood, formerly their father's clerk but now set up for himself, a conceited silly fellow but one they make mightily of – my Cosen Roger Pepys and his wife and two daughters. And I had a noble dinner for them as I almost ever had, and mighty merry; and perticularly, myself pleased with looking on Betty Turner – who is mighty pretty. After dinner we fell one to one talk, and another to another, and looking over my house and closet and things, and The[ophila] Turner to write a letter to a lady in the country, in which I did now and then put in half a dozen words, and sometimes five or six lines, and then she as much, and made up a long and good letter, she being mighty witty really, though troublesome humoured with it. And thus till night, that our music came and the office ready, and candles; and also W. Batelier and his sister Susan came, and also Will How and two gentlemen more, strangers, which at my request yesterday he did bring to dance, called Mr Ireton and Mr Starkey; we fell to dancing and continued, only with intermission for a good supper, till 2 in the morning, the music being Greeting and another most excellent violin and theorbo, the best in town; and so, with mighty mirth and pleased with their dancing of jiggs afterward, several of them, and among others Betty Turner, who did it mighty prettily; and lastly, W. Batelier's blackmore and blackmore maid, and then to a country dance again; and so broke up with extraordinary pleasure, as being one of the days and nights of my life spent with the greatest content, and that which I can but hope to repeat again a few times in my whole life. This done, we parted, the strangers home, and I did lodge my cousin Pepys and his wife in our blue chamber – my cousin Turner, her sister, and The[ophila] in our best chamber – Babb, Betty, and Betty Turner in our own chamber; and myself and my wife in the maid's bed, which is very good – our maids in the coachman's bed – the coachman with the boy in his settle-bed; and Tom where he uses to lie; and so I did to my great content lodge at once in my house, with great ease, fifteen, and eight of them strangers of quality.

My wife this day put on first her French gown, called a *sac*, which becomes her very well, brought her over by W. Batelier.

4 March. Walked to Deptford, where I have not been I think these twelve months; and there to the [Navy] Treasurer's house, where the Duke of York is, and his Duchesse; and there we find them at dinner in the great room, unhung, and there was with them my Lady Duchess of Monmouth, the Countess of Falmouth, Castlemayne, Henrietta Hide, my Lady Hinchingbrooke's sister, and my Lady Peterbrough. I did find the Duke of York and Duchess with all the great ladies, sitting upon a carpet on the ground, there being no chairs, playing at 'I love my love with an A because he is so and so; and I hate

. . . .

'My wife this day put on first her French gown . . . which becomes her very well.'
(2 March 1669.) French fashions of 1670.

him with an A because of this and that'; and some of them, but perticularly the Duchess herself and my Lady Castlemaine, were very witty. This done, they took barge, and I with Sir J. Smith to Captain Cox's and there to talk, and left them and other company to drink while I slunk out to Bagwell's and there saw her and her mother and our late maid Nell, who cried for joy to see me; but I had no time for pleasure there nor could stay; but after drinking, I back to the yard, having a month's mind para have had a bout with Nell – which I believe I could have had – and may another time.

Sir William Coventry, a Commissioner of the Treasury and for long Pepys's friend and mentor, has just been disgraced and committed to the Tower on the ground that he had (allegedly) challenged the Duke of Buckingham to a duel. He had for some time been losing ground to Buckingham and his faction. He retires into private life to grow peaches in Oxfordshire.

6 March. Up and to the office, where all the morning. Only before the office, I stepped to Sir W. Coventry at the Tower and there had a great deal of discourse with him – among others, of the King's putting him out of the Council yesterday – with which he is well contented, as with what else they can strip him of – he telling me, and so hath long, that he is weary and surfeited of business. But he joins with me in his fears that all will go to naught as matters are now managed. This day, my wife made it appear to me that my late entertainment this week cost me above 12*l*, a expense which I am almost ashamed of, though it is but once in a great while, and is the end for which in the most part we live, to have such a merry day once or twice in a man's life.

7 March. Lords Day. Up and to the office, busy till church time; and then to church, where a dull sermon; and so home to dinner all alone with my wife, and then to even my journall to this day; and then to the Tower to see Sir W. Coventry, who had H. Jermin and a great many more with him, and more, while I was there, came in; so that I do hear that there was not less than sixty coaches there yesterday and the other day. I hear that tomorrow the King and Duke of York set out for Newmarket by 3 in the morning to some foot and horse races, to be abroad ten or twelve days.

8 March. To the Privy Seal Office to examine what records I could find there for my help in the great business I am put upon, of defending the present constitution of the Navy.

9 March. Up, and to the Tower and there find Sir W. Coventry alone, writing down his journall, which he tells me he now keeps of the material things; [upon] which I told him, and he is the only man that I ever told it to I think, that I have kept it most strictly these eight or ten years; and I am sorry almost that I told it him – it not being necessary, nor may be convenient to have it known. Hence by and by away, and with my wife and Bab and Betty Pepys and W. Hewers, whom I carried all this day with me, to my Cosen Stradwicks. Here, which I never did before, I drank a glass, of a pint I believe, at one draught, of the juice of oranges of whose peel they make comfits; and here they drink the juice as wine, with sugar, and it is very fine drink; but it being new, I was doubtful whether it might not do me hurt.

11 March. Up and to Sir W. Coventry to the Tower, where I walked and talked with him an hour alone, from one good thing to another; who tells me that he hears that the commission is gone down to the King with a blank to fill for his place in the Treasury; and he believes it will be filled with one of our Treasurers of the Navy, but which he knows not, but he believes it will be Osborne. We walked down to the Stone Walk, which is called, it seems, 'My Lord of Northumberland's Walk', being paved by some of that title that was prisoner there; and at the end of it there is a piece of iron upon the wall with his armes upon it, and holes to put in a peg for every turn that they make upon that walk. So away to the office, where busy all the morning, and so to dinner; and so very busy all the afternoon at my office late, and then home, tired, to supper, with content with my wife; and so to bed – she pleasing me, though I dare not own it, that she hath hired a chambermaid; but she, after many commendations, told me that she had one great fault, and that was that she was very handsome; at which I made nothing, but let her go on; but many times tonight she took occasion to discourse of her handsomeness and the danger she was in by taking her, and that she did doubt yet whether it would be fit for her to take her. But I did assure her of my resolutions to having nothing to do with her maids, but in myself I was glad to have the content to have a handsome one to look on.

12 March. Up, and abroad with my own coach to Auditor Beales house; and thence with W. Hewer to his office and there with great content spent all the morning, looking over the Navy accounts of several years and the several patents of the Treasurers, which was more then I did hope to have found there. About noon I ended there, to my great content; and giving the clerks there 20*s* for their trouble, and having sent for W. How to me to discourse with him about the Patent Office records, wherein I remembered his brother to be concerned, I took him in my coach with W. Hewer and myself toward Westminster, and there he carried me to Nott's, the famous bookbinder that bound for my Lord Chancellor's library. And here I did take occasion for curiosity to bespeak a book to be bound, only that I might have one of his binding. Thence back to Grayes Inn; and at the next door, at a cook's-shop of How's acquaintance, we bespoke dinner, it being now 2 a-clock; and in the meantime he carried us into Gray's Inn to his chamber, where I never was before; and it is very pretty, and little and neat, as he was always. And so after a little stay and looking over a book or two there we carried a piece of my Lord Cooke with us, and to our dinner, where after dinner he read at my desire a chapter in my Lord Cooke about perjury, wherein I did learn a good deal touching oaths. And so away to the Patent Office in Chancery Lane, and here I did set a clerk to look out for some things for me in their books, while W. Hewers and I to the Crowne Office, where we met with several good things that I most wanted and did take short notes of the dockets; and so back to the Patent Office and did the like there, and by candlelight ended; and so home, where thinking to meet my wife with content, after my pains all this day, I find her in her closet, alone in the dark, in a hot fit of railing against me, upon some news she hath this day heard of Deb's living very fine, and with black spots, and speaking ill words of her mistress; but God knows, I know nothing of her nor what she doth nor what becomes of her; though God knows, my devil that is within me doth wish that I could. Yet God I hope will prevent me therein – for I dare not trust myself with it, if I should know it. But what with my high words, and slighting it and then serious, I did at last bring her to very good and kind terms, poor heart; and I was heartily glad of [it], for I do see there is no man can be happier then myself, if I will, with her. But in her fit she did tell me what vexed me all the night, that this had put her upon putting off her handsome maid and hiring another that was full of the smallpox – which did mightily vex me, though I said nothing, and doth still. So down to supper, and she to read to me, and then with all possible kindness to bed.

13 March. To the office, where all the morning; and then home to dinner with my people and so to the office again. And there all the afternoon till night, when comes by mistake my cousin Turner and her two daughters (which loves such freaks) to eat some anchoves and ham of bacon with me, by mistake instead of noon at dinner, when I expected them; but however, I had done my business before they came and so was in good humour enough to be with them; and so home to them to supper, and pretty merry. But that which put me in good humour, both at noon and night, is the fancy that I am this day made a Captain of one of the King's ships, Mr Wren having this day sent me the Duke of York's commission to be Captain of the *Jerzy*, in order to my being of a court martiall for examining the loss of the *Defyance*, and other things.

14 March. Before I went from my office this night, I did tell Tom my resolution not to keep him after Jane was gone, but shall do well by him – which pleases him; and I think he will presently marry her and go away out of my house with her.

15 March. Up, and by water with W. Hewer to the Temple; and thence to the Chapel of Rolles, where I made enquiry for several rolles and was soon informed in the manner of it; and so spent the whole morning with W. Hewer, he taking little notes in shorthand, while I hired a clerk there to read to me about twelve or more several rolls which I did call for: and it was great pleasure to me to see the method wherein their rolles are kept; that when the Master of the Office, one Mr Case, doth call for them (who is a man that I have heretofore known by coming to my Lord Sandwiches) he did most readily turn to them. At noon they shut up, and W. Hewer and I did walk to the Cocke at the end of Suffolke Street, where I never was, a great ordinary, mightily cried up, and there bespoke a pullet; which while dressing, he and I walked into St James's Park, and thence back and dined very handsome, with a good soup and a pullet, for 4s 6d the whole. Thence back to the Rolles and did a little more business; and so by water from Whitehall, whither I went to speak with Mr Williamson (that if he hath any papers relating to the Navy, I might see them, which he promises me); and so by water home, with great content for what I have

. . . .

(*Opposite*) 'To the coffee-house, where excellent discourse with Sir W. Petty; who proposed it, as a thing that is truly questionable, whether there really be any difference between waking and dreaming.' (2 April 1664.) London coffee-house, *c*. 1690.
(*Overleaf*) '[Mr Dancre] took measure of my panels in my dining room, where . . . I intend to have the four houses of the King.' (22 January 1669.) This painting of Greenwich by Hendrik Danckerts is said to be one of the pictures Pepys ordered. If so, the figures in the foreground may be Pepys and his wife.

this day found, having got almost as much as I desire of the history of the Navy from 1618 to 1642, when the King and Parliament fell out. So home, and did get my wife to read, and so to supper and to bed.

16 March. At noon home, where my wife and Jane gone abroad, and Tom, in order to their buying of things for their wedding, which, upon my discourse the last night, is now resolved to be done upon the 26 of this month, the day of my solemnity for my cutting of the stone, when my Cosen Turner must be with us. After dinner I away down by water with W. Hewer to Woolwich, where I have not been I think more then a year or two; and here saw, but did not go on board, my ship the *Jerzy*, she lying at the wharf under repair. But my business was to speak with Ackworth about some old things and passages in the Navy, for my information therein in order to my great business now, of stating the [hi]story of the Navy. This I did, and upon the whole do find that the late times, in all their management were not more husbandly then we, and other things of good content to me. Thence, to Greenwich by water, and there landed at the King's house, which goes on slow, but is very pretty. I to the park, there to see the prospect of the hill to judge of Dancre's picture which he hath made thereof for me; and I do like it very well – and is a very pretty place.

19 March. With Commissioner Middleton and Kempthorne to a court martiall to which, by virtue of my late captainshipp, I am called, the first I was ever at – where many commanders, and Kempthorne president. Here was tried a difference between Sir L. van Hemskirke, the Dutch captain who commands the *Nonsuch*, built by his direction, and his lieutenant; a drunken kind of silly business. We ordered the lieutenant to ask him pardon, and have resolved to lay before the Duke of York what concerns the captain, which was striking of his lieutenant and challenging him to fight, which comes not within any article of the laws-martiall. But upon discourse the other day with Sir W. Coventry, I did advise Middleton, and he and I did forbear to give judgment; but after the debate, did withdraw into another cabin (the Court being held in one of the yachts, which was on purpose brought up over against St Katharines), it being to be feared that this precedent of our being made captains in order to the trying of the loss of the *Defyance*, wherein we are the proper persons to enquire out the want of instructions while ships do lie in harbour, evil use might be hereafter made of the precedent, by putting the Duke of Buckingham or any of these rude fellows that now are uppermost to make packed courts, by captains made on purpose to serve their turns. The other cause was of the loss of the *Providence* at Tanger; where the Captain's being by chance on shore may prove very inconvenient to him, for example sake, though the man be a good man.

20 March. Up and to the Tower to W. Coventry, and there walked with him alone on the Stone Walk till company came to him; and there about the business of the Navy discoursed with him, and about my Lord Chancellor and Treasurer; that they were

. . . .

(*Opposite*) 'Spent the evening mighty well in good music, to my great content.'
(19 May 1667.) The music lesson, by G. ter Borch *c.* 1670.

against the war at first – declaring, as wise men and statesmen at first to the King, that they thought it fit to have a war with them at some time or other, but that it ought not to be till we found the Crowns of Spain and France together by the eares.

21 March. Up and down [Whitehall]; met with Mr May, who tells me the story of his being put by Sir John Denham's place (of Surveyor of the King's Works, who it seems is lately dead) by the unkindness of the Duke of Buckingham, who hath brought in Dr Wren – though he tells me he hath been his servant for twenty years together, in all his wants and dangers, saving him from want of bread by his care and management, and with a promise of having his help in his advancement, and an engagement under his hand for 1000*l* not yet paid; and yet the Duke of Buckingham is so ungrateful as to put him by – which is an ill thing, though Dr Wren is a worthy man.

22 March. Up and by water with W. Hewer to Whitehall, there to attend the Lords of the Treasury; but before they set I did make a stop to see Sir W. Coventry at his house, where, I bless God, he is come again. [He] told me that he was going to visit Sir Jo. Trevor, who hath been kind to him; and he showed me a long list of all his friends that he must this week make visits to, that came to visit him in the Tower. And seems mighty well satisfied with his being out of business; but I hope he will not long be so. At least, do believe that all must go to wrack, if the King doth not come to see the want of such a servant.

23 March. Up and to my office to do a little business there; and so my things being all ready, I took coach with Commissioner Middleton, Captain Tinker, and Mr Huchinson, a hackney-coach, and over the bridge, and so out towards Chatham; and dined at Dartford, where we stayed an hour or two, it being a cold day; and so on and got to Chatham just at night, with very good discourse by the way; but mostly of matters of religion, wherein Huchinson his vein lies. After supper we fell to talk of spirits and apparitions, whereupon many pretty perticular stories were told, so as to make me almost afeared to lie alone, but for shame I could not help it; and so to bed, and being sleepy, fell soon to rest and so rested well.

24 March. A mighty cold and windy, but clear day, and had the pleasure of seeing the Medway running, winding up and down mightily, and a very fine country; and I went a little way out of the way to have visited Sir Jo. Bankes, but he at London; but here I had a sight of his seat and house, the outside, which is an old abbey just like Hinchingbrooke, and as good at least, and mighty finely placed by the river; and he keeps the grounds about it, and walls and the house, very handsome – I was mightily pleased with the sight of it. Thence to Maydstone, which I had a mighty mind to see, having never been there; and walked all up and down the town, and up to the top of the steeple and had a noble view, and then down again and in the town did see an old man beating of flax, and did step into the barn and give him money and saw that piece of husbandry, which I never saw, and it is very pretty. In the street also, I did buy and send to our inne, the Bell, a dish of fresh fish; and so having walked all round the town, and find it very pretty as most towns I ever saw, though not very big, and people of good fashion in it, we to our inne to dinner, and had a good dinner.

25 March. Up, and by and by, about 8 a-clock, comes Rere-Admirall Kempthorne and seven captains more by the Duke of York's order, as we expected, to hold the court-martiall about the loss of the *Defyance*; and so presently, we by boat to the *Charles*, which lies over against Upnor Castle, and there we fell to the business; and there I did manage the business, the Duke of York having by special order directed them to take the assistance of Commissioner Middleton and me, forasmuch as there might be need of advice in what relates to the government of the ship in harbour; and so I did lay the law open to them, and rattle the Maister-Attendants out of their wits almost, and I made the trial last till 7 at night, not eating a bit all the day; only, when we had done examination and I given my thoughts that the neglect of the gunner of the ship was as great as I thought any neglect could be, which might by the law deserve death, but Commissioner Middleton did declare that he was against giving the sentence of death, we withdrew, as not being of the court, and so left them to do what they pleased; and while they were debating it, the bosun of the ship did bring us out of the kettle a piece of hot salt beef and some brown bread and brandy; and there we did make a little meal, but so good as I never would desire to eat better meat while I live – only, I would have cleaner dishes. By and by they had done, and called us down from the quarterdeck; and there we find they do sentence that the gunner of the *Defyance* should stand upon the *Charles* three hours, with his fault writ upon his breast and with a halter about his neck, and so be made uncapable of any office. The truth is, the man doth seem, and is I believe, a good man; but his neglect, in trusting a girle to carry fire into his cabin, is not to be pardoned.

26 March. Up and with Middleton all the morning at the docke, looking over the storehouses and Comissioner Pett's house, in order to Captain Cox's coming to live there in his stead, as Commissioner. But it is a mighty pretty house; and pretty to see how everything is said to be out of repair for this new man, though 10*l* would put it into as good condition in everything as it ever was in – so free everybody is of the King's money. And so to dinner at the Hill House; and after dinner, till 8 at night, close, Middleton and I examining the business of Mr Pett about selling a boat, and we find him a very knave; and some other quarrels of his, wherein, to justify himself, he hath made complaints of others. This being done, we to supper and so to talk, Commissioner Middleton being mighty good company upon a journy; and so to bed – thinking how merry my people are at this time, putting Tom and Jane to bed, being to have been married this day, it being also my feast for my being cut of the stone; but how many years I do not remember, but I think it to be about ten or eleven.

27 March. Up, and did a little business, Middleton and I; then after drinking a little buttered ale, he and Huchinson and I took coach, and exceeding merry in talk, to Dartford, Middleton finding stories of his own life at Berbados and up and down, at Venice and elsewhere, that are mighty pretty and worth hearing; and he is a strange good companion and droll upon the road, more then ever I could have thought to have been in him. Here we dined and met Captain Allen of Rochester, who dined with us and so went on his journey homeward. And we by and by took coach again, and got home about 6 at night, it being all the morning as cold, snowy, windy, and rainy day as any in the whole winter past, but pretty clear in the afternoon. I find all well, but my wife abroad with Jane, who was married yesterday; and I to the office busy, till by and by my wife comes home; so home and there hear how merry they were yesterday; and I glad at it, they being married it seems very handsomely, at Islington, and dined at the old house and lay in our blue chamber, with much company and wonderful merry. The[ophila] Turner and Mary Battalier bridemaids, and Talb. Pepys and W. Hewers bridemen. Anon to supper and to bed, my head a little troubled with the muchness of business I have upon me at present.

28 March. Lords Day. Lay long, talking with pleasure with my wife, and so up and to the office with Tom, who looks mighty smug upon his marriage, as Jane also doth, both of whom I did give joy.

29 March. I to Sir T. Clifford's and there, after an hour's waiting, he being alone in his closet, I did speak with him and fell to talk of the business of the Navy; and giving me good words, did fall foul of the constitution, and did then discover his thoughts that Sir J. Mennes was too old, and so was Collonell Middleton, and that my Lord Brouncker did mind his mathematics too much. I did not give much encouragement to that of finding fault with my fellow officers, but did stand up for the constitution, and did say that what faults there was in our office would be found not to arise from the constitution, but from the failures of the officers in whose hands it was. This he did seem to give good ear to. But did give me of myself very good words; which pleased me well, though I shall not build upon them anything.

· ·

Lord Brouncker, President of the Royal Society and Navy Commissioner, after Lely.

2 April. Up and by water to Whitehall; and there with the office attended the Duke of York, and stayed in Whitehall till about noon; and so with W. Hewer to the Cock, and there he and I dined alone with great content, he reading to me, for my memory sake, my late collections of the history of the Navy, that I might represent the same by and by to the Duke of York; and so after dinner he and I to Whitehall and there to the Duke of York's lodgings, whither he by and by, by his appointment, came; and alone with him an hour in his closet, telling him mine and W. Coventry's advice touching the present posture of the Navy, as the Duke of Buckingham and the rest do now labour to make changes therein; and that it were best for him to suffer the King to be satisfied with the bringing in of a man or two which they desire. I did also give the Duke of York a short account of the history of the Navy, as to our Office, wherewith he was very well satisfied; but I do find that he is pretty stiff against their bringing in of men against his mind. This night I did bring home from the King's potticary's in Whitehall, by Mr Cooling's direction, a water that he says did him mighty good for his eyes; I pray God it may do me good, but by his description, his disease was the same as mine, and this doth encourage me to use it.

4 April. At noon by appointment comes Mr Sheres, and he and I to Unthankes, where my wife stays for us in our coach, and Betty Turner with her; and we to the Mullberry Garden, where Sheres is to treat us with a Spanish *oleo* by a cook of his acquaintance that is there, that was with my Lord in Spain. And without any other company, he did do it, and mighty nobly; and the *oleo* was endeed a very noble dish, such as I never saw better, or any more of. This, and the discourse he did give us of Spain, and description of the Escuriall, was a fine treat. So we left other good things that would keep till night for a collation – and with much content took coach again and went five or six miles towards Branford: the Prince of Tuscany, who comes into England only to spend money and see our country, comes into the town today, and is much expected; and we met him, but the coach passing by apace, we could not see much of him, but he seems a very jolly and good comely man.

6 April. To Whitehall, where the Board waited on the Duke of York to discourse about the disposing of Sir Tho. Allen's fleet, which is newly come home to Portsmouth; and here Middleton and I did in plain terms acquaint the Duke of York what we thought and had observed in the late court⁄martiall, which the Duke of York did give ear to; and though he thinks not fit to revoke what is already done in this case by a court⁄martiall, yet it shall bring forth some good laws in the behaviour of captains to their under⁄officers for the time to come.

11 April. Lords Day. Easter Day. Up, and to church, where Alderman Backewell's wife and mother and boy and another gentlewoman did come and sit in our pew – but no women of our own there, and so there was room enough. Our parson made a dull sermon; and so home to dinner, and after dinner my wife and I out by coach, and Balty with us, to Loton the lanskip⁄drawer, a Dutchman living in St James's Market, but there saw no good pictures; but by accident he did direct us to a painter that was then in the house with him, a Dutchman newly come over, one Everelst, who took us to his lodging

Still life, by S. Verelst.

. . . .

close by and did show us a little flowerpott of his doing, the finest thing that ever I think I saw in my life – the drops of dew hanging on the leaves, so as I was forced again and again to put my finger to it to feel whether my eyes were deceived or no. He doth ask 70*l* for it; I had the vanity to bid him 20*l* – but a better picture I never saw in my whole life, and it is worth going twenty miles to see. Thence, leaving Balty there, I took my wife to St James's and there carried her to the Queen's Chapel, the first time I ever did it. And going out of the Chapel, I did see the Prince of Tuskany come out, a comely black, fat man, in a mourning suit. So home; and to my office and there set down my journal, with the help of my left eye through my tube, for fourteen days past; which is so much, as I hope I shall not run in arrear again, but the badness of my eyes doth force me to it. So home to supper and to bed.

13 April. By hackney coach to the Spittle and heard a piece of a dull sermon to my Lord Mayor and Aldermen and then saw them all take horse and ride away, which I have not seen together many a day; their wifes also went in their coaches – and endeed the sight was mighty pleasing. I away home; and there sent for W. Hewer and he and I by water to Whitehall. But here, being with him in the courtyard, as God would have it, I spied Deb, which made my heart and head to work; and I presently could not refrain, but sent W. Hewer away to look for Mr Wren (W. Hewer, I perceive, did see her, but whether he did see me see her I know not, or suspect my sending him away I know not) but my heart could not hinder me. And I run after her and two women and a man, more ordinary people, and she in her old clothes; and after hunting a little, find them in the lobby of the Chapel below stairs; and there I observed she endeavoured to avoid me, but I did speak to her and she to me, and did get her para docere me ou she demeures now. And did charge her para say nothing of me that I had vu elle – which she did promise; and so, with my heart full of surprize and disorder, I away; and meeting with Sir H. Cholmley, walked into the park with him and back again, looking to see if I could spy her again in the park, but I could not. And so back to Whitehall, and then back to the park with Mr May, but could see her no more; and so with W. Hewer, who I doubt by my countenance might see some disorder in me, we home by water. But, God forgive me, I hardly know how to put on confidence enough to speak as innocent, having had this passage today with Deb, though only, God knows, by accident. But my great pain is lest God Almighty shall suffer me to find out this girl, whom endeed I love, and with a bad amour; but I will pray to God to give me grace to forbear it.

So home to supper, where very sparing in my discourse, not giving occasion of any enquiry where I have been today, or what I have done; and so, without any trouble tonight more then my fear, we to bed.

15 April. Going down Holburn Hill by the Conduit, I did see Deb on foot going up the hill; I saw her, and she me, but she made no stop, but seemed unwilling to speak to me; so I away on, but then stopped and light and after her, and overtook her at the end of Hosier Lane in Smithfield; and without standing in the street, desired her to fallow me, and I led her into a little blind alehouse within the walls; and there she and I alone fell to talk and besar la and tocar su mamelles; but she mighty coy, and I hope modest; but however, though with great force, did hazer ella con su hand para tocar mi thing, but ella was in great pain para be brought para it. I did give her in a paper *20s*, and we did agree para meet again in the Hall at Westminster on Monday next; and so, giving me great hopes by

· ·

'I took my wife to St James's . . . to the Queen's Chapel . . . and heard excellent music.'
(11 April 1669.) The Queen's Chapel (now Marlborough House Chapel), *c.* 1687.

her carriage that she continues modest and honest, we did there part, she going home and I to Mrs Turner's; but when I came back to the place where I left my coach, it was gone, I having stayed too long, which did trouble me to abuse a poor fellow so; but taking another coach, I did direct him to find out the fellow and send him to me.

16 April. Was in great pain about yesterday still, lest my wife should have sent her porter to enquire anything; though for my heart, I cannot see it possible how anything could be discovered of it; but yet, such is fear, as to render me full of doubt and disquiet. At night, to supper and to bed.

18 April. Lords Day. Up, and all the morning till 2 a'clock at my office with Gibson and Tom, about drawing up fair my discourse of the administracion of the Navy. And then Mr Spong being come to dine with me, I in to dinner and then out to my office again to examine the fair draft; and so borrowing Sir J. Mennes's coach, he going with Commissioner Middleton, I to Whitehall, where we all met and did sign it; and then to my Lord Arlington's, where the King and Duke of York and Prince Rupert, as also Ormond and the two Secretaries, with my Lord Ashly and Sir T. Clifford, was; and there, by and by being called in, Mr Williamson did read over our paper, which was in a letter to the Duke of York, bound up in a book with the Duke of York's book of Instructions. He read it well, and after read, we were bid to withdraw, nothing being at all said to it. And by and by we were called in again, and nothing said to that business but another begun, about the state of this year's action and our wants of money, as I had stated the same lately to our Treasurers – which I was bid, and did largely and with great content, open; and having so done, we all withdrew and left them to debate our supply of money; after which, being called in and referred to attend on the Lords of the Treasury, we all departed; and I only stayed in the House till the Council rose, and then to the Duke of York, who in the Duchess's chamber came to me and told me that the book was there left with my Lord Arlington, for any of the Lords to view that had a mind, and to prepare and present to the King what they had to say in writing to any part of it; which is all we can desire, and so that rested.

19 April. Up, and with Tom (whom, with his wife, I and my wife had this morning taken occasion to tell that I did intend to give him 40*l* for himself and 20*l* to his wife toward their setting out in the world, and that my wife would give her 20*l* more, that so she might have as much to begin with as he) by coach to Whitehall; and there having set him work in the robe chamber, I to Westminster Hall and there walked from 10 a'clock to past 12, expecting Deb; but whether she had been there before, and missing me went away, or is prevented in coming and hath no mind to come to me (the last whereof, as being most pleasing, as showing most modesty, I should be most glad of) I know not; but she not then appearing, I being tired with walking went home; and my wife being all day at Jane's, helping her as she said to cut out linning and other things belonging to her new condition, I after dinner out again; and call[ed] for my coach, which was at the coachmaker's and hath been for these two or three days, to be new painted and the window frames gilt against May Day.

20 April. In the afternoon we walked to the old Artillery ground near the Spitalfields, where I never was before; but now, by Captain Deanes invitation, did go to see his new gun tryed, this being the place where the Officers of the Ordnance do try all their great guns; and when we came, did find that the trial had been made, and they going away with extraordinary report of the proof of his gun, which, from the shortness and bigness, they do call 'Punchinello'. But I desired Collonell Legg to stay and give us a sight of her performance, which he did; and there, in short, against a gun more then as long and as heavy again, and charged with as much powder again, she carried the same bullet as strong to the mark, and nearer and above the mark at a point-blank then theirs, and is more easily managed and recoyls no more then that – which is a thing so extraordinary, as to be admired for the happiness of his invention, and to the great regret of the old gunners and Officers of the Ordinance that were there.

21 April. Walking with Sir H. Cholmly in the Court, talking of news; where he told me that now the great design of the Duke of Buckingham is to prevent the meeting, since he cannot bring about with the King the dissolving, of this Parliament, that the King may not need it; and therefore my Lord St Albans is hourly expected, with great offers of a million of money, to buy our breach with the Dutch; and this they do think may tempt the King to take the money, and thereby be out of a necessity of calling the Parliament again – which these people dare not suffer to meet again. But this he doubts, and so do I, that it will be to the ruin of the nation if we fall out with Holland. This we were discoursing, when my boy comes to tell me that his mistress was at the gate with the coach; whither I went and there find my wife and the whole company; so she and Mrs Turner and The[ophila] and Talbot in mine, and Joyce, W. Batelier, and I in a hackney to Hyde Park, where I was ashamed to be seen; but mightily pleased, though troubled with a drunken coachman that did not remember, when we came to light, where it was that he took us up; but said at Hammersmith, and thither he was carying of us when we came first out of the Park. So I carried them all to Hercules Pillars and there did treat them; and so about 10 at night parted, and my wife and I and W. Batelier home; and he gone, we to bed.

24 April. Up and to the office, where all the morning; and at noon home to dinner, Mr Sheres dining with us by agreement, and my wife, which troubled me, mighty careful to have a handsome dinner for him. But yet I see no reason to be troubled at it, he being a very civil and worthy man I think; but only, it doth seem to imply some little neglect of me.

After dinner to the King's House and there saw *The Generall* revived, a good play, that pleases me well; and thence, our coach coming for us, we parted and home, and I busy late at the office and then home to supper and to bed – well pleased tonight to have Lead the vizard-maker bring me home my vizard with a tube fastened in it, which I think will do my business, at least in a great measure, for the easing of my eyes.

25 April. Abroad with my wife in the afternoon to the park – where very much company, and the weather very pleasant. I carried my wife to the Lodge, the first time this year, and there in our coach eat a cheesecake and drank a tankard of milk. I showed her this day also first the Prince of Tuscany, who was in the park – and many very fine ladies. And so home, and after supper to bed.

26 April. My wife and [Creed] and I out, and I set him down at Temple Bar, and myself and wife went down the Temple upon seeming business, only to put him off. And just at the Temple Gate, I spied Deb with another gentlewoman, and Deb winked on me and smiled, but undiscovered, and I was glad to see her.

28 April. Up, and was called upon by Sir H. Cholmly to discourse about some accounts of his of Tanger; and then to other talk, and I find by him that it is brought almost to effect, the late endeavours of the Duke of York and Duchess, the Queen Mother and my Lord St Albans, together [with] some of the contrary faction, my Lord Arlington, that for a sum of money we shall enter into a league with the King of France; wherein he says my Lord Chancellor is also concerned, and he believes that in the doing hereof, it is meant that he shall come in again, and that this sum of money will so help the King as that he will not need the Parliament; and that in that regard, it will be forwarded by the Duke of Buckingham and his faction, who dread the Parliament; but hereby, we must leave the Dutch, and that I doubt will undo us, and Sir H. Cholmly says he finds W. Coventry to think the like. My Lady Castlemayne is instrumental in this matter and, he says, never more great with the King then she is now. But this is a thing that will make the Parliament and kingdom mad, and will turn to our ruine – for with this money the King shall wanton away his time in pleasures, and think nothing of the main till it be too late.

He gone, I to the office, where busy till noon; and then home to dinner, where M. Batelier dined with us, and pretty merry; and so I to the office again.

30 April. To my tailor's and then to the belt-maker's, where my belt cost me 55*s*, of the colour of my new suit; and here, understanding that the mistress of the house, an oldish woman in a hat, hath some water good for the eyes, she did dress me, making my eyes smart most horribly, and did give me a little glass of it, which I will use and hope it will do me good. This morning I did visit Mr Oldenburgh and did see the instrument for perspective made by Dr Wren, of which I have one making by Browne; and the sight of this doth please me mightily. Thence to the frame-maker's, one Norris in Long Acre – who showed me several forms of frames to choose by; which was pretty, in little bits of mouldings to choose by. This done, I to my coachmaker's, and there vexed to see nothing yet done to my coach at 3 in the afternoon; but I set it in doing, and stood by it till 8 at night and saw the painter varnish it; which is pretty, to see how every doing it over doth make it more and more yellow. And it dries as fast in the sun as it can be laid on almost. Here I did make the workmen drink, and saw my coach cleaned and oyled; and staying among poor people there in the ally, did hear them call their fat child 'punch'; which pleased me mightily, that word being become a word of common use for all that is thick and short.

1 May. Up betimes, called up by my tailor, and there first put on a summer suit this year – but it was not my fine one of flowered tabby vest and coloured camelott tunic, because it was too fine with the gold lace at the hands, that I was afeared to be seen in it – but put on the stuff suit I made the last year, which is now repaired; and so did go to the office in it and sat all the morning, the day looking as if it would be fowle. At noon home to dinner, and there find my wife extraordinary fine with her flowered tabby gown that she made two years ago, now laced exceeding pretty, and endeed was fine all over – and mighty earnest to go, though the day was very lowering, and she would have me put on my fine suit, which I did; and so anon we went alone through the town with our new liverys of serge, and the horses' maines and tails tied with red ribbon and the standards thus gilt with varnish and all clean, and green raynes, that people did mightily look upon us; and the truth is, I did not see any coach more pretty, or more gay, then ours all the day. But we set out out of humour; I because Betty, whom I expected, was not come to go with us; and my wife, that I would sit on the same seat with her, which she liked not, being so fine; and then expected to meet Sheres, which we did in the Pell Mell, and against my will I was forced to take him into the coach, but was sullen all day almost, and little complaisant; the day also being unpleasing, though the park full of coaches; but dusty and windy and cold, and now and then a little dribbling rain; and what made it worst, there were so many hackney coaches as spoiled the sight of the gentlemen's, and so we had little pleasure. But here was W. Batelier and his sister in a borrowed coach by themselfs, and I took them and we to the Lodge, and at the door did give them a sullabub and other things, cost me 12s, and pretty merry; and so back to the coaches and there till the evening; and then home, leaving Mr Sheres at St James's gate, where he took leave of us for altogether, he being this night to set out for Portsmouth post, in his way to Tanger – which troubled my wife mightily, who is mighty, though not I think too fond of him. But she was out of humour all the evening, and I vexed at her for it; and she did not rest almost all the night, so as in the night I was forced to take her and hug her to put her to rest.

2 May. Lords Day. Up, and by water to Whitehall and there visit my Lord Sandwiches, who, after about two months absence at Hinchingbrooke, came to town last night. I saw him, and very kind; and I am glad he is so, I having not wrote to him all the time, my eyes endeed not letting me. Here, with Sir Ch. Herbert and my Lord Hinchingbrooke and Sidny, we looked upon the picture of Tanger designed by Ch. Herberd and drawn by Dancre, which my Lord Sandwich admires, as being the truest picture that ever he saw in his life – and it is endeed very pretty, and I will be at the cost of having one of them.

5 May. At noon with Sir Tho. Allen and Sir Ed. Scott and Lord Carlingford to the Spanish Embassadors, where I dined the first time – the *oleo* not so good as Shere's. There was at the table, himself and a Spanish Countess, a good, comely, and witty lady, three fathers, and us. Discourse good and pleasant; and here was an Oxford scholar in a Doctor's of Laws gowne, where the Embassador lay when the Court was there, to salute him from the college before his return to Spain. This man, though a gentle sort of scholar, yet sat like a fool for want of French or Spanish; but only Latin, which he spoke like a Englishman to one of the fathers. And by and by, he and I to talk, and the company very merry at my defending Cambridge against Oxford; and I made much use of my French and Spanish here, to my great content.

View of Tangier, by Hendrik Danckerts 1669. Pepys was long involved in the affairs of Tangiers as Treasurer of the Tangier Committee, and in 1683–4 sailed there with Lord Dartmouth to supervise its abandonment.

8 May. At the office all the morning; and this day the first time did alter my side of the table, after above eight years sitting on that next the fire. But now I am not able to bear the light of the windows in my eyes, I do go there; and I did sit with much more content then I had done on the other side for a great while, and in winter the fire will not trouble my back.

At noon home to dinner; and after dinner, all the afternoon within with Mr Hater, Gibson, and W. Hewer, reading over and drawing up new things in the instructions of commanders; which will be good, and I hope to get them confirmed by the Duke of York, though I perceive nothing will effectually perfect them but to look over the whole body of the instructions of all the officers of a ship, and make them all perfect together. By and by also comes Browne the mathematical-instrument maker, and brings me home my instrument for perspective, and he hath made it, I think, very well; and that that I believe will do the thing, and therein give me great content, but that I fear all the contents that must be received by my eyes are almost lost.

So to the office and there late at business, and then home to supper and to bed.

10 May. Troubled, about 3 in the morning, with my wife's calling her maid up, and rising herself, to go with her coach abroad to gather May dew – which she did; and I troubled for it, for fear of any hurt, going abroad so betimes, happening to her. But I to sleep again, and she came home about 6 and to bed again, all well.

To my Lord Crew, whom I have not seen since he was sick, which is eight months

Lambeth Palace, 1697. 'With Mr Wren to Lambeth, with the Archbishop of Canterbury; the first time I was ever there . . . where a noble house, and well furnished with good pictures and furniture.' (14 May 1669.)

· ·

ago I think – and there dined with him. He is mightily broke. A stranger, a country gentleman, was with him, and he pleased with my discourse accidentally about the decay of gentlemen's families in the country, telling us that the old rule was that a family might remain 50 miles from London 100 year, 100 mile off from London 200 years, and so, farther or nearer London, more or less years. He also told us that he hath heard his father say that in his time it was so rare for a country gentleman to come to London, that when he did come, he used to make his will before he set out.

12 May. My brother John tells me the first news that my sister is with child and far gone; which I know not whether it did more trouble or please me, having no great care for my friends to have children, though I love other people's.

14 May. Up, and to St James's to the Duke of York and thence to Whitehall, where we met about office business; and then at noon to dinner with Mr Wren to Lambeth, with the Archbishop of Canterbury; the first time I was ever there, and I have long longed for it – where a noble house, and well furnished with good pictures and furniture, and noble attendance in good order, and great deal of company, though an ordinary day, and exceeding great cheer, nowhere better, or so much that ever I think I saw for an ordinary table. And the Bishop mighty kind to me, perticularly desiring my company another time, when less company there. Most of the company gone, and I going, I heard by a gentleman of a sermon that was to be there; and so I stayed to hear it, thinking it serious, till by and by the gentleman told me it was a mockery by one Cornet Bolton, a very gentleman-like man, that behind a chair did pray and preach like a Presbyter-Scot that ever I heard in my life, with all the possible imitation in grimaces and voice till it made us all burst; but I did wonder to have the Bishop at this time to make himself sport with things of this kind, but I perceive it was shown him as a rarity. And he took care to have the room door shut, but there was about twenty gentlemen there – and myself infinitely pleased with the novelty.

16 May. Lords Day. My wife and I at church, our pew filled (which vexed me at her confidence) with Mrs Backwell and six more that she brought with her. Dined at home, and W. Batelier with us, and I all the afternoon drawing up a foul draft of my petition to the Duke of York about my eyes, for leave to spend three or four months out of the office, drawing it so as to give occasion to a voyage abroad; which I did to my pretty good liking. And then with my wife to Hyde Park, where a good deal of company, and good weather; and so home to supper and to bed.

19 May. With my coach to St James, and there, finding the Duke of York gone to muster his men in Hyde Park, I alone with my boy thither; and there saw more, walking out of my coach as other gentlemen did, of a soldier's trade then ever I did in my life – the men being mighty fine, and their commanders, perticularly the Duke of Monmouth; but methought their trade but very easy, as to the mustering of their men, and the men but indifferently ready to perform what was commanded in the handling their arms. Thence by and by to Whitehall, and there I waited upon the King and Queen all dinner-time in the Queen's lodgings, she being in her white pinner and apern, like a woman with child; and she seemed handsomer, plain so, then dressed. And by and by, dinner done, I out and to walk in the gallery for the Duke of York's coming out; and there meeting Mr May, he took me down about 4 a-clock to Mr Chevins's lodgings, and all alone did get me a dish of cold chickens and good wine, and I dined like a prince, being before very hungry and empty. By and by the Duke of York comes, and readily took me to his closet and received my petition, and discoursed it about my eyes and pitied me, and with much kindness did give me his consent to be absent, and approved of my proposition to go into Holland to observe things there of the Navy, but would first ask the King's leave; which he anon did, and did tell me that the King would be 'a good maister to me' (these were his words about my eyes) and doth like of my going into Holland, but doth advise that nobody should know of my going thither – but pretend that I did go into the country somewhither – which I liked well.

20 May. Up and to the office, where all the morning. At noon, the whole office, Brouncker, J. Mennes, T. Middleton, S. Pepys, and Captain Cox, to dine with the parish at the Three Tuns, this day being Ascension Day – where exceeding good discourse among the merchants. And thence back home, and after a little talk with my wife, to my office and did a great deal of business; and so, with my eyes mighty weary and my head full of care how to get my accounts and business settled against my journy, home to supper and to bed.

31 May. [Up] very betimes, and so continued all the morning, with W. Hewer, upon examining and stating my accounts, in order to the fitting myself to go abroad beyond sea, which the ill condition of my eyes, and my neglect for a year or two, hath kept me behindhand in, and so as to render it very difficult now, and troublesome to my mind to do it; but I this day made a satisfactory entrance therein. Dined at home, and in the afternoon by water to Whitehall, calling by the way at Michell's, where I have not been many a day till just the other day; and now I met her mother there and knew her husband to be out of town. And here yo did besar ella, but have not opportunity para hazer mas with her as I would have offered if yo had had it. And thence had another meeting with the Duke of York at Whitehall; and so being called by my wife, we to the park, Mary Batelier, [and] a Duch gentleman, a friend of hers, being with us. Thence to the World's End, a drinking-house by the park, and there merry; and so home late.

And thus ends all that I doubt I shall ever be able to do with my own eyes in the keeping of my journall, I being not able to do it any longer, having done now so long as to undo my eyes almost every time that I take a pen in my hand; and therefore, whatever comes of it, I must forbear; and therefore resolve from this time forward to have it kept by my people in longhand, and must therefore be contented to set down no more then is fit for them and all the world to know; or if there be anything (which cannot be much, now my amours to Deb are past, and my eyes hindering me in almost all other pleasures), I must endeavour to keep a margin in my book open, to add here and there a note in shorthand with my own hand. And so I betake myself to that course which [is] almost as much as to see myself go into my grave – for which, and all the discomforts that will accompany my being blind, the good God prepare me.

May.31.1669.   S.P.

POSTSCRIPT

Pepys never kept another diary on the same scale as this, although his eyes quickly recovered from the worst effects of the strain which had led him to end it. He composed four other diaries for specific (mostly official) purposes. Two were written from his notes or at his dictation by his clerks: a journal of 1670 recording his examination by the Privy Council about the report of the Brooke House Committee ('the Accounts Committee'); the other a journal of 1679–80 designed to help him in his defence against the accusation of high treason brought against him during the Popish Plot. Neither covers more than a few weeks. Two others were journals kept in his own hand and in shorthand. One was a series of pencilled notes of Commons' debates on navy business in 1677. The other was his Tangier journal of 1683–4, which he kept, also in shorthand but in ink, when he went as secretary to the expedition sent to supervise the evacuation of the colony. Although by far the fullest and most personal of these later diaries, it is not much more than a travel journal: Pepys does not attempt in its pages to lay bare his life. It is the only one of these later diaries to have been published. Three editions have appeared since 1841: the best is that by E. Chappell (1935). What readers of the great diary must regret is that Pepys did not resume it in the 1670s and '80s. His version of the ten critical years from the Exclusion Crisis to the Glorious Revolution of 1688, told in diary form and in Pepysian detail by one who knew James II so well, would be an historical source of incomparable value. It must rank as one of the most important books never written.

1633 23 February: Born in Salisbury Court, Fleet Street
3 March: Baptized in St Bride's, Fleet Street

c. 1644 At the grammar school, Huntingdon

c. 1646–50 At St Paul's School, London

1649 Saw Charles I beheaded

1650 Awarded leaving exhibition

1651–4 At Magdalene College, Cambridge
1651, 1653 Awarded scholarships

1654 Takes his B.A.
?1654 Appointed secretary or domestic steward to Edward Mountagu in Whitehall Palace
?1654 Appointed clerk to George Downing, Teller of the Receipt in the Exchequer

1655 1 December: Married to Elizabeth St Michel in St Margaret's, Westminster

1658 26 March: Operated on for the stone
c. August: Moves to Axe Yard

1659 May: Carries letters to Mountagu in the Baltic

1660 1 January: Begins diary
April–May: Accompanies Mountagu's fleet to Holland to bring over Charles II
28 June: Resigns clerkship in Exchequer
29 June: Appointed Clerk of the Acts to the Navy Board
23 July: Sworn in as Mountagu's deputy as clerk in Privy Seal Office
24 September: Sworn in as J.P.

1661 *23 April: Coronation of Charles II*
5 July: Uncle Robert Pepys dies

1662 15 February: Admitted as Younger Brother of Trinity House
17 August: Resigns deputy-clerkship in Privy Seal
20 November: Appointed to Tangier Committee

1664 15 March: His brother Tom dies
8 April: Appointed to Corporation for the Royal Fishery

1665 15 February: Elected Fellow of the Royal Society

22 February: Second Dutch War begins
20 March: Appointed Treasurer of Tangier Committee
Spring: Great Plague begins in London
3 June: Battle of Lowestoft
5 July: Moves family to Woolwich
21 August: The Navy Office moves to Greenwich
October: Takes lodgings at Greenwich
4 December: Appointed Surveyor-General of the Victualling

1666 January: Navy Office and Pepys household move back to London
March: Sandwich arrives in Spain as Ambassador
1–4 June: Four Days Fight
25 July: St James's Day Fight
2–5 September: The Great Fire of London

1667 25 March: His mother dies at Brampton
10–13 June: Dutch raid on Thames and Medway
13 June: Sends his gold to Brampton
28 July: Resigns Surveyorship of Victualling
31 July: End of Second Dutch War
7–12 October: Visits Brampton to recover his gold
22 October: Defends Navy Board before parliamentary Committee on Miscarriages

1668 27 February: His sister Paulina marries John Jackson
5 March: Defends Navy Board before House of Commons
5–17 June: His holiday tour to West Country
September: Sandwich returns
25 October: Elizabeth discovers him *in flagrante* with Deb

1669 31 May: Discontinues his diary
June–October: Travels to France and Low Countries
10 November: Elizabeth dies; he erects a monument to her in St Olave's, Hart Street

1670 30 March: His brother John appointed Clerk to Trinity House

1672 24 January: Admitted as Elder Brother of Trinity House
17 March: Third Dutch War begins
28 May: Death of Sandwich in Battle of Sole Bay

1673 29 January: Navy Office destroyed by fire; he moves to Winchester Street
15 June: Duke of York resigns as Lord High Admiral under terms of Test Act (March) excluding Roman Catholics; office put in commission
18 June: Appointed Secretary to Admiralty Commission; is succeeded at Navy Board by his brother John and Thomas Hayter as joint Clerks
4 November: Elected M.P. for Castle Rising, Norfolk

1674 January: Moves to Derby House, new headquarters of Admiralty
19 February: End of Third Dutch War

1676 1 February: Appointed the Governor of Christ's Hospital
22 May: Elected Master of Trinity House

1677 15 March: His brother John buried
8 August: Elected Master of Clothworkers' Company

1679 5 February: Elected M.P. for Harwich
21 May: Resigns as Secretary to Admiralty and Treasurer for Tangier
22 May–9 July: In Tower on suspicion of treasonable correspondence with France
July: Moves to W. Hewer's house in York Buildings, Buckingham Street

1680 30 June: Proceedings against him abandoned
c. September: His brother-in-law John Jackson dies
3, 5 October: Takes down at King's dictation story of his escape after Battle of Worcester
4 October: His father buried at Brampton

1682 May: Accompanies Duke of York to Edinburgh

1683 30 July: Sets out for Tangier as secretary to expedition under Lord Dartmouth to evacuate colony
1683–4 December–February: Visits Spain

1684 30 March: Returns to England
10 June: Appointed King's Secretary for Naval Affairs
1 December: Elected President of Royal Society

1685 *6 February: Death of Charles II; accession of Duke of York as James II*

19 May: Takes seat as M.P. for Harwich, having been elected for both Harwich and Sandwich
20 July: Nominated Master of Trinity House by King under new charter

1686 March: Special Commission 'for the Recovery of the Navy' begins to sit
30 November: Resigns Presidency of Royal Society

1688 29 June: Called as witness in Trial of Seven Bishops
October: Special Commission dissolved
5 November: William of Orange lands
23 December: James II takes flight to France

1689 16 January: Defeated in parliamentary election at Harwich
13 February: William and Mary become joint sovereigns
20 February: Resigns his Secretaryship
May–July: Detained on suspicion of Jacobitism
26 August: Resigns Mastership of Trinity House

1690 25–30 June: Imprisoned on suspicion of Jacobitism
Publishes his *Memoires Relating to the State of the Royal Navy* [*1679–88*]

1699 27 April: Made freeman of city of London for services to Christ's Hospital

1701 *c.* June: Retires to Hewer's house at Clapham

1703 26 May: Dies at Clapham
4 June: Buried at St Olave's, Hart Street

1723 His nephew and heir, John Jackson, dies

1724 July: His library moved from Clapham to Magdalene College, Cambridge

1766 His account of the King's escape after the Battle of Worcester first published by Sir David Dalrymple

1825 His diary first published by Lord Braybrooke from the transcription by John Smith

1841 His Tangier Journal first published by John Smith

1884 His monument erected in St Olave's

1903 The Samuel Pepys Club founded in his honour

ILLUSTRATION ACKNOWLEDGMENTS

The publishers would like to thank the following for permission to reproduce illustrations:

Her Majesty the Queen, Copyright Reserved, facing page 24, page 130, facing page 161, page 228.

Crown Copyright Reserved, reproduced with permission of the Controller of Her Majesty's Stationery Office, page 18.

Austrian National Library, Vienna, page 188.

The Marquess of Bath, page 41 (*Coventry*).

His Grace the Duke of Beaufort KG, facing page 105 (photo Derrick Witty).

The British Library, page 47, page 81 (centre), page 103, page 159 (right).

The Trustees of the British Museum, page 23, page 138 (photo Derrick Witty), page 143 (photo Derrick Witty), page 183, facing page 216 (photo Michael Holford Library).

The Governors of Christ's Hospital, facing page 144 (photo Derrick Witty).

Richard Green, London, page 222.

Guildhall Library, page 182, page 193.

Iveagh Bequest, Kenwood, between pages 104–5 (top), (photo Cooper-Bridgeman Library).

R. Malet de Carteret, page 41 (*Carteret*).

The Mansell Collection, page 72 (left), page 173.

Victor Montagu, page 185.

Museum of London, page 35, page 50 (left), page 73 (left), page 76 (left), page 87, between pages 104–5 (bottom), page 122, page 124 (left), page 131 (right), page 142.

The Trustees of the National Gallery, London, facing page 217.

National Maritime Museum, London, page 41 (*J. Mennes and W. Penn*), page 56, page 57 (left), pages 116–17, facing page 145, page 201, between pages 216–17.

National Portrait Gallery, London, page 37, facing page 104, page 220.

Pepys Library, by permission of the Master and Fellows, Magdalene College, Cambridge, page 14, page 16, page 31, page 45, page 57 (right), page 68, page 72 (right), page 74, page 76 (centre and right), page 98, page 99, page 101, page 118, page 124 (right), page 131 (left), page 135 (left), page 154, page 157, page 159 (left), page 167, page 171, page 194, page 195, page 213, page 223, page 229.

Private Collection, page 139.

Radio Times Hulton Picture Library, page 50 (right), page 51, page 65, page 81 (left and right), page 181 (left).

Rijksmuseum, Amsterdam, page 109.

His Grace the Duke of Roxburghe, facing page 160.

Lord Sackville, facing page 25.

His Grace the Duke of St Albans, between pages 24–5 (photo Cooper-Bridgeman Library).

Society of Antiquaries of London, page 40, page 67, page 186, page 209.

Victoria and Albert Museum, London, Crown Copyright, page 18 (right), page 73 (right), page 135 (right), page 181 (right).

INDEX AND GLOSSARY

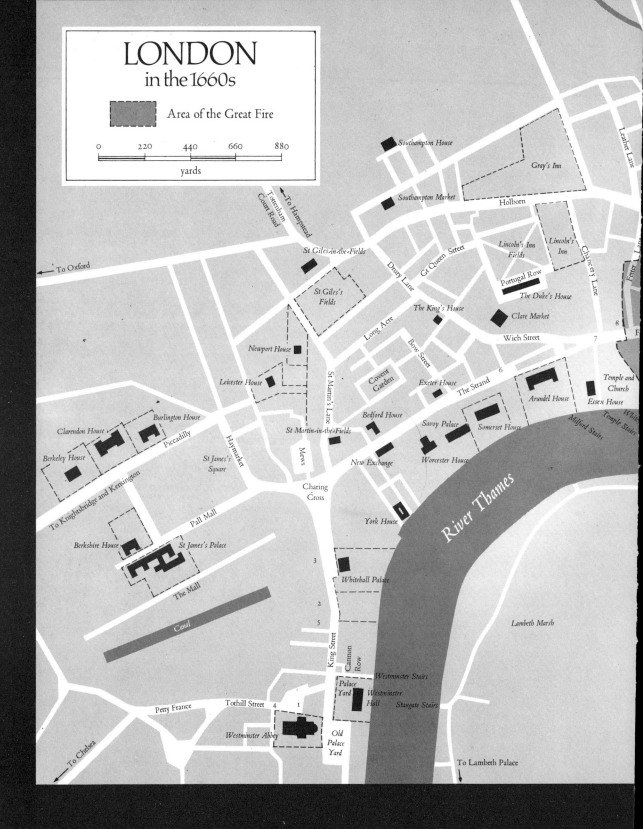

LONDON
in the 1660s

Area of the Great Fire

0   220   440   660   880
yards

Southampton House

Gray's Inn

Southampton Market

Holborn

To Hampstead

Tottenham Court Road

St Giles-in-the-Fields

Drury Lane

Gt Queen Street

Lincoln's Inn Fields

Lincoln's Inn

Chancery Lane

To Oxford

St Giles's Fields

Portugal Row

The Duke's House

Fetter Lane

Leather Lane

Long Acre

The King's House

Clare Market

Wich Street

8

7

Newport House

Bow Street

Covent Garden

Exeter House

The Strand

6

Temple and Church

Essex House

Leicester House

St Martin's Lane

Bedford House

Arundel House

Burlington House

Clarendon House

Piccadilly

St Martin-in-the-Fields

Mews

Savoy Palace

Somerset House

Worcester House

Milford Stairs

Temple Stairs

Berkeley House

New Exchange

St James's Square

Haymarket

Charing Cross

York House

To Knightsbridge and Kensington

River Thames

Pall Mall

Berkshire House

St James's Palace

3

Whitehall Palace

Lambeth Marsh

The Mall

Canal

2

5

King Street

Cannon Row

Westminster Stairs

Palace Yard

Westminster Hall

Stangate Stairs

Petty France

Tothill Street

4

1

Westminster Abbey

Old Palace Yard

To Chelsea

To Lambeth Palace

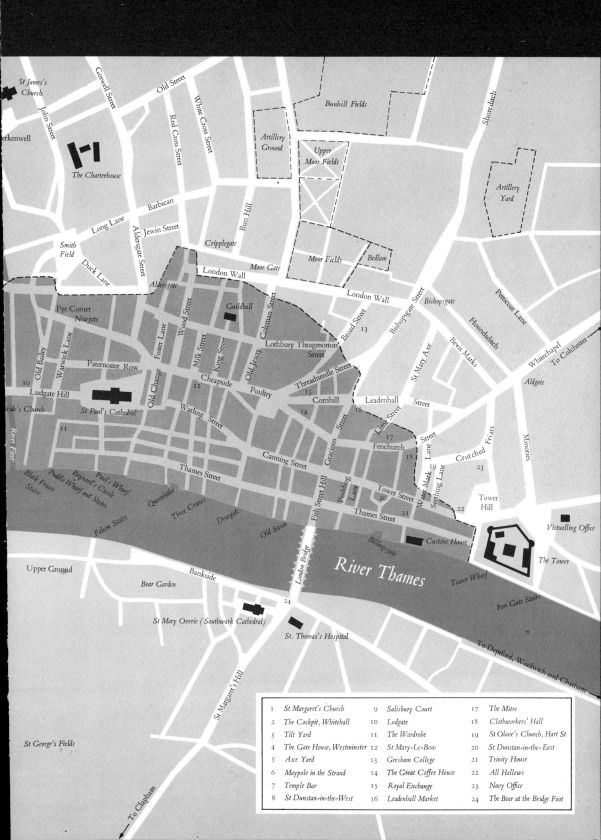

St James's
Church

Clerkenwell

John Street

Goswell Street

Old Street

White Cross Street

Red Cross Street

Shoreditch

Bunhill Fields

The Charterhouse

Artillery
Ground

Upper
Moor Fields

Artillery
Yard

Long Lane

Barbican

Aldersgate Street

Jewin Street

Bun Hill

Cripplegate

Moor Gate

Moor Fields

Bedlam

Petticoat Lane

Smith
Field

Duck Lane

Aldersgate

London Wall

London Wall

London Wall

Bishopsgate

Bishopsgate

Houndsditch

Whitechapel

To Colchester

Pye Corner
Newgate

Wood Street

Guildhall

Coleman Street

Broad Street

13

St Mary Axe

Bevis Marks

Aldgate

Old Bailey

Warwick Lane

Paternoster Row

Foster Lane

Milk Street

King Street

Old Jewry

Lothbury Throgmorton'
Street

Threadneedle Street

Leadenhall

Street

Crutched Friars

Minories

10

Ludgate Hill

St Bride's Church

Cheapside

12

Old Change

Poultry

15

Cornhill

14

16

Lime Street

Street

17

Fenchurch

18

23

St Paul's Cathedral

Watling Street

11

River Fleet

Black Friars
Stairs

Puddle Wharf and Stairs

Baynard's Castle

Paul's Wharf

Thames Street

Canning Street

Gracious
Street

Fish Street Hill

Pudding
Lane

Tower Street

19

Water Mark Lane

Seething Lane

Tower Street

22

Tower
Hill

Queenhithe

Three Cranes

Dowgate

Old Swan

20

Thames Street

21

Custom House

Victualling Office

Felton Stairs

London Bridge

Billingsgate

The Tower

Upper Ground

Bankside

Bear Garden

St Mary Overie (Southwark Cathedral)

24

St. Thomas's Hospital

Tower Wharf

Iron Gate Stairs

River Thames

To Deptford, Woolwich and Chatham

St George's Fields

St Margaret's Hill

To Clapham

1	St Margaret's Church	9	Salisbury Court	17	The Mitre
2	The Cockpit, Whitehall	10	Ludgate	18	Clothworkers' Hall
3	Tilt Yard	11	The Wardrobe	19	St Olave's Church, Hart St
4	The Gate House, Westminster	12	St Mary-le-Bow	20	St Dunstan-in-the-East
5	Axe Yard	13	Gresham College	21	Trinity House
6	Maypole in the Strand	14	The Great Coffee House	22	All Hallows
7	Temple Bar	15	Royal Exchange	23	Navy Office
8	St Dunstan-in-the-West	16	Leadenhall Market	24	The Bear at the Bridge Foot